Windows® 10

for dummies®
A Wiley Brand

2nd edition

by Andy Rathbone

for dummies®
A Wiley Brand

Windows® 10 For Dummies®, 2nd Edition

Published by **John Wiley & Sons, Inc.,** 111 River Street, Hoboken, NJ 07030-5774, www.wiley.com

Copyright © 2016 by John Wiley & Sons, Inc., Hoboken, New Jersey

Media and software compilation copyright © 2016 by John Wiley & Sons, Inc. All rights reserved.

Published simultaneously in Canada

For general information on our other products and services, please contact our Customer Care Department within the U.S. at 877-762-2974, outside the U.S. at 317-572-3993, or fax 317-572-4002. For technical support, please visit https://hub.wiley.com/community/support/dummies.

Wiley publishes in a variety of print and electronic formats and by print-on-demand. Some material included with standard print versions of this book may not be included in e-books or in print-on-demand. If this book refers to media such as a CD or DVD that is not included in the version you purchased, you may download this material at http://booksupport.wiley.com. For more information about Wiley products, visit www.wiley.com.

Library of Congress Control Number: 2016947152

ISBN: 978-1-119-31104-1

ISBN (ePDF): 978-1-119-31105-8; ISBN (ePub): 978-1-119-31106-5

Manufactured in the United States of America

10 9 8 7 6 5 4 3 2 1

Contents at a Glance

Table of Contents

Introduction

Welcome to *Windows 10 For Dummies*, the world's best-selling book about the newest — and supposedly last — Windows version, Windows 10!

This book's popularity probably boils down to this simple fact: Some people want to be Windows whizzes. They love interacting with dialog boxes. Some randomly press keys in the hope of discovering hidden, undocumented features. A few memorize long strings of computer commands while washing their hair.

And you? Well, you're no dummy, that's for sure. But when it comes to Windows and computers, the fascination just isn't there. You want to get your work done, stop, and move on to something more important. You have no intention of changing, and there's nothing wrong with that.

That's where this book comes in handy. Instead of making you a whiz at Windows, it merely dishes out chunks of useful computing information when you need them. Instead of becoming a Windows expert, you'll know just enough to get by quickly, cleanly, and with a minimum of pain so that you can move on to the more pleasant things in life.

And you'll be able to do that whether you're dealing with a touchscreen tablet, laptop, or desktop computer.

About This Book

Don't try to read this book in one sitting; there's no need. Instead, treat this book like a dictionary or an encyclopedia. Turn to the page with the information you need and say, "Ah, so that's what they're talking about." Then put down the book and move on.

Don't bother trying to memorize all the Windows jargon, such as Select the Menu Item from the Drop-Down List Box. Leave that stuff for the computer enthusiasts. In fact, if anything technical comes up in a chapter, a road sign warns you well in advance. Depending on your mood, you can either slow down to read it or speed on around it.

TIP

HOW I WROTE THIS BOOK

How did this book arrive in your hands so quickly after Microsoft released its big Summer update? No, I didn't crank it out in two weeks. While building Windows 10, Microsoft ships early releases to people who've signed up for its Windows Insider's program (https://insider.windows.com). This gives Microsoft a way to test new features before shipping them to the public. And it gives me a chance to write about features before they're released.

I spent many months poring over early releases, writing up sections of the book in advance. Then, when Microsoft released its final, approved version to the Windows Insider members, I went over every section and step-by-step instruction to make sure the book's instructions matched Microsoft's final release.

A few weeks later, when Microsoft released the final version of Windows to the public, the publisher was able to release this book, as well.

Instead of fancy computer jargon, this book covers subjects like these, all discussed in plain English:

>> Keeping your computer safe and secure

>> Making sense of the new Windows 10 Start menu

>> Finding, starting, and closing programs and apps

>> Locating the file you saved or downloaded yesterday

>> Setting up a computer or tablet for the whole family to share

>> Copying information to and from a disc or flash drive

>> Saving and sharing files from your smartphone or digital camera

>> Printing or scanning your work

>> Creating a network between two or more computers to share the Internet, files, or a printer

>> Fixing Windows when it's misbehaving

There's nothing to memorize and nothing to learn. Just turn to the right page, read the brief explanation, and get back to work. Unlike other books, this one enables you to bypass the technical hoopla and still complete your work.

How to Use This Book

Windows 10 will most definitely leave you scratching your head at some point. It's the most complicated version of Windows ever released to the public, so take pride in the fact that you're strong enough to persevere.

When something in Windows leaves you stumped, use this book as a reference. Find the troublesome topic in this book's table of contents or index. The table of contents lists chapter and section titles and page numbers. The index lists topics and page numbers. Page through the table of contents or index to the spot that deals with that particular bit of computer obscurity, read only what you have to, close the book, and apply what you've read.

If you're feeling adventurous and want to find out more, read a little further in the bulleted items below each section. You can find a few completely voluntary extra details, tips, or cross-references to check out. There's no pressure, though. You aren't forced to discover anything that you don't want to or that you simply don't have time for.

If you have to type something into the computer, you'll see easy-to-follow bold text like this:

Type **Media Player** into the Search box.

In the preceding example, you type the words *Media Player* and then press the keyboard's Enter key. Typing words into a computer can be confusing, so a description follows that explains what you should be seeing on the screen.

When I describe a key combination you should press, I describe it like this:

Press Ctrl+B.

That means to hold down your keyboard's Control key while pressing your keyboard's B key. (That's the shortcut key combination that applies bold formatting to selected text.)

Whenever I describe an email address or filename, I present it this way:

notepad.exe

And website addresses appear like this:

www.andyrathbone.com

This book doesn't wimp out by saying, "For further information, consult your manual." Windows doesn't even *come* with a manual. This book also doesn't contain information about running specific Windows software packages, such as Microsoft Office. Windows is complicated enough on its own! Luckily, other *For Dummies* books mercifully explain most popular software packages.

Don't feel abandoned, though. This book covers Windows in plenty of detail for you to get the job done. Plus, if you have questions or comments about *Windows 10 For Dummies,* feel free to drop me a line on my website at www.andyrathbone.com. I answer a reader's question on my website each week.

Finally, keep in mind that this book is a *reference.* It's not designed to teach you how to use Windows like an expert, heaven forbid. Instead, this book dishes out enough bite-sized chunks of information so that you don't *have* to learn Windows.

Touchscreen Owners Aren't Left Out

Although Windows 10 comes preinstalled on all new Windows desktop PCs and laptops, Microsoft also aims this bold new version of Windows at owners of *touchscreens.* Tablets, phones, and some laptops and desktop monitors come with screens you can control by touching them with your fingers.

If you're a new touchscreen owner, don't worry. This book explains where you need to touch, slide, or tap your fingers in all the appropriate places.

If you find yourself scratching your head over explanations aimed at mouse owners, remember these three touchscreen rules:

>> **When told to *click,* you should *tap.*** Quickly touching and releasing your finger on a button is the same as clicking it with a mouse.

>> **When told to double-click, *tap twice.*** Two touches in rapid succession does the trick.

>> **When told to *right-click* something, *hold down your finger on the item.* Then, when an icon appears, *lift your finger.*** The right-click menu appears onscreen. (That's what would have happened if you'd right-clicked the item with a mouse.) While you're looking at the pop-up menu, tap any of its listed items to have Windows carry out your bidding.

REMEMBER

If you find touchscreens to be cumbersome while you're sitting at a desk, you can always add a mouse and keyboard to your touchscreen tablet. They work just fine. In fact, a mouse and keyboard almost always work better than fingers on the Windows desktop, even in Windows 10. (They're almost mandatory on small Windows tablets.)

And What about You?

Chances are good that you already own Windows 10, or you're thinking about upgrading. You know what *you* want to do with your computer. The problem lies in making the *computer* do what you want it to do. You've gotten by one way or another, perhaps with the help of a computer guru — for instance, a friend at the office, a relative, or perhaps a neighbor's teenager.

But when your computer guru isn't around, this book can be a substitute during your times of need.

Icons Used in This Book

It just takes a glance at Windows to notice its *icons*, which are little push-button pictures for starting various programs. The icons in this book fit right in. They're even a little easier to figure out.

TECHNICAL STUFF

Watch out! This signpost warns you that pointless technical information is coming around the bend. Swerve away from this icon to stay safe from awful technical drivel.

TIP

This icon alerts you about juicy information that makes computing easier: a new method for keeping the cat from sleeping on top of your tablet, for example.

REMEMBER

Don't forget to remember these important points (or at least dog-ear the pages so that you can look them up again a few days later).

WARNING

The computer won't explode while you're performing the delicate operations associated with this icon. Still, wearing gloves and proceeding with caution is a good idea.

NEW

Are you moving to Windows 10 from an older Windows version? This icon alerts you to areas where Windows 10 behaves quite differently from its predecessors.

Beyond the Book

Like every Windows For Dummies book, this one comes with a free Cheat Sheet that brings together some of the most commonly needed information for people struggling with Windows. It describes how Microsoft changed Windows 10 one year after its release, and offers keyboard shortcuts as well as tips on using Windows 10 on a touchscreen. To get the Cheat Sheet, head for www.dummies.com and using the Search box, search for **Windows 10 For Dummies 2nd Edition Cheat Sheet**.

Where to Go from Here

Now you're ready for action. Give the pages a quick flip and scan a section or two that you know you'll need later. Please remember, this is *your* book — your weapon against the computer nerds who've inflicted this whole complicated computer concept on you. Please circle any paragraphs you find useful, highlight key concepts, add your own sticky notes, and doodle in the margins next to the complicated stuff.

REMEMBER

The more you mark up your book, the easier it will be for you to find all the good stuff again.

1

Windows 10 Stuff Everybody Thinks You Already Know

Chapter 1

What Is Windows 10?

C hances are good that you've heard about *Windows:* the boxes and windows that greet you whenever you turn on your computer. In fact, millions of people worldwide are puzzling over Windows as you read this book. Almost every new computer and laptop sold today comes with Windows preinstalled, ready to toss colorful boxes onto the screen.

This chapter helps you understand why Windows lives inside your computer, and I introduce Microsoft's latest Windows version, *Windows 10.* I explain how Windows 10 differs from previous Windows versions and help you determine whether you should upgrade your computer to Windows 10.

Finally, I explain what's new in Windows 10 and how to install this upgrade onto your Windows 7 or 8.1 computer.

What Is Windows, and Why Are You Using It?

Created and sold by a company called Microsoft, Windows isn't like your usual software that lets you calculate income taxes or send angry emails to politicians. No, Windows is an *operating system*, meaning it controls the way you work with your computer. It's been around for 30 years, and the latest incarnation is called *Windows 10*, shown in Figure 1-1.

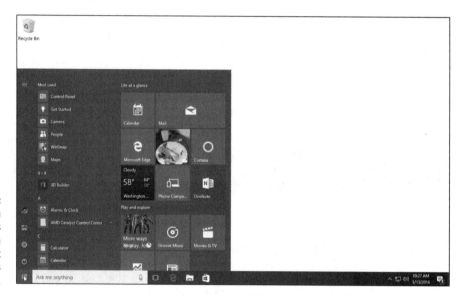

FIGURE 1-1:
Although
Windows 10 looks
different on
different PCs, it
usually looks
much like this.

The name *Windows* comes from all the little windows it places on your computer screen. Each window shows information, such as a picture, a program, or a baffling technical reprimand. You can place several windows onscreen simultaneously and jump from window to window, visiting different programs. Or, you can enlarge one window to fill the entire screen.

When you turn on your computer, Windows jumps onto the screen and begins supervising any running programs. When everything goes well, you don't really notice Windows; you simply see your programs or your work. When things don't go well, though, Windows often leaves you scratching your head over a perplexing error message.

In addition to controlling your computer and bossing around your programs, Windows comes with a bunch of free programs and *apps* — mini-programs. These programs and apps let you do different things, such as write and print letters, browse the Internet, play music, and send your friends dimly lit photos of your latest meal.

And why are you using Windows? Well, you probably didn't have much choice. Nearly every computer, laptop, or Windows tablet sold after July 2015, comes with Windows 10 preinstalled. A few people escaped Windows by buying Apple computers (those nicer-looking computers that cost a lot more). But chances are good that you, your neighbors, your boss, and millions of other people around the world are using Windows.

TIP

SEPARATING THE ADS FROM THE FEATURES

Microsoft touts Windows as a helpful companion that always keeps your best interests in mind, but that description isn't really true. Windows always keeps *Microsoft's* interests in mind. You'll find that out as soon as you call Microsoft for help with a Windows problem. Microsoft charges $100 an hour for phone support.

Microsoft also uses Windows to plug its own products and services. *Microsoft Edge,* the new Windows web browser opens with links to Microsoft's own websites, for example. The browser's Favorites area, a place for you to add *your* favorite web destinations, comes stocked with *Microsoft* websites.

Windows 10 places a link to OneDrive, its online storage service, in every folder. But Microsoft isn't as quick to mention that you must pay an annual fee when you reach your storage limit.

Ads appear on the Start menu, as well as the Windows *Lock Screen,* the screen that appears when you haven't used your PC for a while.

The Maps app uses the Microsoft Bing mapping service, rather than Google Maps or another competitor.

Microsoft also wants you to start buying *apps* rather than traditional programs. Apps are sold only through the Windows Store, and Microsoft takes a cut of each sale.

The list goes on.

Simply put, Windows not only controls your computer but also serves as a huge Microsoft advertising vehicle. Treat these built-in advertising flyers as a salesperson's knock on your door.

>> Microsoft wants Windows 10 to run on PCs, laptops, tablets, *and* phones. (It looks and behaves quite similarly on all of them.) That's why Windows 10 includes many large buttons for easier poking with fingers on touchscreens. Windows 10 can also run *apps,* small programs usually found on smartphones and tablets, in windows on a desktop PC.

>> To confuse everybody, Microsoft never released a Windows 9. Microsoft skipped a version number when moving from Windows 8.1 to Windows 10.

>> The desktop's traditional Start menu, missing from Windows 8 and 8.1, returns in Windows 10. Microsoft has tinkered with the popular menu since Windows 10's initial release, making it a little easier to understand. (I explain how to customize the new Start menu to your liking in Chapter 2.)

What's New in Windows 10?

Microsoft views Windows 10 as a one-size-fits-all computing solution that runs on laptops and desktop PCs (shown earlier in Figure 1-1) as well as phones and tablets, shown in Figure 1-2.

FIGURE 1-2:
Windows 10
behaves almost
identically on
laptops and
desktop PCs
(shown earlier),
phones (left), and
tablets (right).

Windows 10 can even run on your TV through Microsoft's Xbox One game console. Windows 10 behaves almost identically on every device, and it brings a huge bonus: Apps known as *universal apps* will run on a Windows 10 phone, tablet, PC, laptop, and Xbox One.

NEW

Besides aiming to run on everything but clock radios, Windows 10 brings these changes to your computer:

» **Start button and menu:** Removed from Windows 8 and half-heartedly tacked back onto Windows 8.1, the Start button and Start menu triumphantly return to the desktop in Windows 10. The revamped Start menu sports a column of icons, as well as fingertip-sized tiles for launching apps. (Tile haters find instructions for removing them in Chapter 2.)

» **Apps on the desktop:** *Apps,* which are small programs from the world of phones and tablets, consumed the full screen in Windows 8 and 8.1. Windows 10 now lets you choose whether to run apps full screen or within desktop windows.

» **Continuum:** This buzzword simply means that Windows 10 senses how you're using a device and behaves accordingly. When Windows 10 runs on a tablet, for example, Continuum enlarges the Start menu and apps to fill the screen with larger buttons, sized appropriately for fingertips to tap. But when you attach a mouse or keyboard to your tablet, your tablet switches away from Tablet mode; the Start menu retreats to a small corner of your screen, and apps begin to run in desktop windows. Continuum lets your tablet switch quickly into a desktop PC and then back to a tablet when needed.

» **Cortana:** The digital assistant in Windows 10, Cortana, helps you manage your computing by fetching lost files, stocking your calendar with appointments, grabbing up-to-date traffic information about your commute, and extracting informational tidbits from the Internet. Controlled through either your voice or keyboard, Cortana works from the Search box adjacent to the Start button.

» **OneDrive:** Formerly called *SkyDrive,* Microsoft's online file storage service comes built into the Windows 10 desktop. However, OneDrive no longer stores your files on both your PC *and* the Internet (sometimes called the "cloud"). Instead, OneDrive asks you to choose which files and folders should live *only* on the cloud and which should live on both the cloud *and* your computer.

» **More Apps:** The Windows Store offers more than 700,000 apps. That's nowhere near the number of apps found for the iPhone, iPad, or Android phones and tablets, but you can find plenty of big names like Facebook and Netflix, with more on the way.

» **Multiple desktops:** Windows 10 lets you create extra desktops, and you can switch between them with a click or tap. You can set up one desktop for work and another for gaming, for example. (Or, you can completely ignore the feature.)

>> **Windows Hello:** This welcome security update allows you to sign into your computer without typing in a password. With the right fingerprint reader or camera, your computer can recognize either your face, fingerprint, or iris and automatically let you in. You can even access supported websites without having to type in your username and password.

>> **Windows Ink:** This big update lets you write on your tablet's screen with a special pen, letting you add handwritten notes and drawings to apps like Maps, the Microsoft Edge browser, and Office.

>> **Windows 10 is now a service:** Perhaps most important, Microsoft treats Windows 10 as a constantly changing *service* rather than a finished product. Microsoft plans to keep adding new apps, features, and updates to Windows 10 for as long as you own the device.

Unlike Windows 8 and 8.1, Windows 10 no longer feels like two operating systems crammed into one computer. It feels like a single operating system that brings out the best in both tablets and desktop PCs.

TIP

For its first year of release, Windows 10 was a free upgrade for people owning fully patched Windows 7 or 8.1 computers. The upgrade is no longer free, but it still keeps all of your files, apps, and programs in place. Owners of older PCs can also upgrade to Windows 10, but the upgrade will wipe out all of your files and programs. You'll need to reinstall everything from a backup. (If your old computer is a slow crawler, it will *still* be a slow crawler after upgrading to Windows 10. You're probably better off buying a new PC with Windows 10 preinstalled.)

TECHNICAL
STUFF

Windows no longer comes in a Windows RT version. If you bought a Windows RT tablet, such as the Surface RT or Surface 2, you can't upgrade it to Windows 10.

Should I Bother Upgrading to Windows 10?

If you're happy with your current version of Windows, don't bother upgrading to Windows 10. Most people stick with the Windows version that came preinstalled on their computers. That way they avoid the chore of figuring out a new version. Windows 10 comes with a steep learning curve because it's quite different from earlier Windows versions.

Also, many of the biggest changes in Windows 10 work best with *touchscreens* — those fingertip-controlled screens found on expensive cellphones, tablets, and some of the latest laptops and desktop monitors. Most desktop PC owners don't need that feature.

TIP

HISTORY FOR WINDOWS 7 UPGRADERS

Windows 7 diehards missed a lot of hubbub by skipping Windows 8 and 8.1. Those two poorly received Windows versions affected Windows 10 quite a bit, so here's a wee bit of history so you'll understand Windows 10 a little better.

For years, Microsoft had watched helplessly as hordes of people bought iPhones, iPads, and *apps* — small and simple programs for lightweight touchscreen tasks. To compete, Microsoft designed Windows 8 for touchscreen tablets and unleashed it in 2012. Like the competition, Windows 8 opened to a screen full of touchable colorful tiles, each representing an app.

Even the desktop was relegated to an app, a tiny tile on the screen. But when opened, the Desktop app lacked its Start button and menu. Microsoft expected people to return to the tile-filled opening screen to launch their desktop programs.

Most desktop owners hated Windows 8. And because very few people bought Windows 8 tablets, Windows 8 bombed in the marketplace. Windows 8.1 made a few amends, but not enough.

With Windows 10, Microsoft aims to placate desktop lovers by bringing back a more traditional Start button and Start menu. To please tablet owners, the Start menu can fill the screen on command, making it easier to control with fingertips.

Best of all, Windows 10 is smart enough to change shape depending on what device it's installed on. On a tablet, Windows 10 presents the tile-filled, full-screen Start menu, which subtly changes its spacing to accommodate finger taps. On desktop PCs, Windows 10 shows the traditional desktop, Start menu, and Start button. And the menus remain small, which works well for the pinpoint clicks of a mouse.

With Windows 10, Microsoft hopes Windows will finally serve the needs of both desktop traditionalists *and* tablet owners.

Instead of upgrading, stick with the masses and stay with your current Windows version. When you're ready to buy a new computer, Windows 10 will be installed and waiting for you.

But if you're running Windows 8.1, and you're unhappy with it, you may enjoy upgrading to Windows 10. The update smooths over many of the rough edges of those Windows versions, especially on desktop PCs and tablets that convert into PCs.

If you're one of the few people with a Windows cell phone, then move to Windows 10. The two work together quite smoothly.

After Windows 7, Microsoft ended its support for *Windows XP mode,* a popular way to run a Windows XP desktop within Windows 7. If you rely on Windows XP mode in Windows 7, stick with Windows 7. The same holds true for *Windows Media Center,* a popular way to record TV shows and watch DVDs. If you rely on either of those two programs, don't upgrade to Windows 10.

What's So Different About Windows 10?

Today, computing falls into two camps: creating and consuming. People turn to their desktop PC for *creating* things. They write papers, send email, prepare tax returns, update blogs, edit videos, or, quite often, tap whichever keys their boss requires that day.

But when *consuming,* people often walk away from their desktop PCs. They pull out their smartphone or tablet to read email, watch videos, listen to music, and browse the web.

That split creates a problem. Desktop PCs, phones, and tablets all work differently; each offers different screen sizes, programs, and commands. What works well with fingers doesn't always work well with a mouse and keyboard. Sharing files among gadgets can be a nightmare.

Windows 10 aims to fix those problems by creating one operating system that works well on *everything,* letting both consumers and creators work on a single device. To do that, Windows 10 includes two different modes:

» **Tablet mode:** For on-the-go information grabbers with touchscreen tablets, the Windows 10 Start menu fills the entire screen with large, colorful tiles that constantly update to show the latest stock prices, weather, email, Facebook updates, and other tidbits. Shown earlier in Figure 1-2, that information appears before you touch a button. And *touch* is a keyword: The full-screen Start menu works best with a touchscreen monitor or tablet.

» **Desktop mode:** When it's time for work, the traditional Windows desktop brings all its power — as well as its more powerful and detailed menus.

Some people like the convenience of having both types of computers built into one: a touchscreen laptop, for example, or a tablet with a docking station that lets you plug in a mouse and keyboard. Others find the two experiences to be oddly disjointed.

>> If you can stomach the initial confusion, Windows 10 may offer you the best of both worlds: You can stay on the full-screen Start menu for quick, on-the-go browsing. And when work beckons, you can head for the desktop, where your traditional Windows programs await.

>> If you're sitting at a desktop PC, Windows 10 should automatically open to the desktop. Windows 10 tablets usually open to a full-screen Start menu.

>> If Windows 10 doesn't open to the mode you prefer, click the Action Center icon (shown in the margin) found on the taskbar at the bottom of the screen; when the Action Center pane appears, click the Tablet mode toggle button. Your Start menu should quickly return to its proper size.

TECHNICAL
STUFF

>> Microsoft's game console, the Xbox One, runs in Tablet mode. The Xbox One's game controller serves as your finger, letting you move from tile to tile by pressing the controller's arrow keys. (If you've attached a Kinect controller, you can control the Xbox One with your hands, as well.)

>> I explain the new Windows 10 Start menu in Chapter 2; the Windows desktop awaits your attention in Chapter 3.

Why Does Windows 10 Keep Changing?

Microsoft calls Windows 10 a *service* rather than an operating system. Like any other service, it's subject to changes. Every month or two, Microsoft changes Windows 10 slightly. Some of Microsoft's changes occur more quickly: Your apps, for example, can update weekly. Some update daily.

Other changes arrive packed into large groups. For example, Microsoft released a large update in November 2015, that changed Windows 10 in a variety of ways. An update in mid 2016 called the *Anniversary Update* changed Windows yet again. (This edition of the book includes all of those updates.)

You may not notice any changes made by the updates. Indeed, most of them just fix hundreds of annoying bugs, making Windows 10 run and install more smoothly.

But if you're curious, here are some visible ways that Microsoft has changed Windows 10 since its release in late July 2015:

» Microsoft's Edge browser now remembers your Favorites, Reading list items, and settings. It stores them with your Microsoft account, along with your other settings. When you sign into another Windows PC, tablet, or phone, Edge will behave just like it did on your old PC.

» Before the update, Windows 10 painted white across every window's title bar. That sea of white title bars made it difficult to find your active window at a glance. Now you can splash an accent color on the title bars by clicking the Start menu, choosing Settings, and clicking Personalization. In the Colors section, click the toggle called Show Color on Start Taskbar, Action Center and Title Bar.

» You can install apps to a memory card, a boon for owners of small tablets with limited memory.

» Windows 10 includes several new apps: Messaging, Phone, and Skype Video. Each one includes access to Skype, a system that lets you make voice and video calls over the Internet.

» Once limited to Microsoft account holders, Cortana now works with local accounts, as well. While reading your mail, Cortana can remind you of upcoming movies and shows, even offering to book you a ride to the event. Cortana also lets you search within PDF files, too, letting you highlight words or phrases, right-clicking and choosing Ask Cortana for more information.

Microsoft sends these updates automatically to your computer through Windows Update; you don't need to jump through hoops to find and install them.

Your apps update themselves automatically through the Windows Store. That's why the Music app automatically changed its name to the Groove Music app, for example. The Photos app suddenly added a way to search your photos by folder.

So, when something suddenly changes with Windows 10, don't think it's your fault. Microsoft constantly changes Windows 10, and Windows will keep changing for years to come.

Can My Current PC Still Run Windows 10?

If you want to upgrade to Windows 10, your computer probably won't complain. Windows 10 should run without problem on any PC currently running Windows 7, 8, or 8.1.

If your PC runs Windows Vista or Windows XP, it may still run Windows 10, but not very well. I don't recommend it.

If you have a technogeek in your family, have him or her translate Table 1-1, which shows the Windows 10 hardware requirements you can find written in the fine-print for new computers.

In common language, Table 1-1 simply says that nearly any computer sold in the past five years can be upgraded to Windows 10 with little problem.

TABLE 1-1

The Windows 10 Hardware Requirements

Architecture	x86 (32-bit)	x86 (64-bit)
Processor	1 GHz or faster	
Memory (RAM)	At least 1GB	At least 2GB
Graphics Card	DirectX 9 graphics device with Windows Display Driver Model (WDDM) driver	
HDD free space	At least 16GB	At least 20GB
Firmware	Unified Extensible Firmware Interface (UEFI) 2.3.1 with secure boot enabled	

Windows 10 runs nearly any program that runs on Windows Vista, Windows 7, Windows 8, and Windows 8.1. It even runs some Windows XP programs as well. Some older programs, however, won't work, including older games and most security-based programs, such as antivirus, firewall, and security suites. You'll need to contact the program's manufacturer for an upgraded version.

Don't know what version of Windows runs on your current PC? If clicking the Start button brings a Start menu, right-click the menu's Computer entry, and choose Properties. The screen that appears lists your Windows version.

If there's no Start button, you're running Windows 8. And if clicking your Start button fills the screen with a bunch of colorful tiles, you're running Windows 8.1.

The Different Flavors of Windows 10

Microsoft offers several different versions of Windows 10, but you'll probably want only one: the aptly titled "Home" version.

Small businesses will choose Windows 10 Pro, and larger businesses will want Windows 10 Enterprise.

Here are some guidelines for choosing the version you need:

>> If you'll be using your PC at home or small business, pick up **Windows Home.**

>> If you need to connect to a domain through a work network — and you'll know if you're doing it — you want **Windows Pro.**

>> If you're a computer tech who works for businesses, go ahead and argue with your boss over whether you need **Windows Pro** or **Windows Enterprise.** The boss will make the decision based on whether it's a small company (Windows Pro) or a large company (Windows Enterprise).

For more details about upgrading to Windows 10, visit Microsoft's Windows website at www.windows.com.

Chapter 2

Starting with the Start Menu

First, the big news: Windows 10 brings back the Start menu! Now the bad news: The new Start menu doesn't look much like the Start menu in your earlier version of Windows. In fact, it doesn't even look like Windows 10's original Start menu from last year.

The basic mechanics remain the same, though. Click the Start button in the screen's bottom-left corner, and the Start menu rises, listing the apps and programs installed on your PC. Click an app or program, and it leaps to the screen, ready for action.

In this chapter, I explain how to figure out this odd, shape-shifting Start menu. On touchscreen tablets, the Start menu fills the entire screen. Its large tiles make them easy to tap with your fingertips. On a desktop computer, however, the Start menu retreats to a corner of the screen, where you can click its tiny buttons and menus with your mouse pointer.

Whether you're using a tablet or desktop PC, this chapter shows how to make the Start menu do its main job: launch your apps and programs.

TIP

If you're using a touchscreen computer, substitute the word *tap* when you read the word *click*. Tapping twice works like *double-clicking*. And when you see the term *right-click*, touch and hold your finger on the glass; lift your finger when the right-click menu appears.

Being Welcomed to the World of Windows

Starting Windows is as easy as turning on your computer — Windows leaps onto the screen automatically with a flourish. But before you can begin working, Windows stops you cold: It displays a locked screen, shown in Figure 2-1, with no entrance key dangling nearby.

FIGURE 2-1:
To move past this lock screen, press a key on the keyboard or drag up on the screen with your mouse or finger.

Introduced back in Windows 8, the lock screen appears before you can sign into your computer with your account name and password.

How do you unlock the lock screen? The answer depends on whether you're using a mouse, keyboard, or touchscreen:

>> **Mouse:** On a desktop PC or laptop, click any mouse button.

>> **Keyboard:** Press any key, and the lock screen slides away. Easy!

>> **Touch:** Touch the screen with your finger and then slide your finger *up* the glass. A quick flick of the finger will do.

When you're in the door, Windows wants you to *sign in*, as shown in Figure 2-2, by clicking your name and typing in a password.

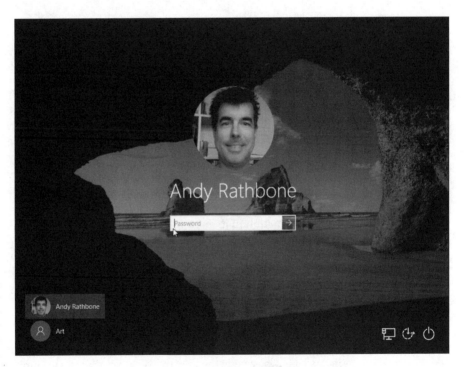

FIGURE 2-2:
Click your user account name and then type your password on the next screen.

I've customized my lock screen and Sign In screen. Yours will look different. When facing the Sign In screen, you have several options:

>> **If you see your name or email address listed, type your password.**
Windows lets you in and displays your Start menu, just as you last left it.

>> **If you don't see your name, but you have an account on the computer, look in the screen's bottom-left corner.** There, Windows displays a list of all the account holders. You may see the computer owner's name.

>> **If you bought a new computer, use the account you created when turning on your computer for the first time**. As part of its setup process, Windows guides you through creating an account on your computer.

>> **No account?** Then find out who owns the computer and beg that person to set up an account for you.

If you need more information about user accounts, including creating new ones and managing old ones, flip ahead to Chapter 14.

Don't *want* to sign in at the Sign In screen? Two of the screen's bottom-corner buttons offer these other options:

>> **The little wheelchair-shaped button,** shown in Figure 2-2 and the margin, customizes Windows for people with physical challenges in hearing, sight, or manual dexterity, all covered in Chapter 12. If you choose this button by mistake, click or touch on a different part of the screen to avoid changing any settings.

>> **The little round button,** shown in Figure 2-2 and the margin, lets you shut down or restart your PC, as well as put it to sleep — a power-saving state that quickly awakes. (If you've accidentally clicked the button and shut down your PC, don't panic. Press the power button on your PC's case, and your PC returns to this screen.)

Even while locked, as shown earlier in Figure 2-1, your computer's screen displays current information in its bottom-left corner. Depending on how your PC is configured, you can see the time and date; your wireless Internet signal strength (the more radio waves in the icon, the better your connection); battery strength (the more colorful the icon, the better); your next scheduled appointment; a count of unread email; and other items.

Understanding user accounts

Windows allows several people to work on the same computer, yet it keeps everybody's work separate. To do that, it needs to know who's currently sitting in front of the keyboard. When you *sign in* — introduce yourself — by clicking your username and typing your password, as shown in Figure 2-2, the Windows Start menu and desktop appear as you just left them, ready for you to make your own personalized mess.

When you're through working or just feel like taking a break, sign out (explained at this chapter's end) so that somebody else can use the computer. Later, when you sign back in, your own files will be waiting for you.

Although you may turn your work area into a mess, it's your own mess. When you return to the computer, your letters will be just as you saved them. Jerry hasn't accidentally deleted your files or folders while playing *Words with Friends.* Tina's Start menu still contains links to her favorite scrapbooking websites. And nobody will be able to read your email.

Until you customize your username picture, you'll be a silhouette, like the account listed in the bottom-left corner of Figure 2-2. To add a photo to your user account, click the Expand icon (shown in the margin) in the Start menu's upper-left corner. Then click your username in the column that appears, and choose Change Account Settings from the pop-up menu. When the Settings menu's Your Info section appears, click the Camera icon to take a quick shot with your computer's built-in camera. Still wearing your pajamas? Then choose the Browse For One link to choose a photo already stored in your Pictures folder

Keeping your account private with a password

Because Windows lets many people use the same computer, how do you stop Diane from reading Rob's love letters to Miley Cyrus? How can Grace keep Josh from deleting her *Star Wars* movie trailers? Using a *password* solves some of those problems.

In fact, a password is more important than ever in Windows 10 because some accounts can be tied to a credit card. By typing a secret password when signing in, you enable your computer to recognize *you* and nobody else. If you protect your username with a password, nobody can access your files. And nobody can rack up charges for computer games while you're away from home.

Also, if your computer is ever stolen, a password keeps the thieves from logging onto your account and connecting to any websites with your account.

To set up or change the password on your account, follow these steps:

1. **Click the Start button and then click the Settings icon.**

When the Start menu appears, click the Settings icon near the menu's bottom-left corner. (It's the little gear directly above the Power icon.) The Settings app appears.

2. **Click the Accounts icon (shown in the margin). When the Accounts pane appears, click the words Sign-in Options along the pane's left edge.**

Options for signing into your computer appear on the right.

3. **From the Password section on the app's right side, click the Change button, shown in Figure 2-3. Don't have a password? Click the Add button instead.**

You may need to type your existing password to gain entrance.

FIGURE 2-3:
Click the
Password
section's Change
button.

4. **Type a password that will be easy to remember.**

TIP

Choose something like the name of your favorite vegetable, for example, or your dental floss brand. To beef up its security level, capitalize some letters and embed a number or two in the password, like **TurnipsR4Me** or **Floss2BKleen**. (Don't use these exact two examples, though, because they've probably been added to every password cracker's arsenal by now.)

5. **If asked, type that same password into the Retype Password text box so Windows knows you're spelling it correctly.**

6. **In the Password Hint box, type a hint that reminds you — and only you — of your password.**

Windows won't let you type in your exact password as a hint. You have to be a bit more creative.

7. **Click the Next button and click Finish.**

Do you suspect you've botched something during this process? Click Cancel to return to Step 3 and either start over or exit.

After you've created the password, Windows begins asking for your password whenever you sign in.

>> Passwords are case-sensitive. The words Caviar and caviar are considered two different passwords.

>> Afraid that you'll forget your password someday? Protect yourself now: Flip ahead to Chapter 14, where I describe how to make a Password Reset Disk, which is a special way of resetting forgotten passwords for local accounts. (You can reset a lost Microsoft account password online at http://live.com.)

REMEMBER

>> When you change your Microsoft account password on your PC, you also change it on your Windows phone, your Xbox, and every other device where you sign in with a Microsoft account. (I cover Microsoft accounts in this chapter's next section.)

>> Windows also allows you to create a picture password in Step 4, where you drag a finger or mouse over a photo in a certain sequence. Then, instead of entering a password, you redraw that sequence on the sign-in picture. (Picture passwords work much better on touchscreen tablets than desktop monitors.)

>> Another option in Step 4 is Create a PIN. A *PIN* is a four-or-more character code like the ones you punch into Automated Teller Machines (ATMs). The disadvantage of a PIN? There's no password hint. Unlike Microsoft accounts, your PIN only works on the computer where it was created.

NEW

>> Tired of constantly entering your password? Connect a Windows 10 compatible fingerprint reader or camera to your PC. (Some laptops, tablets, and keyboards have them built in.) Your computer quickly lets you in after you either scan your fingertip or gaze into your PC's camera. I describe how to sign in with Windows Hello in Chapter 14.

>> Forgotten your password *already?* When you type a password that doesn't work, Windows automatically displays your hint (if you created one) which should help to remind you of your password. Careful, though — anybody can read your hint, so make sure that it's something that makes sense only to you. As a last resort, insert your Password Reset Disk, a job I cover in Chapter 14.

I explain lots more about user accounts in Chapter 14.

Signing up for a Microsoft account

Whether you're signing in to Windows for the first time, trying to access some apps, or just trying to change a setting, you'll eventually see a screen similar to the one in Figure 2-4.

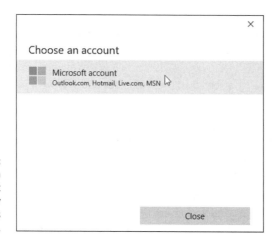

FIGURE 2-4:
You need a
Microsoft account
to access many
Windows
features.

You can sign in to your computer with either a *Microsoft* account or a *Local* account. Although a Microsoft account makes Windows much easier to work with, each type of account serves different needs:

>> **Local account:** This account works fine for people using traditional Windows programs on the Windows desktop. However, Local account holders can't store files on OneDrive. They can't download apps from the Windows Store, either.

>> **Microsoft account:** Required to access many of Microsoft's services, this consists of simply an email address and a password. Microsoft account holders can store files on the Internet with OneDrive, download apps from the Windows Store, and monitor their children's online activities.

You can sign in with a Microsoft account in one of two ways, ranked according to simplicity:

>> **Use an existing Microsoft account.** If you already have an account with Hotmail, MSN, Xbox Live, Outlook.com, or Windows Messenger, you already have a Microsoft account and password. Type in that email address and password at the screen shown in Figure 2-4, and then click the Sign In button.

>> **Sign up for a new Microsoft account.** Click the words Microsoft Account, shown in Figure 2-4. Click the Create One! link, and Microsoft takes you to a website where you can create your own Microsoft account. You can use any email address for a Microsoft account. You simply enter that email address, create a new password to go with it, and wham: You've created a Microsoft account.

If you're signing into Windows on a newly purchased computer for the first time and don't want a Microsoft account, click the words Skip This Step near a screen's bottom, left corner. On the next screen, Windows 10 walks you through creating a Local account, which is limited to your own computer.

But until you sign in with a Microsoft account, the nag screen in Figure 2-4 will haunt you whenever you try to access a Windows feature that requires a Microsoft account. (I explain how to convert a Local account into a Microsoft account in Chapter 14.)

TIP

When you first sign into your new account, Windows may ask whether you want to find other PCs, devices, and content on your network. If you're using a home or work network, click the Yes button. (That lets you print to network printers, as well as share files with other networked computers.) If you're connecting to a *public* network, perhaps at a hotel, coffee shop, or airport, click the No button.

Figuring Out the New Windows 10 Start Menu

In Windows, everything starts with the Start button and its Start menu. Whether you're ready to blow up spaceships, do your taxes, or read the news, you start by clicking the Start button in the screen's bottom-left corner: The Start menu leaps up with a list of your apps and programs.

In theory, you spot the name or tile for your desired app or program and click it; the app launches, and you're off to work. In reality, it's a little more confusing.

On a desktop PC, for example, the Start menu's right edge is filled with a row of tiles, shown in Figure 2-5. Each tile represents an *app* (a small program designed mainly for touchscreens). On the left edge, the menu lists your most recently accessed apps and programs, as well as frequently accessed places on your PC.

NEW

Recently updated in Windows 10, the desktop PC's Start menu now sports a strip of five unlabeled icons along its left edge:

>> **Expand:** A click on this icon reveals the labels of the mysterious icons I'm describing now.

>> **User Account:** This icon looks like your user account picture. Click it to change your account's settings to lock your PC to prevent access while you leave your desk, or to sign out of your account.

Your user account

Your most-used apps

Show titles of icons below   Customizable list of favored apps and programs

FIGURE 2-5:
A desktop PC's
Start menu stays
in the screen's
bottom-left
corner.

Start button

Power

Settings

File Explorer

>> **File Explorer:** A quick click on this folder icon jumps to the desktop and opens File Explorer for you to browser your files.

>> **Settings:** Clicking this little gear icon takes you quickly to the Settings app (formerly known as the PC Settings app) for changing how your PC behaves.

>> **Power:** When you're through working, click this to put your computer to sleep, shut it down, or restart it (handy when it's misbehaving).

The Start menu changes drastically when switched to Tablet mode, commonly used on tablet PCs. The Start menu's tiles fill the entire screen, shown in Figure 2-6. The menu also hides the left pane shown earlier in Figure 2-5.

View alphabetical list of apps

Return to Tablet mode Start menu

Show left panel's icon labels

FIGURE 2-6:
A tablet's Start menu fills the entire screen with easy-to-touch buttons.

>> **Expand:** Just as when in desktop mode, a click on this icon reveals labels for other icons along the screen's left edge.

>> **Pinned Tiles:** The default option, this displays the Start menu's tiles across the entire screen.

>> **All Apps:** Can't find a favorite app? Click this to see an alphabetical list of all of your installed apps and programs.

Despite the Start menu's latest remodel, it still offers a way to start programs; adjust Windows settings; find help for sticky situations; or, thankfully, shut down Windows and get away from the computer for a while.

TIP

The tiles along the Start menu's right edge may be new, but they're not mere visual baggage. For example, the Calendar tile constantly updates to show the current date and day, as well as your next appointment. The Mail tile cycles through the first words of your latest emails.

Your Start menu will change as you add more programs and apps to your computer. That's why the Start menu on your friend's computer, as well as in this book, is probably arranged differently than your computer's Start menu. And if the tiles don't meet your needs, you can remove them completely, as I describe later in this chapter.

WHERE'S THE CHARMS BAR?

Windows 8 and Windows 8.1 sported a hidden menu called a *Charms bar* that popped into view alongside the screen's right edge. The Charms bar offered handy menus for sharing what you're seeing, adding a new device, searching for something, or changing your currently viewed app's settings.

Windows 10 removed the Charms bar. But because some older apps still rely on it, the Charms bar's commands are still available by tapping the *App menu*, which you can access by clicking those three little lines or dots in an older app's upper corner. (If the app fills the screen, right-click inside it or slide your finger down from the screen's top edge to reveal the App menu.) With a touch of that little three-lined icon, the App menu drops down to offer Windows 8-era options like these, including some former Charms bar options:

- **App Commands:** Tap this to fetch the app's menu bar, which lists options for controlling your app.

- **Search:** This brings up the app's Search box. Type your search term in the box, and Windows searches for it, displaying the results.

- **Share:** This fetches options for sharing what's currently on your screen. (Not all apps support this feature, however.)

- **Print:** Choose this to send your current screen's information to your printer, which I cover in Chapter 8.

- **Settings:** Unlike the Charms bar's Settings icon, which controlled your entire computer's settings, this area brings up settings for your currently open app. (To change your PC's settings, click the Start button and then choose Settings.)

Try the following tricks to make the Start menu feel a little more like home:

>> To launch a program or app, click or tap its name or tile. The program leaps to the screen.

>> Keyboard fans can fetch the Start menu by pressing the ⊞ key on their keyboard.

>> Were you unable to spot your desired program or app listed on the Start menu? Then scroll down the list of alphabetically sorted apps. (I describe how to scroll down lists in Chapter 4.)

>> On a touchscreen, navigate the Start menu with your finger: Pretend the Start menu is a piece of paper lying on a table. As you move your finger, the Start menu's items move along with it.

 >> If the Start menu fills the entire screen on your desktop, you're in Tablet mode. To turn off Tablet mode, click the Action Center icon in the screen's bottom-right corner (shown in the margin). When the Action Center pane appears, click the Tablet mode tile in the pane's bottom-left corner. The Start menu will retreat to its normal corner.

Toggling Between Tablet and Desktop Mode

Much of the confusion around Windows 10 centers on one thing: Tablet mode. With Tablet mode turned on, Windows 10 works great on touchscreen tablets. The buttons and menus are bigger, making them easier to control with fingers.

But when a desktop PC runs in tablet mode, confusion reigns. Desktop owners who face Tablet mode on their screens will see these anomalies:

>> **Start button failure.** Pressing the Start button won't fetch the familiar Start menu. Pressing the Start button won't seem to do anything, in fact. That's because Tablet mode stretches the Start menu across the entire screen, where it looks and behaves quite differently than the desktop's corner-bound Start menu.

>> **Everything runs fullscreen.** Apps and programs will run, but they consume the entire screen. You never see the traditional desktop, either, because an app or program always runs fullscreen on top of it.

>> **The Restore button doesn't work.** Desktop programs still include their Minimize, Restore, and Close buttons in their top, right corner. But clicking the Restore button doesn't restore the fullscreen program to a window. The Restore button no longer works because Tablet mode forces app and program to remain fullscreen.

>> **Missing app list:** In Tablet mode, the Start menu lacks the alphabetically sorted list of tiles along the left edge.

For many people, the Tablet mode screen just doesn't look right. And unless you know how to turn off Tablet mode, you'll feel like nothing matches what you're expecting — or what you're seeing in this book.

To turn off Tablet mode and return to the regular desktop Start menu, follow these steps:

1. **Click or tap the Action Center icon (shown in the margin) near the taskbar's right end.**

   The Action Center lists *notifications* — bits of information you should take action on, like newly received emails and news tidbits. When you receive a new notification, the Action Center's icon fills with lines.

2. **When the Action Center pane appears along the screen's right edge, click or tap the Tablet mode icon.**

   Your computer will toggle Tablet mode on or off with each press.

Press it a few times so you can get the feel for the two types of Start menu in Windows 10. Then you'll know what to do when you're facing the menu you don't want.

Launching a Start menu program or app

Windows stocks your Start menu's right edge with *apps,* which are small programs for performing simple tasks. In fact, Windows now refers to *all* Windows programs as apps. To see all the apps and programs installed on your PC, click the Start button in the screen's bottom-left corner. An alphabetical list of every installed program and app appears. (If your computer is in Tablet mode, you also need to tap the All Apps icon shown in the margin.)

Each name or tile on the Start menu is a button for starting an app or a traditional Windows program. Of course, Windows complicates things by offering several ways to launch an app or a program:

>> **Mouse:** Point at the tile and click the left mouse button.

>> **Keyboard:** Press the arrow keys until a box surrounds the desired tile. Then press the Enter key.

>> **Touchscreen:** Tap the tile with your finger.

No matter which app you've chosen, it jumps onto the screen, ready to inform you, entertain you, or, if you're lucky, do both.

I explain the Start menu's built-in apps later in this chapter. If you feel like digging in, you can begin downloading and installing your own by clicking the Start menu's Store tile. (I explain how to download apps in Chapter 6.)

WHAT'S AN APP?

Short for *application*, apps herald from the world of *smartphones*, which is what people call cellphones that are powerful enough to run small programs. The new-fangled Windows apps differ from traditional Windows programs in several ways:

- Unless preinstalled on your computer, Windows apps come from one place: the Windows Store. The Store app, one of several apps preinstalled on Windows, lets you download more apps. Once downloaded, the apps automatically install themselves on your computer. Lots of apps are free, but others cost money.

- Only Windows apps can run on Windows. Apps found on iPhones, iPads, and Android phones and tablets won't run on your Windows computer. Even if you've already bought a favorite Android or iPhone app, you have to pay again to buy that app's Windows version.

- On the positive side, Windows 10 apps will run on your Windows 10 PC, laptop, and tablet. If they're universal Windows apps, they'll also run on your Windows 10 phone and Xbox One video game console.

- Most apps perform small tasks, usually in a way that works well on touchscreens. Some apps make it easier to visit websites such as Facebook. Others let you play games, listen to Internet radio, track your car's mileage, or find nearby restaurants that are still open.

- Although most apps are fairly simple to use, simplicity brings limitations. Unlike desktop programs, many apps don't let you copy words, photos, files, or web links. There's often no way to share an app's contents with a friend.

In an effort to sound young and hip, Windows now refers to traditional desktop programs as *apps*. Don't be surprised to hear most people still use the term *program* to describe older software designed for the Windows desktop, such as Photoshop or TurboTax.

Finding something on the Start menu

You can scour the Start menu until your eagle eyes spot the program or tile you need, and then you can pounce on it with a quick mouse click or finger tap. But when the thrill of the hunt wanes, Windows offers several shortcuts for finding apps and programs hidden inside a crowded Start menu.

In particular, look for these Start menu sections:

>> **Recently Added:** When you view your list of alphabetically sorted apps, the Start menu automatically stocks the list's top edge with recently installed apps or programs. (This area eventually disappears until you add more apps from the Windows Store.)

>> **Most Used:** Your most frequently visited apps and programs appear hear. Look here first to find your favorite computing destinations.

>> **All Apps:** In desktop mode, the Start menu *always* displays a list of alphabetically sorted apps. Tablet mode viewers must first click the All Apps icon (shown in the margin) to see an alphabetical list of *all* of their installed apps and programs.

TIP

Chances are good that you'll spot your desired item on the Start menu without much digging. But when an app or programs proves to be particularly elusive, try these tricks:

>> After opening the Start menu, keyboard owners can simply begin typing the name of their desired app or program, like this: **facebook.** As you type, Windows lists all the apps matching what you've typed so far, eventually narrowing down the search to the runaway.

>> Don't spot your desired app listed as a Start menu tile along the right edge? That right column is scrollable with an upward flick of your finger. Or, point your mouse at the column, and flick the mouse's scroll wheel that lives between the mouse's two buttons. No scroll wheel? Then drag down the scroll bar along the right edge of the Start menu's column of tiles. Either way, more tiles — if there are any — will scroll into view.

>> If the tiles you see don't reflect the way you work, it's time to customize the Start menu to meet your needs. Head for this chapter's later "Customizing the Start menu" section for a heads up.

Viewing or closing your open apps

On a desktop PC, it's fairly easy to move from one app to another. Because they're all in windows on your desktop, you just click the app you want: It pops to the forefront, ready for work. (For more detail about the desktop, flip ahead to Chapter 3.)

On a tablet, apps and programs hog the entire screen when running, making it difficult to switch between them.

Whether you're running Windows on a PC, laptop, or tablet, you can bring any missing app to the forefront by following these two quick steps:

1. **Click or tap the Task View button.**

   The screen clears, and Windows displays miniature views of your open apps and programs, shown in Figure 2-7.

2. **Tap or click any thumbnail to return the app or program to full size.**

FIGURE 2-7:
Click the Task
View button to
see thumbnail
views of each of
your currently
running apps and
programs.

TIP

These three tips can help you keep track of your running apps as well as close down the ones you no longer want open:

>> Currently running apps and programs also appear as icons on the *taskbar,* the narrow strip along the bottom of the screen. (I cover the taskbar in Chapter 3.)

>> To close an unwanted app shown in thumbnail view, click or tap the X in its upper right corner (shown in the margin). With a mouse, you can also right-click the app's thumbnail, and choose Close from the pop-up menu.

>> After·you close an app, the miniature views of the other running apps remain onscreen, letting you either switch to them or close them. Or, to leave the Task View mode, click or tap the desktop.

Getting to know your free apps

The Windows Start menu comes stocked with several free apps, each living on its own square or rectangular tile. Every tile is labeled, helping you know what's what.

The tiles for some apps, known as *live tiles,* change constantly. The Money app tile, for example, constantly updates with the stock market's latest swings, and the Weather tile always tells you what to expect when you walk outdoors.

Here are Windows 10's most popular apps, ready to be launched at the click of a mouse or touch of a finger:

- » **Alarms & Clock:** This offers a world clock, timer, and stopwatch, but you'll probably visit for the alarm clock. It lets you set different wakeup times for every day of the week.

- » **Calculator:** With a toggle between standard, scientific, and converter modes, this app will please grade schoolers, math majors, chefs, and physicists.

- » **Calendar:** This app lets you add your appointments or grab them automatically from any calendars you've already created through your online accounts.

- » **Camera:** Covered in Chapter 17, the Camera app lets you snap photos with your computer's built-in camera or webcam.

- » **Contact Support:** Click here to begin your journey through Microsoft's official technical support channels.

- » **Cortana:** This fetches Cortana, your personal search assistant, who responds to your commands, both verbal and typed into the Search box.

- » **Get Started:** Discussed in Chapter 21, this app describes the most basic features in Windows 10.

- » **Groove Music:** Covered in Chapter 16, this app plays music stored on your PC. But Microsoft hopes you'll buy or rent music from its store, as well.

- » **Mail:** Covered in Chapter 10, the Mail app lets you send and receive email. If you enter a Windows Live, Yahoo!, AOL, or Google account, the Mail app sets itself up automatically and stocks your People list with your contacts.

- » **Maps:** Handy for trip planning, the Maps app brings up a version of Microsoft Bing Maps.

- » **Microsoft Edge:** Microsoft's new browser, Microsoft Edge, arrives in Windows 10, ready to replace Internet Explorer.

- » **Microsoft Solitaire Collection:** This app replaces the card games found in previous Windows versions.

- » **Money:** This live tile opens with business headlines. Scroll to the right to see a 30-minute delay of the Dow, NASDAQ, and S&P with the usual charts depicting fear and uncertainty.

- » **Movies & TV:** Microsoft's video storefront lets you rent or buy movies and TV shows, as covered in Chapter 17. The app also lets you watch videos you've taken with your camera or smartphone.

- » **News:** Visit here to read the news of the day, compiled from news services around the world. (Techie alert: You can add RSS feeds from your favorite websites.)

- >> **OneDrive:** This term describes the Microsoft Internet cubbyhole where you can store your files. By storing them online in OneDrive, covered in Chapter 5, you can access them from nearly any Internet-connected computer, phone, or tablet.

- >> **OneNote:** This popular note-taking app receives an entry on the Start menu in Windows 10.

- >> **People:** Windows 10's People app simply collects your friends' names and contact info.

- >> **Phone Companion:** This app helps you link your Windows, Android, or Apple phone with Windows so they can share information.

- >> **Photos:** Covered in Chapter 17, the Photos app displays photos stored in your computer, as well as on OneDrive, your Internet storage space.

- >> **Settings:** This takes you to the Windows 10 Settings app, which contains almost all of the settings found in the Control Panel from earlier Windows versions. (I cover the Settings app in Chapter 12.)

- >> **Sports:** You can find sports news and scores here, as well as a way to add listings for your favorite sports teams.

- >> **Store:** Covered in Chapter 6, the Windows Store is the only way to add more apps on your Start menu. The Windows Store also carries some programs you can install on your Windows desktop, covered in Chapter 3.

- >> **Weather:** This weather station forecasts a week's worth of weather in your area, but only if you grant it permission to access your location information. (Unless your computer has a GPS — Global Positioning System — the app narrows down your location by closest major city rather than street address.)

- >> **Xbox:** Coveted mostly by owners of Microsoft's Xbox One video game console, this lets you track high scores (for both you and your gaming buddies), chat with other gamers, view your achievements, and visit the Store app to buy more games.

The bundled Windows apps work best when running full screen on a tablet, and they're not as powerful as normal desktop programs. But for some odd reason, Microsoft configured the Windows *desktop* to use some of these Start menu apps rather than standard desktop programs.

TIP

I explain in Chapter 3 how to choose which apps and programs handle which tasks, but here's a temporary hint: On the desktop, right-click a file and choose Open With. A menu appears, letting you choose which program should handle the job. To stay on the desktop, choose your desktop program from the menu, not the currently assigned Start menu app.

Adding or removing Start menu items

Microsoft dumped a random assortment of items on the Windows 10 Start menu. The resulting jumble of tiles consumes a lot of real estate, and is certainly not tailored to *your* personal interests or work habits. This section lets you fix that shortcoming.

TIP

Removing tiles from the Start menu is easy, so you can begin there. To remove an unwanted or unused tile from the Start menu, right-click it and choose Unpin from Start from the pop-up menu. The unloved tile slides away without fuss.

On a touchscreen, hold down your finger on the unwanted tile. When the Unpin icon appears, tap it to remove the tile.

After removing the unwanted items, spend some time *adding* items to the Start menu, making them as easy to reach as a pencil holder on an office desk.

To add programs or apps to the Start menu, follow these steps:

1. **Click the Start button; on a desktop PC, an alphabetical list of apps appears along the Start menu's left side. (In Tablet mode, click the All Apps icon, shown in the margin.)**

The Start menu presents an alphabetical list of all your installed apps and programs.

2. **Right-click the item you want to appear on the Start menu; then choose Pin to Start.**

Each selected item appears as a new Start menu tile. Repeat until you've added all of the items you want. Unfortunately, you must right-click and pin each item separately. Windows 10 doesn't let you select and add several items simultaneously.

3. **From the desktop, right-click desired items and choose Pin to Start.**

The Start menu tiles aren't limited to apps and programs. From the desktop, right-click any folder, file, library, or other item you want added to the Start menu and then choose Pin to Start from the pop-up menu. Newly attached items appear at the Start menu's bottom-right corner. (On well-stuffed Start menus, you may need to scroll down to see them.)

When you're through, your Start menu will have grown considerably with all your newly added destinations.

TIP

Can't find a newly installed app? Chances are good that it's hiding in the Start menu's All Apps area. Windows places newly downloaded apps in the All Apps area rather than as a tile on the Start menu. If you want it visible as a tile along the Start menu's right edge, you need to pin it there yourself.

After you've stuffed your Start menu with your favorite desktop destinations, head to this chapter's "Customizing the Start menu" section to finish organizing. When you finish, you'll have created a Start menu that meets your needs.

Customizing the Start menu

The Start menu contains mostly tiles — clumps of tiles arranged in rectangles. The clumps of tiles consume a lot of space, but they're not very organized. How can you find your favorite stuff?

Give yourself a fighting chance by organizing your Start menu. The following steps begin with a small dose of organization: purging unwanted tiles and adding tiles for your favorites.

Keep following these steps, and you'll eventually reach organizational nirvana: A Start menu full of neatly labeled *groups* (collections of related tiles) that match *your* interests.

You can organize the tiles any way you want, into any number of groups with any names. For example, you may want to organize the Start menu tiles into four groups: People, Work, Play, and Web. (For a quick peek at what organized and labeled groups look like, page ahead to Figure 2-9.)

But no matter how organized you want to be, follow these steps to begin turning that haphazard Start menu into your *own* piles o' tiles:

1. **Remove tiles you don't need.**

   Spot a tile you don't need? Right-click it and choose Unpin from Start from the pop-up menu. Repeat until you've removed all the tiles you don't use. (On a touchscreen, hold your finger down on an unwanted app and then tap the Unpin icon.)

REMEMBER

   Choosing Unpin from Start doesn't *uninstall* the app or program; removing the tile merely removes that item's "start" button from the Start menu. In fact, if you accidentally remove the tile for a favorite app or program, you can easily put it back in Step 3.

2. **Move related tiles next to each other.**

   As an example, you might want to keep your people-oriented apps — Mail, People, and Calendar — next to each other. To move an app to a new location, point at its tile with your mouse and then hold down your left mouse button as you drag the tile to the desired spot. As you drag the tile, other tiles automatically move out of the way to make room for newcomer.

TIP

On a touchscreen, hold down your finger on the app; when the pop-up menu appears, drag the app to its new position.

When you've dragged an app's tile to the desired spot, lift your finger or release the mouse button to set the tile into its new place.

TIP

To conserve screen real estate, shrink a wide rectangular tile to a small square tile: Right-click the wide tile, choose Resize from the pop-up menu, and choose a smaller size from the second menu. (You can also enlarge an app's tile, turning it into a live tile that shows updated information about the app's contents.)

3. **Add tiles for apps, programs, folders, and files you need.**

    I explain how to add tiles for apps, programs, folders, and files earlier, in this chapter's earlier "Adding or removing Start menu items" section.

    After you've purged any unwanted tiles, rearranged the remaining tiles, and added new tiles for items you need, your Start menu may meet your needs. If so, stop. You're done!

    But if your Start menu still sprawls below the Start menu's bottom edge and you can't find important items, keep reading.

    Still here? Okay. Look closely at the Start menu, and you see two groups of tiles. Windows labels them "Life at a Glance," and "Play and Explore." If you're like most people, you probably didn't notice the subtle gap separating the two groups. And that brings you to the next step.

4. **To create a new group, drag and drop any tile away from the two existing groups.**

    Drag and hold a tile away from the existing groups. A horizontal bar appears, as shown in Figure 2-8, creating an empty space below it for your incoming tile. Drop the tile, and the tile forms a *new* group of one lonely tile, located below the two other groups.

5. **To add more tiles to your newly created group, drag and drop additional tiles into the group.**

    Drag and drop new tiles next to your new group's first tile to keep it company. After you drop a tile into a group, you can drag the tile around to a new position within the group.

    Want to create yet another group? Then repeat Steps 4 and 5, dragging and dropping a tile away from the existing groups to create yet another group.

    You might find groups of related tiles to be enough organization for you. If so, stop. But if you want to label the groups, go to the next step.

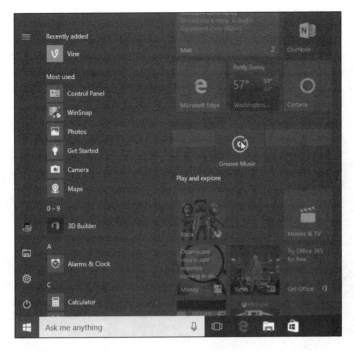

FIGURE 2-8:
To create a new group, drag and hold a tile away from the two groups. When the bar appears, drop the tile.

6. **Name the groups.**

Click in the blank space directly above any group of tiles, and a box appears, ready for you to type in a name or replace the existing name. After typing the name, press Enter, and the box disappears, leaving your tile group bearing its new name.

Type in names (or click on existing names to change those) for any other tile groups, as well.

When you've finished naming the tile groups, you can finally bask in your organizational prowess, as shown in Figure 2-9.

REMEMBER

>> There's no right or wrong way to organize the Start menu. Just as in real life, be as organized or as messy as you want. You can move groups, as well, by dragging and dropping them by their titles.

>> As you install new apps and desktop programs, remember to look for them in the *All Apps* area, not on the Start menu itself. To keep things organized, right-click the newcomers and choose Pin to Start menu. After you place your new apps as tiles on the Start menu, you can drag and drop them into your existing groups or make new groups for the new tiles.

>> Feel free to create a group for your favorite websites, as well, making it easy to get to them straight from the Start menu. (To pin a website to the Start menu, click the More icon (three dots) in the Edge browser and choose Pin this Page to Start from the drop-down menu.)

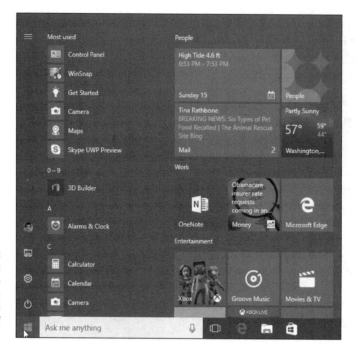

FIGURE 2-9:
Your Start menu
may be easier to
work with when
organized into
labeled groups of
related tiles.

TIP

PERSONALIZING THE START MENU

Windows 10's Settings app offers additional ways to tweak the Start menu. I cover the Settings app in Chapter 12, but this section applies particularly to the Start menu.

To find the Start menu settings, click the Start button, choose the Settings icon, and click the Settings app's Personalization tile. When the Personalization page appears, click Start in the left pane, and the Start menu's options spill out to the right.

The Start menu offers these options:

- **Show more tiles:** If you've added a lot of tiles to the Start menu, turn this on to widen the Start menu and see more tiles.

- **Occasionally show suggestions in Start:** Turn this off to remove the Start menu's "Suggested" apps. (It's actually an advertisement.)

- **Show most used apps:** Leave this on to let the Start menu automatically stock your Start menu's Most Used section.

- **Show recently added apps:** Leave this on, and newly installed apps appear in their own section.

- **Use Start full screen:** This turns on Tablet mode for the desktop, making the Start menu fill the screen.

- **Show recently opened items in Jump Lists on Start or the taskbar:** Leave this turned on so you can return to favorite destinations, both listed in the Start menu and on the taskbar's jump lists, covered in Chapter 3.

- **Choose which folders appear on Start:** The Start menu normally offers links to File Explorer and Settings. Click here to stock that section with other destinations, including Documents, Downloads, Music, Pictures, Videos, HomeGroup, and Network.

There's no right or wrong way to set these settings. Stick with the default settings or experiment to see which settings work for you. They're all toggle switches, so you can always return and flip the toggle again if a settings change doesn't meet your needs.

Exiting from Windows

Ah! The most pleasant thing you'll do with Windows all day could very well be to stop using it. Exiting Windows brings a hurdle to the process, however: You must decide whether to Lock, Sign Out, Shut Down, Restart, or Sleep your computer.

The answer depends on how long you're abandoning your computer. Are you simply stepping away from the computer for a few moments, or are you through working for the day?

I cover both scenarios — a temporary sojourn and leaving your computer for the day — in the next two sections.

But if you don't want to trudge through a manual in order to turn off your PC, here's the quickest way to turn it off:

1. **Click the Start button and then click the Power icon near the Start menu's lower-left corner.**

2. **Choose Shut Down from the drop-down menu.**

3. **If the computer protests, saying you'll lose unsaved work, choose Sleep instead.**

The following two sections deal with the finer points of what's become an alarmingly complex chore.

Power users know this quick shut down trick: Right-click the Start button, choose Shut Down or Sign Out from the pop-up menu, and choose Shut Down from the submenu.

TIP

Temporarily leaving your computer

Windows offers three options when you're leaving your computer temporarily, perhaps to reheat some fish in the office microwave and sneak back to your cubicle before anybody notices. To make the right choice among the various "temporary leave" scenarios in Windows, follow these steps:

1. **Click the Start button to fetch the Start menu.**

2. **Click your user account picture from the Start menu's left edge.**

   There, as shown in Figure 2-10, you can choose one of these options:

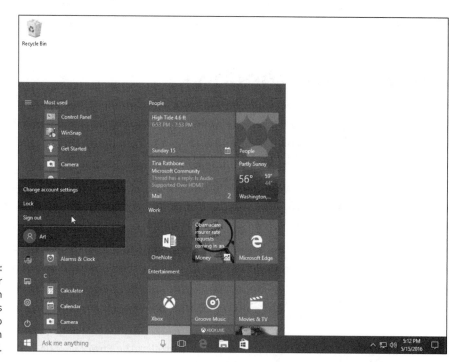

FIGURE 2-10:
Click your account name in the Start menu's top-left corner to choose from these options.

- **Change account settings:** This option whisks you straight to the Settings app, where you can tweak your account's settings. You can change your photo, for example, or change the password of a Local account.

- **Lock:** Meant to add privacy while you take short trips to the water cooler, this option locks your PC, veiling your screen with the Lock screen picture. When you return, unlock the screen by pressing any key and then typing your password. Windows quickly displays your work, just as you left it.

- **Sign Out:** Choose this option when you're through working at the PC and somebody else wants to have a go at it. Windows saves your work and your settings and then returns to the Lock screen, ready for the next person to log on.

- **Another account:** Below your name, as shown earlier in Figure 2-10, Windows lists names of any other accounts on the computer. If one of those people wants to borrow the computer for a few minutes while you're grabbing some coffee, let him choose his name from the list. When he types in his password, his customized screen appears, ready for him to work. When he signs out and you log back in, all your work reappears, just as you left it.

Each of these options lets you give up your computer for a little while, but leaves it waiting for your return.

If you're finished for the day, though, you're ready for the next section.

Leaving your computer for the day

When you're done computing for the day — or perhaps you just want to shut down the laptop while on the subway or that flight to Rome — Windows offers three ways to handle the situation.

Follow this step to choose from the available options:

 Click the Start button and click the Power icon (shown in the margin).

The Power icon's pop-up menu offers three settings, as shown in Figure 2-11.

Here's the rundown on your options:

- » **Sleep:** The most popular choice, this saves your work in your PC's memory *and* on its hard drive and then lets your PC slumber in a low-power state. Later, when you return to your PC, Windows quickly presents everything — even your unsaved work — as if you'd never left. And if the power goes out, your PC will still wake up with everything saved, but it will take a few more seconds.

- » **Shut Down:** This option turns off your computer completely. It's just like Restart but without turning back on again. And, if you're worried about preserving battery life on a laptop or tablet, it's your best choice.

- » **Restart:** Choose this option as a first cure when something weird happens (a program crashes, for example, or Windows seems dazed and confused). Windows turns off your computer and then starts itself anew, hopefully feeling better. (Patches from Windows Update, as well as newly installed programs, occasionally ask you to restart your PC.)

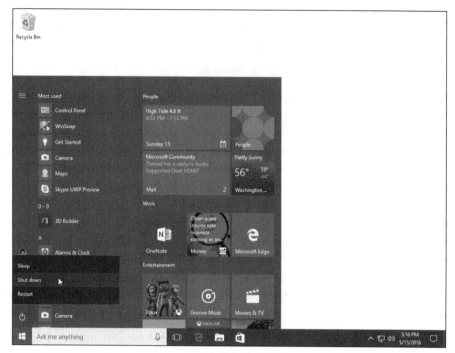

FIGURE 2-11:
Choosing Sleep
makes your
computer wake
up more quickly
when turned back
on. Choosing
Shut Down turns
off the power
completely.

That should be enough to wade through. But if you have a little more time, here are some other facts to consider:

REMEMBER

You don't *have* to shut down your computer each night. In fact, some experts leave their computers turned on all the time, saying it's better for their computer's health. Other experts say that their computers are healthier if they're turned *off* each day. Still others say the Sleep mode gives them the best of both worlds. How-ever, *everybody* says to turn off your monitor when you're done working. Monitors definitely enjoy cooling down when not in use.

Want your laptop or tablet to wake up in Airplane mode, cut off from Internet access? Then switch to Airplane mode and use Sleep rather than Shut Down. When your laptop or tablet wakes back up on your transatlantic flight, it stays in Airplane mode, disconnected from the Internet. (I cover Airplane mode in Chapter 23.)

TIP

To turn off your computer as quickly as possible, right-click the Start button, choose Shut Down or Sign Out from the pop-up menu, and choose Shut Down from the pop-out menu.

Chapter 3

The Traditional Desktop

The Tablet mode in Windows 10 works well for couch-top computing. When the Start menu fills the screen with finger-friendly apps, you can easily listen to music, check your email, watch the latest funny cat videos, and track your friends' misadventures on Facebook.

But when Monday morning inevitably rolls around, it's time to switch gears. Working usually requires ditching the simple Windows apps and firing up more full-featured programs. Employers prefer that you work with spreadsheets and word processors rather than play *Words with Friends.*

That's when the second half of Windows, the desktop, comes into play. When you turn off Tablet mode, the Windows 10 desktop appears, ready to work the same way it's worked for the past decade. Optimized for a mouse and keyboard, it's where you arrange your work in windows and make things happen.

The Windows 10 Start menu and its gang of apps bring many changes, but the desktop works much like the familiar workhorse of yesteryear. This chapter shows you how to transform your computer from an entertainment device back into an office.

Finding the Desktop and the Start Menu

Windows 8 did its best to hide the desktop, but Windows 10 enthusiastically announces its return. There's more good news. Shown in Figure 3-1, the desktop is almost indistinguishable from the one in Windows 7.

Recycle Bin

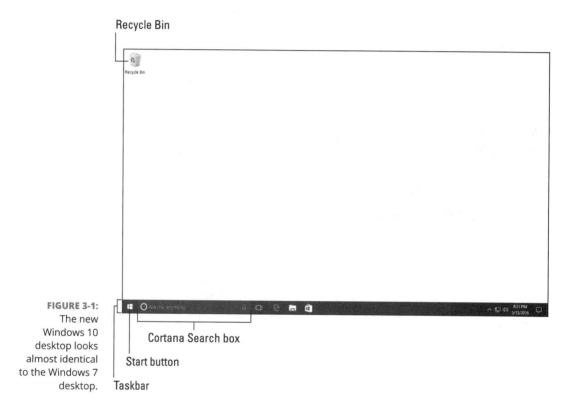

FIGURE 3-1:
The new
Windows 10
desktop looks
almost identical
to the Windows 7
desktop.

Cortana Search box

Start button

Taskbar

The Windows 10 desktop will run nearly all the Windows programs that ran on your old Windows Vista, Windows 7, Windows 8, or Windows 8.1 computer. Exceptions are antivirus programs, security suites, high-performance video games, and some utility programs. Those don't usually transfer well from one Windows version to another.

Fingers work well for tapping the Start menu's extra-large tiles. And if you have especially dainty fingertips, your touchscreen's touch controls will still work on the desktop's buttons and borders. Here's how to control the desktop with your fingers:

- **Select:** To select something on the desktop, tap it with a fingertip; the pad of your finger may be too large.

- **Double-click:** To double-click something, tap it twice. Again, your fingertip works best.

- **Right-click:** To right-click an item, press your fingertip gently on it and wait for a small square to appear onscreen. When the square appears, remove your finger, and the pop-up menu stays on the screen. Then you can tap your desired option on the menu.

If your fingertip seems too wide for delicate desktop window maneuvers, buy a Bluetooth mouse and keyboard for your tablet. They turn your tablet into two computers: one that uses lightweight apps for casual computing and the other with a full Windows desktop for doing some *real* work.

One word of caution: When run in Tablet mode, apps and programs always cover the entire screen; they never run inside desktop windows. If you need to view and right-click the desktop *itself*, you must first turn off Tablet mode.

Note: Only Windows tablets with screens of 8 inches or larger include the desktop. Smaller tablets (and phones) run Windows 10 Mobile, which doesn't include the desktop; those devices can only run apps.

Windows 10 runs apps within a window on the desktop. If they don't run inside a window, turn off Tablet mode, which I describe in the "Toggling between Tablet mode and the desktop" section later in this chapter.

Working with the Desktop

The desktop lets you run several apps and programs simultaneously, each living within its own little *window*. That separation lets you spread several programs across the screen, sharing bits of information among them.

When first installed, Windows starts with the freshly scrubbed, nearly empty desktop shown earlier in Figure 3-1. After you've been working for a while, your desktop will fill up with *icons* — little buttons that load your files with a quick double-click. Many people leave their desktops strewn with icons for easy access.

Other people organize their work: When they finish working on something, they store their files in a *folder*, a task covered in Chapter 4.

But no matter how you use the desktop, it comes with four main parts, labeled earlier in Figure 3-1:

>> **Start button:** To launch a program, click the Start button in the desktop's lower-left corner. When the Start menu appears, click the name or tile for the app or program you want to run.

>> I cover the Start menu and all its quirks in Chapter 2. (Flip back to that chapter if you want to strip the Start menu of its app tiles.) For easy access to your favorite programs, place them on your desktop's taskbar (described next).

>> **Cortana Search box:** Also known as *Cortana*, this combination search box and digital assistant lets you search both your computer and the Internet for files and information. I describe Cortana in Chapter 7.

>> **Taskbar:** Resting lazily along the bottom edge of your screen, the taskbar shows icons for the apps and programs you currently have open, as well as icons for launching a few favored programs. (Point at a program's icon on the taskbar to see the program's name or perhaps a thumbnail photo of that program in action.) I describe how to add your favorite programs' icons to the taskbar in this chapter's later "Customizing the taskbar" section.

>> **Recycle Bin:** The desktop's *Recycle Bin,* that wastebasket-shaped icon, stores your recently deleted files and folders for easy retrieval. Whew!

I cover those items later in this chapter and throughout the book, but these tips will help you until you page ahead:

>> PC and laptop owners can start new projects directly from the Windows desktop: Right-click a blank part of the desktop, choose New, and choose the project of your dreams from the pop-up menu, be it loading a favorite program or creating a folder to store new files. (The New menu lists most of your computer's programs, sparing you a journey back to the Start menu.) In Tablet mode, by contrast, you can start projects only from the Start menu.

>> Are you befuddled about some desktop object's reason for being? Timidly rest the pointer over the mysterious doodad, and Windows pops up a little box explaining what that thing is or does. Right-click the object, and the ever-helpful Windows usually tosses up a menu listing nearly everything you can

do with that particular object. This trick works on most icons and buttons found on your desktop and its programs.

WARNING

>> All the icons on your desktop may suddenly disappear. To bring your work back to life, right-click your empty desktop and choose View from the pop-up menu. Then make sure the Show Desktop Icons menu option has a check mark so everything stays visible. If that doesn't work, try turning off Tablet mode: Tap the Action Center icon next to the clock in the screen's bottom-right corner. Then click or tap the Tablet mode button to toggle it off. (Tablet mode hides everything on the desktop.)

Launching apps with the Start menu

The Start button never strays from your desktop's bottom-left corner. A click or tap of the Start button fetches the Start menu, which lists all of your installed apps and programs. When the Start menu appears, you click the app or program you'd like to run.

I cover the Start menu in Chapter 2, but here's a quick step-by-step on how to open the Start menu and launch an app or program:

1. **Click the mouse pointer on the Start button in your screen's bottom-left corner.**

   The Start menu appears, as shown in Figure 3-2. (If your PC is running in Tablet mode, described later in this chapter, the Start menu fills the screen.)

FIGURE 3-2:
If you spot your desired app or program on the Start menu, launch it with a click on its name or tile.

The Start menu automatically lists names of your most recently accessed apps and programs in its top, left corner. To the right, another column displays tiles of popular apps installed on your computer.

2. **If you see your desired app or program listed on the Start menu, click it.**

   Click a name or a tile, and the app or program rises to the top of your desktop, ready for action.

Don't see the name of your desired app or program? The Start menu's left column presents an alphabetical list of all of your apps and programs. That leaves you with several choices:

>> If you don't see your desired app's name, scroll down the list of names by clicking in the bar just to the right of the names. (I describe how to scroll with a scroll box in Chapter 4.)

>> To see an alphabetical list of apps when in Tablet mode, click or tap the All Apps icon (shown in the margin) near the screen's upper-left corner.

>> If your app doesn't appear on the list, chances are good that it's not installed on your computer. To download it, visit the Windows Store, which I cover in Chapter 6.

You can also fetch the Start menu by pressing the ⊞ key on your keyboard or tablet.

After you've opened an app or program, you'll eventually want to close it, a task I cover in Chapter 4. (But here's a spoiler: To close an app, move your mouse pointer to the app's upper-right corner and click the little X, shown in the margin.)

I explain more about the Start menu, including how to customize it to meet your needs, in Chapter 2.

Jazzing up the desktop's background

To jazz up your desktop, Windows covers it with a pretty picture known as a *back-ground*. (Many people refer to the background simply as *wallpaper*.)

When you tire of the built-in scenery, feel free to replace it with a picture stored on your computer:

1. **Click the Start button and choose the Settings icon.**

   Located just above the Power button, the Settings icon resembles a gear. Click it, and Windows 10's Settings app appears.

2. **Click the Personalization icon (shown in the margin).**

   The Settings app's Personalization section opens to the Background page.

3. **Click any one of the pictures, shown in Figure 3-3, and Windows quickly places it onto your desktop's background.**

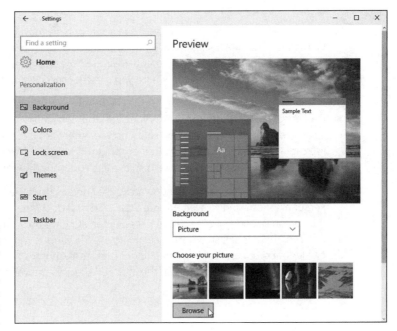

FIGURE 3-3:
Try different backgrounds by clicking them. Click the Browse button to see pictures from different folders.

Found a keeper? Then you're done; your change takes place immediately. Or, if you're still searching, move to the next step.

4. **Click the Browse button to see photos inside your Pictures folder.**

   Most people store their digital photos in their Pictures folder. (I explain browsing folders in Chapter 4.) If you've chosen to sync pictures taken by your tablet or smartphone with OneDrive, they appear in the Picture folder's Camera Roll folder.

5. **Click different pictures to see how they look as your desktop's background.**

   When you find a background you like, you're done. Exit the program with a click in its upper-right corner, and your chosen photo drapes across your desktop.

Here are some tips on changing your desktop's background:

>> Options listed on the Background page's Choose a Fit drop-down menu let you choose whether the image should be *tiled* repeatedly across the screen, *centered* directly in the middle, or *stretched* to fill the entire screen. The Tile, Fill, and Fit options work best with small photos, such as those taken with cellphones, by repeating or enlarging them to fit the screen's borders.

>> The new Microsoft Edge web browser can easily borrow most pictures found on the Internet for a background. Right-click the website's picture and choose Save Picture As from the pop-up menu. Microsoft sneakily offers to copy the image into your Pictures folder, where you can choose it as a background in Step 4 above.

>> If a background photograph makes your desktop icons too difficult to see, splash your desktop with a single color instead: After Step 2 of the preceding list, click Colors from the Personalization window's left pane. When the colored squares appear, click one to splash it across your desktop.

>> To change the entire *look* of Windows, choose Themes from the Personalization window's left edge in Step 2. Then click Theme Settings from the Personalization window's right pane. Aimed at heavy-duty procrastinators, different themes splash different colors across the various Windows buttons, borders, and boxes. I explain more about themes in Chapter 12. (If you download any themes offered on the Internet, check them with antivirus software, covered in Chapter 11.)

Toggling between Tablet mode and the desktop

Some people work with Windows 10 on a tablet; others prefer a desktop. Still others prefer a tablet that can double as a desktop by adding a keyboard and mouse. Making your tablet work like a desktop PC can introduce a problem, though: Tablets work best with your fingertips, but the desktop is best controlled with a mouse and keyboard.

To please both camps, Windows 10 lets you toggle Tablet mode on and off. Turning on Tablet mode, for example, makes all of your apps and programs fill the screen. (The Start menu runs full screen as well, hiding the desktop.) Tablet mode also subtly increases the spacing between your menus and icons, making them easier to tap with fingers.

In many cases, Windows 10 notices how you're working and automatically turns Tablet mode on and off when necessary. (Microsoft calls that special sense

Continuum.) But if you find Windows 10 working in the wrong mode, follow these steps to toggle between Tablet mode manually:

1. **Click the Taskbar's Action Center icon.**

   The Action Center icon lives near the right edge of the *taskbar,* that strip running along the bottom of every screen.

   The Action Center pane appears, shown in Figure 3-4.

FIGURE 3-4:
The Action Center pane's lower buttons offer easy-to-reach settings, including the Tablet mode toggle.

2. **Click or tap the Tablet Mode button along the bottom left of the Action Center pane.**

   When the Tablet mode button is highlighted with color, Tablet mode is on; when the button's color disappears, Tablet mode is off and the desktop behaves normally.

   TIP

   To fetch the Action Center pane quickly on a tablet, slide your finger in from the screen's right edge. The Action Center pane appears, letting you quickly tap the Tablet mode toggle.

Dumpster diving in the Recycle Bin

 The Recycle Bin, that wastebasket icon in the upper-left corner of your desktop, works much like a *real* recycle bin. Shown in the margin, it lets you retrieve the discarded desktop files you thought you'd never need.

You can dump something from the desktop — a file or folder, for example — into the Recycle Bin in either of these ways:

>> Simply right-click the unwanted item and choose Delete from the pop-up menu. Windows asks cautiously if you're *sure* that you want to delete the item. Click Yes, and Windows dumps it into the Recycle Bin, just as if you'd dragged it there. Whoosh!

>> For a quick deletion rush, click the unwanted object and poke your Delete key.

Want something back? Double-click the Recycle Bin icon to see your recently deleted items. Right-click the item you want and choose Restore. The handy little Recycle Bin returns your precious item to the same spot where you deleted it. (You can also resuscitate deleted items by dragging them to your desktop or any other folder; drag 'em back into the Recycle Bin to delete them again.)

TIP

The Recycle Bin can get pretty crowded. If you're searching frantically for a recently deleted file, tell the Recycle Bin to sort everything by the date and time you deleted it: Right-click an empty area inside the Recycle Bin and choose Sort By. Then choose Date Deleted from the pop-up menu.

TIP

To delete something *permanently,* just delete it from inside the Recycle Bin: Click it and press the Delete key. To delete *everything* in the Recycle Bin, right-click the Recycle Bin icon and choose Empty Recycle Bin.

To bypass the Recycle Bin completely when deleting files, hold down Shift while pressing Delete. Poof! The deleted object disappears, ne'er to be seen again — a handy trick when dealing with sensitive items, such as credit-card numbers or late-night love letters meant for a nearby cubicle dweller.

>> The Recycle Bin icon changes from an empty wastepaper basket to a full one (as shown in the margin) as soon as it's holding any deleted file or files.

>> The Recycle Bin holds only items deleted from the desktop. It doesn't retain information deleted from Start menu apps.

>> Your Recycle Bin keeps your deleted files until the garbage consumes about 5 percent of your computer's available space. Then it purges your oldest deleted files to make room for the new. If you're low on hard drive space, shrink the bin's size by right-clicking the Recycle Bin and choosing Properties.

Decrease the Custom Size number to purge the bin more quickly; increase the number, and the Recycle Bin hangs onto files a little longer.

WARNING

>> The Recycle Bin saves only items deleted from your *own* computer's drives. That means it won't save anything deleted from a CD, memory card, phone, MP3 player, flash drive, or digital camera.

>> Already emptied the Recycle Bin? You might still be able to retrieve the then-trashed-now-treasured item from the Windows File History backup, covered in Chapter 13.

WARNING

>> If you delete something from somebody else's computer over a network, it can't be retrieved. The Recycle Bin holds only items deleted from your *own* computer, not somebody else's computer. (For some awful reason, the Recycle Bin on the other person's computer doesn't save the item, either.) Be careful.

Bellying Up to the Taskbar

Whenever more than one window sits across your desktop, you face a logistics problem: Programs and windows tend to overlap, making them difficult to spot. To make matters worse, programs such as web browsers and Microsoft Word can contain several windows apiece. How do you keep track of all the windows?

The Windows solution is the *taskbar* — a special area that keeps track of your currently running programs and their windows. Shown in Figure 3-5, the taskbar lives along the bottom of your desktop, constantly updating itself to show an icon for every currently running app or desktop program.

NEW

Unlike Windows 8, Windows 10 keeps the taskbar firmly in place, even when run in Tablet mode. The taskbar remains accessible along the screen's bottom edge, even when apps or the Start menu fill the screen. (You can toggle the taskbar's appearance in Tablet mode by right-clicking the taskbar and choosing Settings. The Taskbar settings page appears, where you can toggle whether the taskbar should remain hidden.)

TIP

The taskbar also serves as a place to launch your favorite programs. By keeping your favorite programs' icons in sight and one quick click away, you're spared a detour to the Start menu.

Not sure what a taskbar icon does? Rest your mouse pointer over any of the taskbar icons to see either the program's name or a thumbnail image of the program's contents, as shown in Figure 3-5. In that figure, for example, you can see that the Photos app is displaying three photos.

FIGURE 3-5:
Point at a taskbar
icon to see its
currently running
programs.

From the taskbar, you can perform powerful magic, as described in the following list:

REMEMBER

NEW

>> To play with a program listed on the taskbar, click its icon. The window rises to the surface and rests atop any other open windows, ready for action. Clicking the taskbar icon yet again minimizes that same window.

>> Whenever you load an app or program, its icon automatically appears on the taskbar. If one of your open windows ever gets lost on your desktop, click its icon on the taskbar to bring it to the forefront.

>> To close an app or program listed on the taskbar, right-click its icon and choose Close from the pop-up menu. The program quits, just as if you'd chosen its Exit command from within its own window. (The departing program thoughtfully gives you a chance to save your work before it quits and walks off the screen.)

>> Taskbar icons with a thin underline along their bottom edge let you know that their app or program is currently running.

>> Traditionally, the taskbar lives along your desktop's bottom edge, but you can move it to any edge you want, a handy space saver on extra-wide monitors. (Hint: Try dragging it to your screen's side. If it doesn't move, right-click the taskbar and click Lock the Taskbar to remove the check mark by that option.)

>> Can't find an open app or window? Click on the taskbar's Task View icon (shown in the margin) to see *all* of your open apps and programs. Click the one you want to revisit, and it rises to the top of the screen.

>> If the taskbar keeps hiding below the screen's bottom edge, point the mouse at the screen's bottom edge until the taskbar surfaces. Then right-click the taskbar, choose Properties, and remove the check mark from the option Auto-Hide the Taskbar.

TIP

>> You can add your favorite apps and programs directly to the taskbar: From the Start menu, right-click the favored program's name or tile and choose Pin to Taskbar. The program's icon then lives on the taskbar for easy access, just as if it were running. Tired of the program hogging space on your taskbar? Right-click it and choose Unpin from Taskbar from the pop-up menu.

Shrinking windows to the taskbar and retrieving them

Windows spawn windows. You start with one window to write a letter of praise to your local taco shop. You open another window to check an address, and then yet another to ogle an online menu. Before you know it, four windows are crowded across the desktop.

To combat the clutter, Windows provides a simple means of window control: You can transform a window from a screen–cluttering square into a tiny button on the taskbar along the bottom of the screen. The solution is the Minimize button.

See the three buttons lurking in just about every window's top–right corner? Click the *Minimize button* — the button with the little line in it, shown in the margin. Whoosh! The window disappears, represented by its little button on the taskbar at your screen's bottom.

REMEMBER

To make a minimized program on the taskbar revert to a regular, onscreen window, just click its icon on the taskbar. Pretty simple, huh?

>> Can't find the taskbar icon for the window you want to minimize or maximize? If you hover your mouse pointer over the taskbar button, Windows displays a thumbnail photo of that program or the program's name.

>> When you minimize a window, you neither destroy its contents nor close the program. And when you click the window's name on the taskbar, it reopens to the same size you left it, showing its same contents.

Switching to different tasks from the taskbar's Jump Lists

The Windows taskbar doesn't limit you to opening programs and switching between windows. You can jump to other tasks, as well, by right-clicking the taskbar's icons. Right-clicking the File Explorer icon brings up a quick list of your recently visited folders, as shown in Figure 3-6. Click any folder on the list to make a quick return visit.

FIGURE 3-6: Right-click File Explorer to see a clickable list of recently visited locations.

Called *Jump Lists,* these pop-up menus add a new trick to the taskbar: They let you jump quickly to previously visited locations, letting you work faster.

Jump list items work any time. Even if you haven't opened File Explorer, for example, you right-click its taskbar icon and jump to a listed folder.

The Microsoft Edge browser breaks with tradition by not offering Jump Lists, but Microsoft may add them later.

Clicking the taskbar's sensitive areas

Like a crafty card player, the taskbar comes with a few tips and tricks. For example, here's the lowdown on the icons near the taskbar's right edge, shown in

Figure 3-7, known as the *Action Center.* Different items appear in the Action Center depending on your PC and programs, but you'll probably encounter some of these:

Safely remove USB device

View OneDrive status

Open Windows Defender

Adjust speaker volume

Open Action Center

Time and date

Wired network status

View hidden icons

FIGURE 3-7: Click the arrow to see the taskbar's hidden icons.

» **Minimize Windows:** This small strip hidden against the taskbar's far-right edge instantly minimizes all open windows when you click it. Click it again to put the windows back in place. (This strip disappears in Tablet mode because every app and program runs fullscreen.)

» **Time/Date:** Click the time and date to fetch a handy monthly calendar, clock, and a list of upcoming appointments from the Calendar app. If you want to change the time or date or even add a second time zone, right-click the Time/Date area and choose Adjust Date/Time, a task I cover in Chapter 12.

» **Location:** Your computer is currently sharing your location with an app, often seen when checking maps or other location-specific apps.

» **Bluetooth:** Click this to see your options for connecting wirelessly with Bluetooth, commonly used with mice, keyboards, and speakers.

» **Safely Remove Hardware:** Before unplugging a storage device, be it a tiny flash drive, a portable music player, or a portable hard drive, click here. That tells Windows to prepare the gadget for unplugging.

» **Action Center:** Click this to fetch the Action Center, a strip along the screen's right edge which keeps you up-to-date on your emails and appointments, as well as your computer's performance.

» **Wired Network:** Found mostly on desktop PCs, this icon appears when you're connected to the Internet or other PCs through a wired network. Not connected? A red X appears over the icon.

» **Wireless Network:** This appears when your PC is wirelessly connected to the Internet or other network. The more waves you see on the icon, the more powerful your wireless signal. (I explain how to connect to wireless networks in Chapter 9.)

» **Volume:** Click or tap this ever-so-handy little speaker icon to adjust your PC's volume, as shown in Figure 3-8. (Or right-click the icon and choose Open Volume Mixer to bring up a mixing panel. Mixers let you adjust separate volume levels for each program, so you can keep your music player's volume louder than your other programs' annoying beeps.)

» **Task Manager:** Coveted by computer technicians, this little program can end misbehaving programs, monitor background tasks, monitor performance, and do other stuff of techie dreams.

FIGURE 3-8:
Slide the lever to
adjust the
volume.

» **OneDrive:** When your computer is synchronizing its files with OneDrive (your Internet storage space), little arrows appear beneath this icon.

» **Power, Outlet:** This shows that your laptop or tablet is plugged into an electrical outlet and is charging its battery.

» **Power, Battery:** Your laptop or tablet is running on batteries only. (Rest your mouse pointer over the icon to see how much power remains.)

» **Arrow:** Sometimes the taskbar hides things. If you see a tiny upward-pointing arrow at the start of the taskbar's notification area, click it to see a few hidden icons slide up and out. (Check out the later "Customizing the taskbar" section for tips and tricks on whether icons should hide.)

You can pick and choose which notification icons should always be visible by right-clicking the taskbar, and choosing Settings. When the Taskbar Settings page appears, click the link called Select Which Icons Appear on the Taskbar. A new window appears, with sliding on/off toggles for all of the icons. (I like to leave them all on.)

CHATTING WITH CORTANA

You may notice an odd box on the taskbar, just to the right of the Start button. That's *Cortana*, your new digital assistant bundled with Windows 10. Cortana helps you find information, both on your computer and on the Internet.

For example, type a few words from one of your files into the box, and Cortana should find the file and list its name, ready for you to open it with a click. Cortana should do the same if you type the name of a setting or program.

Cortana also understands speech commands, if your computer's microphone is powerful enough. Click the little microphone in the box and say your command. Or, just preface your command with the words, "Hey Cortana." Cortana listens to what you say and responds.

Or at least, she usually does. Cortana takes some time to grow used to your voice, and you need time to grow used to her limited vocabulary. I cover Cortana in Chapter 7.

Opening the Action Center

The taskbar's right edge is often stuffed with icons. Unless you've memorized the chart in this book's previous section, they're pretty mysterious. Well, just click the Action Center icon, and then the Action Center pane appears, as shown in Figure 3-9, and demystifies that area by giving you more details about both your computer and your personal information.

The Action Center lists information about your latest emails, for example, as well as times of upcoming appointments, and other notifications. It also provides a list of handy buttons along the bottom. Windows 10 usually displays these four buttons:

>> **Tablet mode:** Click or tap this button to toggle Tablet mode. (When it's colored, you're in Tablet mode, which works well only on touchscreens.)

>> **Network:** This displays information about your current network connections, including the Internet.

>> **Note:** Click here to fetch OneNote, an app for taking notes in text, pictures, sound, and video.

>> **All Settings:** This brings up the Windows 10 Settings app, a huge panel of organized switches, which replaces most of the Control Panel found in older Windows versions. (You can also reach the Settings app by clicking the Start button and clicking the Settings icon.)

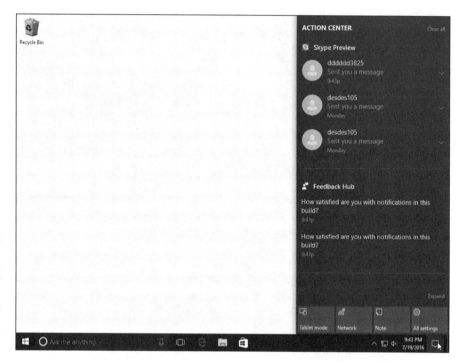

FIGURE 3-9:
Click the Action
Center icon to see
the Action Center
pane, which
displays current
information
about your
computer.

Although the Action Center's bottom usually shows only four buttons, click the word Expand over the right–most button to reveal hidden buttons. The available buttons vary according to your particular model of computer or tablet.

Keep these things in mind to reap the most benefits from the Action Center:

>> The Action Center sometimes goes overboard, reminding you about an appointment from yesterday. To remove an item, point at it and then click the X that appears in its upper-right corner.

>> To clear everything listed in the Action Center, click the words Clear All in its top-right corner.

TIP

>> Tablet owners can quickly fetch the Action Center by sliding their finger inward from the screen's right edge.

>> When the Action Center's icon changes to show lines inside of it, you know you have a notification waiting inside.

TIP

>> To customize the Action Center's bottom buttons, click the All Settings button in the pane's bottom-right corner. When the Settings window appears, click the System section and click that section's Notifications & Actions link. When the Notifications & Actions window appears, you see your four current

buttons listed along its top of a grid of buttons. Drag the buttons to place your four favorite ones on top, and they subsequently replace the Action Center's buttons.

>> While you're at the Settings page listed above, check out the toggles that control which apps may send you notifications. You can turn off notifications for apps you don't particularly care about.

Customizing the taskbar

Windows offers a whirlwind of options for the lowly taskbar, letting you play with it in more ways than a strand of spaghetti and a fork.

And that's especially important if you don't care for the new Start menu: By stocking the taskbar with icons for oft-used programs, you can avoid unnecessary trips to the Start menu.

First, the taskbar's left edge comes preloaded with icons for three apps: Microsoft Edge (the new Windows 10 web browser), File Explorer (your file browser), and the Store app (for downloading apps and programs). Like all your taskbar icons, they're movable, so feel free to drag them to any order you want.

If you spot a favored program's icon or tile on the Start menu, right-click the icon, choose More from the pop-up menu, and choose Pin to Taskbar from the next pop-up menu.

For even more customization, right-click a blank part of the taskbar and choose Settings. The Taskbar's Settings page appears, as shown in Figure 3-10.

Table 3-1 explains the most-used taskbar settings, as well as my recommendations for them.

Feel free to experiment with the taskbar until it looks right for you. Your changes take place immediately. Don't like the change? Click the toggle switch again to reverse your decision.

After you set up the taskbar just the way you want it, turn the Lock the Taskbar toggle to On, described in Table 3-1.

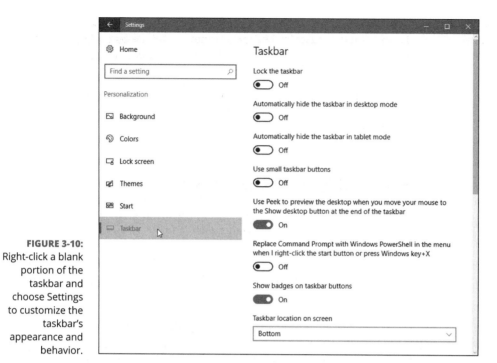

FIGURE 3-10:
Right-click a blank
portion of the
taskbar and
choose Settings
to customize the
taskbar's
appearance and
behavior.

TABLE 3-1   ## Customizing the Taskbar

Setting	My Recommendations
Lock the Taskbar	Turning this on locks the taskbar in place, keeping you from changing its appearance. Keep it locked to protect from accidental changes, but lock the taskbar only after you've set it up to suit your needs.
Automatically Hide the Taskbar	Handy mostly for small screens, this option makes the taskbar automatically hide itself when you're not near it. (Point your cursor at the screen's bottom edge to bring it back into view.) I leave this option toggled Off to keep the taskbar always in view. An adjacent toggle also lets you hide the taskbar in Tablet mode, handy for some tablets.
Use Small Taskbar Buttons	Another helper for the small screens found on some laptops and tablets, this setting shrinks the taskbar to half-height, letting you pack in a few extra tiny icons.
Use Peek	When you activate this feature, pointing at the taskbar's far-right edge makes the windows transparent, letting you peek at your underlying desktop. (Clicking that area minimizes all open windows.)
Show Badges on Taskbar Buttons	Leave this on to see little reminders on your taskbar app's buttons. The Mail app's taskbar icon, for example, will continuously display your number of unread emails.
Taskbar Location On Screen	Your taskbar can live on any edge of your desktop, not just the bottom. Choose any of the four edges here.

Setting	My Recommendations
Combine Taskbar Buttons	When you open lots of windows and programs, Windows accommodates the crowd by grouping similar windows under one button: All open Microsoft Word documents stack atop one Microsoft Word button, for example. To protect the taskbar from overcrowding, select the option called Always, Hide Labels.
Notification Area	This section's two links button let you choose which icons should appear in the Notification area. You can turn off the notification for Battery level, for example, if you're working on a desktop PC.
Multiple Displays	Head here if you hook up a second monitor to your PC. You can then choose whether the taskbar should extend to the other PC. (Choose Off if you watch movies on the second screen, for example; choose On if you simply want to extend your desktop across both displays.)

Setting Up Multiple Desktops

TECHNICAL STUFF

Some people connect two or more monitors to their computer so that they can double their desktop real estate. These computing enthusiasts can then view a spreadsheet on one monitor, for example, while viewing the other to write a report about the spreadsheet. (I describe how to set up two monitors in Chapter 12.)

To accommodate those on a budget, Windows 10 introduces a way to run several desktops on a *single* monitor. Called *virtual* desktops, the desktops can be swapped into view, letting you shift your work from one desktop to another. That can be handy for people with small monitors who want to toggle among several sets of adjacent windows, for example. Instead of juggling windows, they can just switch between desktops.

To create virtual desktops and work between them, follow these steps:

1. **Click the taskbar's Task View button and then click the words New Desktop.**

   A click or tap on the Task View button, shown in the margin, and the screen clears, showing thumbnails of all your open windows. In the bottom-right corner, shown in Figure 3-11, you see the words New Desktop.

   Click the words New Desktop, and a tiny desktop thumbnail immediately appears along the screen's bottom edge, shown in Figure 3-12.

2. **Click the thumbnail of the new desktop, and your second desktop fills the screen.**

   The thumbnail expands into a new desktop. The new desktop is a replica of your original desktop but without any open programs or windows.

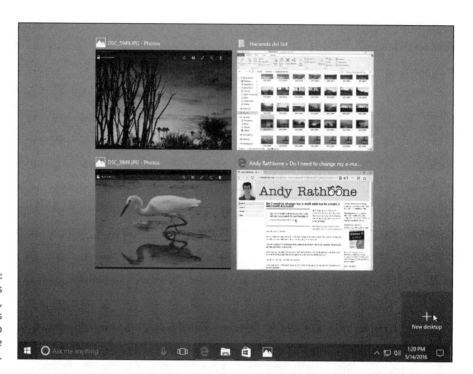

FIGURE 3-11:
Click the taskbar's
Task View button,
and the words
New Desktop
appear above the
taskbar.

FIGURE 3-12:
When the
thumbnail of the
second desktop
appears, switch
to it with a click.

That's it. You've created a second virtual desktop and moved to it. Windows keeps your other desktop tucked away until you want to switch back to it with a return click on the Task View button.

Some people love virtual desktops. Other people find the whole concept needless and confusing. But whether you love or hate virtual desktops, these tips will come in handy:

>> To switch between desktops, click the Task View button. When your miniature virtual desktop windows appear, as shown in Figure 3-12, click the one you want.

>> To see a virtual desktop's currently open windows, click the Task View button. When the miniature desktops appear along the screen's bottom edge, hover your mouse pointer over a miniature desktop; the screen changes to show thumbnails of *that* desktop's open windows. To revisit a window on any desktop, just click the window's thumbnail.

>> To close an unwanted desktop, click the Task View button, and then click the X (shown in the margin) in that desktop's thumbnail. (Hover your mouse pointer over the desktop, and the X appears.) Any open windows on that desktop will be dumped onto your original, "real" desktop. That's important: You won't lose any unsaved work by accidentally closing a virtual desktop.

>> To create even more virtual desktops, click the Task View button. When the screen shown earlier in Figure 3-11 appears, click the plus sign icon (shown in the margin) in the screen's bottom-right corner.

>> Keyboard lovers can add a desktop by holding the Windows key and then pressing Ctrl+D. Your current desktop immediately disappears, replaced by a new, empty desktop. (Pressing ⊞+Tab opens the Task View mode, letting you see all of your open windows, as well as any virtual desktops.)

>> To move an open window from one virtual desktop to another, click the Task View button to see the thumbnails of your open virtual desktops. Then drag the desired window down to the desired desktop thumbnail along the screen's bottom edge. (Right-clicking a desired window fetches a pop-up menu that lists all of your virtual desktop options.)

Making Programs Easier to Find

Whenever you install a new program on your computer, the program usually asks way too many obtuse questions. But perk up your ears when you see this question: "Would you like a shortcut icon placed on your desktop or taskbar?"

Say yes, please, as that will save you from dashing out to the Start menu to find the program's icon or tile.

But if your favorite programs don't yet have icons on the desktop or taskbar, put them there by following these steps:

1. **Head to the Start menu and scroll down the list of apps in the menu's left column.**

As you scroll up or down, an alphabetical list of icons for all of your apps and programs scrolls up or down, as well. (When in Tablet mode, click the All Apps icon, shown in the margin, to see all of your apps.)

2. **Right-click the name of any program or app you want to appear on the taskbar, choose More from the pop-up menu, and choose Pin to Taskbar from the second pop-up menu.**

If you're using a touchscreen, hold down your finger on the desired app icon for a second or two. Then lift your finger, tap the word More, and tap the Pin to Taskbar option on the pop-up menu.

Now, instead of heading to the Start menu, you can launch your oft-used apps with a click on their taskbar icon.

TIP

After you've stocked your taskbar with icons, pretend they're numbered, from left to right, but don't number the Task View icon. Pressing ⊞ +1 from the desktop opens the first program; ⊞ +2 opens the second program; and so on. You've created automatic shortcuts!

Chapter 4

Basic Desktop Window Mechanics

The Windows 10 Start menu boasts bright colors, big letters, and large buttons. It's easy to see what you're poking at with a finger or mouse.

The Windows desktop, by contrast, includes miniscule, monochrome buttons, tiny lettering, unlabeled buttons, and windows with pencil-thin borders. The windows come with way too many parts, many with confusing names that programs expect you to remember. To give you a hand, this chapter provides a lesson in windows anatomy and navigation.

You eventually need to know this stuff because windows tend to cover each other up on the desktop; you need to manually push and prod them into view.

I've dissected each part of a window so you know what happens when you click or touch each portion. By all means, use this book's margins to scribble notes as you move from the fairly simple Start menu to the powerful yet complicated Windows desktop.

Dissecting a Typical Desktop Window

Figure 4-1 places a typical window on the slab, with all its parts labeled. You might recognize the window as your Documents folder, that storage tank for most of your work.

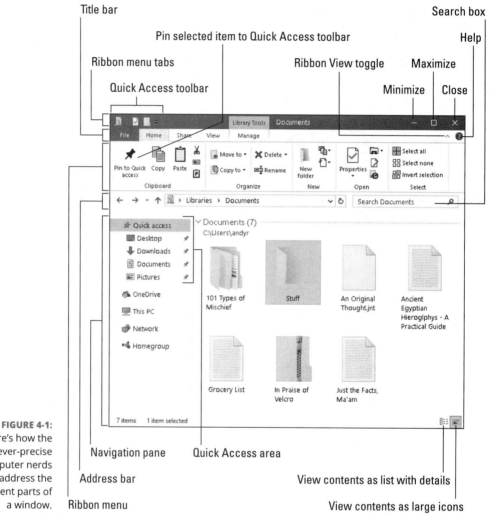

FIGURE 4-1:
Here's how the ever-precise computer nerds address the different parts of a window.

Just as boxers grimace differently depending on where they've been punched, windows behave differently depending on where they've been clicked. The next few sections describe the main parts of the Documents window in Figure 4-1, how to click them, and how Windows jerks in response.

>> Windows veterans remember their My Documents folder, that stash for almost all of their files. Windows 10 calls it simply the Documents folder. (No matter what it's called, you're still supposed to stash your files inside it.)

>> A thick, control-filled panel called the Ribbon lives atop every folder. Some people like the Ribbon's larger buttons and menus; others preferred the older menu system. Don't like the Ribbon? Gaze at the folder's top-right corner and click the tiny arrow next to the question mark, and the Ribbon disappears. (Repeat to put it back.)

>> Windows no longer shows libraries in the Navigation Pane. Most people won't miss them. If you do, put them back: Right-click a blank place inside the Navigation Pane and choose Show Libraries from the pop-up menu.

>> Windows is full of little oddly shaped buttons, borders, and boxes. You don't need to remember all their names, although that would give you a leg up on figuring out the scholarly Windows Help menus. When you spot an odd portion of a window, just return to this chapter, look up its name in Figure 4-1, and read its explanation.

>> You can deal with most things in Windows by clicking, double-clicking, or right-clicking. Hint: When in doubt, always right-click.

>> Navigating desktop windows on a touchscreen computer? For some touching tips, drop by the sidebar in Chapter 3 on touching desktop programs on a Windows tablet.

>> After you click a few windows a few times, you realize how easy it is to boss them around. The hard part is finding the right controls for the *first* time, like figuring out the dashboard on that rental car.

Tugging on a window's title bar

Found atop nearly every desktop window (see examples in Figure 4-2), the title bar usually lists the program name and the file or folder it's currently displaying. For example, Figure 4-2 shows the title bars from the Windows WordPad (top) and Notepad (bottom) programs. The WordPad title bar lists the file's name as Document because you haven't had a chance to save and name the file yet.

Although mild-mannered, the mundane title bar holds hidden powers, described in the following tips:

>> Title bars make convenient handles for moving windows around your desktop. Point at a blank part of the title bar, hold down the mouse button,

and move the mouse around: The window follows along as you move your mouse. Found the right location? Let go of the mouse button, and the window sets up camp in its new spot.

» Double-click a blank portion of the title bar, and the window leaps to fill the entire desktop. Double-click it again, and the window retreats to its original size.

» See the cluster of little icons in the WordPad program's top-left corner? Those icons form the Quick Access Toolbar, which is part of what Microsoft calls a *Ribbon interface.* The icons offer one-click access to common tasks such as saving a file.

» In Windows 10, both programs and apps place three buttons on the right end of every title bar. From left to right, they let you Minimize, Restore (or Maximize), or Close a window, topics all covered in the "Maneuvering Windows Around the Desktop" section, later in this chapter.

» To find the window you're currently working on, look at the title bar along the window's top edge. One title bar will be darker than the other. See how the WordPad title bar (Figure 4-2, top) is darker than the Notepad title bar (Figure 4-2, bottom)? That color distinguishes that window from windows you *aren't* working on. By glancing at all the title bars on the desktop, you can tell which window is awake and accepting anything you type.

FIGURE 4-2:
A title bar from WordPad (top) and Notepad (bottom).

TIP

DRAGGING, DROPPING, AND RUNNING

Although the phrase *drag and drop* sounds as if it's straight out of a Mafia guidebook, it's really a nonviolent mouse trick used throughout Windows. Dragging and dropping is a way of moving something — say, an icon on your desktop — from one place to another.

To *drag,* put the mouse pointer over the icon and *hold down* the left or right mouse button. (I prefer the right mouse button.) As you move the mouse across your desk, the pointer drags the icon across the screen. Place the pointer/icon where you want it and release the mouse button. The icon *drops,* unharmed.

Holding down the *right* mouse button while dragging and dropping makes Windows toss up a helpful little menu, asking whether you want to *copy* or *move* the icon.

Helpful Tip Department: Did you start dragging something and realize midstream that you're dragging the wrong item? Don't let go of the mouse button — instead, press Esc to cancel the action. Whew! (If you've dragged with your right mouse button and already let go of the button, you can take another exit: Choose Cancel from the pop-up menu.)

Navigating folders with a window's Address bar

Directly beneath every folder's title bar or Ribbon lives the *Address bar,* shown near the top of the folder in Figure 4-3. Web surfers will experience déjà vu: The Windows Address bar is lifted straight from the top edge of web browsers like Internet Explorer and glued atop every folder.

FIGURE 4-3:
An Address bar.

The Address bar's four main parts, described from left to right in the following list, perform four different duties:

>> **Backward and Forward buttons:** These two arrows track your path as you forage through your PC's folders. The Backward button backtracks to the folder you just visited. The Forward button brings you back.

>> **Down Arrow button:** Click this extraordinarily tiny arrow to see a drop-down list of folders you've visited previously. You can click any listed folder for a quick revisit.

>> **Up Arrow button:** Click the Up Arrow button to move up one folder from your current folder. For example, if you've been sorting files in your Documents folder's "Stuff" folder, click the Up arrow to return to your Documents folder.

>> **Address:** Just as a web browser's Address bar lists a website's address, the Windows Address bar displays your current folder's address — its location inside your PC. For example, the Address bar shown in Figure 4-3 shows three words: This PC, Documents, and Stuff. Those words tell you that you're looking inside the Stuff folder inside the Documents folder on This PC. (That's *your* PC, as opposed to somebody else's PC.) Yes, addresses are complicated enough to warrant an entire chapter: Chapter 5.

>> **Search box:** Every Windows folder sports a Search box. Instead of searching the Internet, though, it rummages through your current folder's contents. For example, if you type the word **carrot** into a folder's Search box, Windows digs through that folder's contents and retrieves every file or folder mentioning *carrot.*

TIP

In the Address bar, notice the little arrows between the words *This PC, Documents,* and *Stuff.* The arrows offer quick trips to other folders. Click any arrow — the one to the right of the word *Documents,* for example. A little menu drops down from the arrow, letting you jump to any other folder inside your Documents folder.

Finding commands on the Ribbon

The Windows desktop has more menu items than an Asian restaurant. To keep everybody's minds on computer commands instead of seaweed salad, Windows places menus inside a tab-filled *Ribbon* that lives atop every folder. (See Figure 4-4.)

FIGURE 4-4:
The Ribbon's
tabs.

The Ribbon's tabs each offer different options. To reveal the secret options, click any tab — Share, for example. The Ribbon quickly changes, as shown in Figure 4-5, presenting all your options related to *sharing* a file.

Just as restaurants sometimes run out of specials, a window sometimes isn't capable of offering all its menu items. Any unavailable options are *grayed out,* like the Print option in Figure 4-5. (Because you can't print music files, that option is grayed out.)

FIGURE 4-5:
Click any Ribbon
tab to see its
associated
commands.

TIP

If you accidentally click the wrong tab on the Ribbon, causing the wrong commands to leap onto the screen, simply click the tab you *really* wanted. A forgiving soul, Windows displays your newly chosen tab's contents instead.

You needn't know much about the Ribbon because Windows automatically places the correct buttons atop each program. Open your Music folder, for example, and the Ribbon quickly spouts a new Play tab for listening sessions.

If a button's meaning isn't immediately obvious, hover your mouse pointer over it; a little message explains the button's *raison d'être.* My own translations for the most common tabs and buttons are in the following list:

» **File:** Found along every Ribbon's left edge, this tab offers little in rewards: It gives you options for opening new windows; returning to popular locations; and, oddly enough, deleting evidence of folders you've peeked inside.

» **Home:** Found on every folder's Ribbon, the Home tab usually brings pay dirt, so every folder opens showing this tab's options. The Home tab offers tools to select, cut, copy, paste, move, delete, or rename a folder's items.

» **Share:** As the name implies, this tab offers ways to let you share a folder's contents with other people, whether by burning the contents to a CD, emailing them, or sharing them on a network. (I cover network sharing in Chapter 15.)

» **View:** Click here to change how files appear in the window. In your Pictures folder, for example, choose Extra Large Icons to see larger thumbnails of your photos.

» **Manage:** Found only on special folders, this general-purpose tab shows customized ways to handle your folder's items. Atop a folder full of pictures, for example, the Manage tab offers a Slide Show button, as well as buttons to rotate skewed photos or turn them into desktop backgrounds.

REMEMBER

Don't like that thick Ribbon hogging an inch of space atop your window? If you're pressed for space, axe the Ribbon by clicking the tiny upward-pointing arrow next to the blue question mark icon in the Ribbon's upper-right corner. Click it again to bring back the Ribbon.

Quick shortcuts with the Navigation Pane

Look at most "real" desktops, and you'll see the most-used items sitting within arm's reach: the coffee cup, the stapler, and perhaps a few crumbs from the coffee room snacks. Similarly, Windows gathers your PC's most frequently used items and places them in the Navigation Pane, shown in Figure 4-6.

FIGURE 4-6:
The Navigation
Pane offers
shortcuts to
places you visit
most frequently.

NEW

Found along the left edge of every folder, the Navigation Pane contains several main sections: Quick Access, OneDrive, and This PC. (On PCs connected through a network, you'll also see entries for Network and Homegroup.) Click any of those sections — Quick Access, for example — and the window's right side quickly shows you the contents of what you've clicked.

Here's a more detailed description of each part of the Navigation Pane:

>> **Quick Access:** Formerly called *Favorites,* these locations serve as clickable shortcuts to your most frequently accessed locations in Windows.

  • **Desktop:** Your Windows desktop, believe it or not, is actually a folder that's always spread open across your screen. Clicking Desktop quickly shows you the contents of your desktop.

  • **Downloads:** Click this shortcut to find the files you've downloaded with Internet Explorer while browsing the Internet. Ah, that's where they ended up!

  • **Documents:** A perennial favorite, this folder stores most of your work: spreadsheets, reports, letters, and other things you've created.

  • **Pictures:** Another popular destination, this takes you to photos you've shot yourself or saved from the Internet.

- **OneDrive:** This free online storage space was handed to you by Microsoft when you created a Microsoft account. Because it's password-protected and online, it's tempting to fill it with favorite files for access from any PC. But when your stored files exceed your storage limit, Microsoft asks for your credit card to pay for the extra space. I cover OneDrive at the end of Chapter 5.

» **This PC:** This section lets you browse through your PC's folders and hard drives. (Many of these commonly used storage areas also live in the Navigation Pane's Quick Access area, as well.) The This PC section holds these areas:

- **Desktop:** Click this to see the files and folders stored on your desktop. (Or, you can just close the folder and see your desktop in person.)

- **Documents:** This opens the Documents folder, a convenient repository for letters, forms, and reports.

- **Downloads:** Downloaded a file from Internet Explorer? Then look in here to be reintroduced.

- **Music:** Yep, this shortcut jumps straight to your Music folder, where a double-click on a song starts it playing through your PC's speakers.

- **Pictures:** This shortcut opens your Pictures folder, the living quarters for all your digital photos.

- **Videos:** Click here to visit your Videos folder, where a double-click on a video opens it for immediate viewing.

TECHNICAL
STUFF

- **Local Disk (C:):** A holdover for old techies, this entry lets you crawl through any folder on your PC. Unless you know specifically what item you're seeking, though, you probably won't find it. Stick with the other destinations, instead.

- **Disc Drives:** If your PC includes extra disc drives, icons for those appear here. Insert a flash drive into your USB port, and its icon appears here, as well.

- **Network:** Although Homegroups simplify file sharing, old-school networks still work, and any networked PCs — including your Homegroup buddies — appear here.

- **Homegroup:** A convenient way of sharing information among several household computers, Homegroups are two or more PCs that share information through a simple network. Click Homegroup in the Navigation Pane to see folders shared by other networked PCs in your Homegroup. (I cover Homegroups and other networks in Chapter 15.)

Here are a few tips for making the most of your Navigation Pane:

>> To avoid treks back to the Start menu, add your own favorite places to the Navigation Pane's Quick Access area: Right-click the folder and choose Pin to Quick Access from the pop-up menu.

>> If you've connected to a network at home or work, the pane's This PC section may include those other computers' music, video, and photos (which are sometimes referred to as *media*). Click those computers' icons to access those goodies as if they were stored on your own computer.

TECHNICAL STUFF

>> Windows 7 owners may notice that Windows 10 doesn't show libraries in the Navigation Pane. Libraries still exist, but they're hidden in the background. To bring them back into view, click a blank portion of the Navigation Pane and choose Show Libraries from the pop-up menu. (You must also manually add the Public folders to each library in order to return them to the glory days of Windows 7.)

Moving inside a window with its scroll bar

The scroll bar, which resembles a cutaway of an elevator shaft (see Figure 4-7), rests along the edge of all overstuffed windows. You can even find a scroll bar along the side of an extra-long Start menu.

FIGURE 4-7:
A horizontal and vertical scroll bar.

Inside the shaft, a little elevator (technically, the *scroll box*) rides along as you move through the window's contents. In fact, by glancing at the box's position in the scroll bar, you can tell whether you're viewing items in the window's beginning, middle, or end.

By clicking in various places on the scroll bar, you can quickly view different parts of things. Here's the dirt:

NEW

>> Click inside the scroll bar in the direction you want to view. On a *vertical* scroll bar, for example, click above the scroll box to move your view up one page. Similarly, click below the scroll box to move your view down a page.

>> The Start menu's extreme right edge is a difficult-to-see scroll bar, but it appears when the mouse pointer is nearby. Slide the scroll bar's box downward to view any shy apps hiding below the screen's bottom edge.

>> Don't see a scroll bar or a box in the bar? Then you're already seeing all that the window has to offer; there's nothing to scroll.

>> To move around in a hurry, drag the scroll box inside the scroll bar. As you drag, you see the window's contents race past. When you see the spot you want, let go of the mouse button to stay at that viewing position.

>> Are you using a mouse that has a little wheel embedded in the poor critter's back? Spin the wheel, and the elevator moves quickly inside the scroll bar, shifting your view accordingly. It's a handy way to explore a tile-packed Start menu, long documents, and file-filled folders.

Boring borders

A *border* is that thin edge surrounding a window, including desktop windows containing apps. Compared with a bar, it's really tiny.

To change a window's size, drag the border in or out. (When the mouse pointer turns into a two-headed arrow, you're in the right place to start dragging.) Some windows, oddly enough, don't have borders. Stuck in limbo, their size can't be changed — even if they're an awkward size.

Except for tugging on them with the mouse, you won't be using borders much.

WHEN ONE JUST ISN'T ENOUGH

Normally, you can select only one thing at a time in Windows. When you click another file, for example, Windows deselects the first file in order to select the second. If you want to select several files or folders simultaneously, try these tricks:

- To select more than one file or folder, hold down the Ctrl key and click each item you want. Each item stays highlighted. On a tablet, hold your finger down on a file or folder to select it. (You may see check boxes appear around adjacent files or folders, letting you select multiple items by clicking on their check boxes.)

- To select a bunch of adjacent files from a list inside a folder, click the first file you want. Then hold down Shift and click the last file you want. Windows immediately highlights the first file, last file, and every file in between. Pretty sneaky, huh? (To weed out a few unwanted files from the middle, hold down Ctrl and click them; Windows unhighlights them, leaving the rest highlighted.)

- Finally, when grabbing bunches of files or folders, try using the "lasso" trick: Point at an area of the screen next to one item and, while holding down the mouse button, move the mouse until you've drawn a lasso around all the items. After you've high-lighted the files or folders you want, let go of the mouse button, and they remain highlighted. (On tablets, your finger works as a mouse when lassoing items.)

Maneuvering Windows Around the Desktop

A terrible dealer at the poker table, Windows tosses windows around your desktop in a seemingly random way. Programs cover each other or sometimes dangle off the desktop. The following sections show you how to gather all your windows into a neat pile, placing your favorite window on the top of the stack. If you prefer, lay them all down like a poker hand. As an added bonus, you can change their size, making them open to any size you want, automatically.

Moving a window to the top of the pile

Windows says the window atop the pile that's getting all the attention is called the *active* window. Being the active window means that it receives any keystrokes you or your cat happen to type.

You can move a window to the top of the pile so that it's active in any of several ways:

>> Move the mouse pointer until it hovers over any portion of your desired window; then click the mouse button. Windows immediately brings the window to the top of the pile.

>> On the taskbar along the desktop's bottom, click the icon for the window you want. Chapter 3 explains what the taskbar can do in more detail.

TIP

>> Hold down the Alt key while tapping and releasing the Tab key. With each tap of the Tab key, a small window pops up, displaying a thumbnail of each open window on your desktop. (You also see thumbnails of open Start menu apps.) When your press of the Tab key highlights your favorite window, let go of the Alt key, and your window leaps to the forefront.

>> A click of the Task View button (shown in the margin), also places miniature views of each window on the screen, even if they're on different virtual desktops. Click the desired miniature window, and it rises to the top, ready for action. I cover the Task View button and virtual desktops in Chapter 3.

TIP

Is your desktop too cluttered for you to work comfortably in your current window? Then hold down your mouse pointer on the window's title bar and give it a few quick shakes; Windows drops the other windows down to the taskbar, leaving your main window resting alone on an empty desktop.

Moving a window from here to there

Sometimes you want to move a window to a different place on the desktop. Perhaps part of the window hangs off the edge, and you want it centered. Or maybe you want one window closer to another.

In either case, you can move a window by dragging and dropping its *title bar,* that thick bar along its top. (If you're not sure how dragging and dropping works, see the sidebar "Dragging, dropping, and running," earlier in this chapter.) When you *drop* the window in place, the window not only remains where you've dragged and dropped it, but it also stays on top of the pile — until you click another window, that is, which brings *that* window to the pile's top.

Making a window fill the whole desktop

Sooner or later, you'll grow tired of all this multiwindow mumbo jumbo. Why can't you just make one window fill the screen? Well, you can.

To make any desktop window grow as large as possible, double-click its *title bar*, that bar along the window's topmost edge. The window leaps up to fill the entire desktop, covering up all the other windows.

To reduce the pumped-up window back to its former size, double-click its title bar once again. The window quickly shrinks to its former size, and you can see things that it covered.

>> If you're morally opposed to double-clicking a window's title bar to expand it, you can click the Maximize button. Shown in the margin, it's the middle of the three buttons in the upper-right corner of every window.

>> When a window is maximized to fill the desktop, the Maximize button turns into a Restore button, shown in the margin. Click the Restore button, and the window returns to its smaller size.

>> Need a brute force method? Then drag a window's top edge until it butts against the top edge of your desktop. The shadow of the window's borders will expand to fill the desktop; let go of the mouse button, and the window's borders fill the desktop. (Yes, simply double-clicking the title bar is faster, but this method impresses any onlookers from neighboring cubicles.)

TIP

>> Too busy to reach for the mouse? Maximize the current window by holding down the ⊞ key and pressing the up-arrow key. (Hold down the ⊞ key and press the down-arrow key to return to normal size.)

Closing a window

When you're through working in a window, close it: Click the little X in its upper-right corner. Zap! You're back to an empty desktop.

If you try to close your window before finishing your work, be it a game of Solitaire or a report for the boss, Windows cautiously asks whether you'd like to save your work. Take it up on its offer by clicking Yes and, if necessary, typing in a filename so that you can find your work later.

Making a window bigger or smaller

Like big lazy dogs, windows tend to flop on top of one another. To space your windows more evenly, you can resize them by *dragging and dropping* their edges inward or outward. It works like this:

1. **Point at any corner with the mouse arrow. When the arrow turns into a two-headed arrow, you can hold down the mouse button and drag the corner in or out to change the window's size.**

2. **When you're happy with the window's new size, release the mouse button.**

   The window settles down into its new position.

Placing two windows side by side

The longer you use Windows, the more likely you are to want to see two windows side by side. For example, you may want to copy things from one window into another or compare two versions of the same file. By spending a few hours with the mouse, you can drag and drop the windows' corners until they're in perfect juxtaposition.

If you're impatient, Windows lets you speed up this handy side-by-side placement several ways:

>> For the quickest solution, drag a window's title bar against one side of your desktop; when your mouse pointer touches the desktop's edge, let go of the mouse button. Repeat these same steps with the second window, dragging it to the opposite side of the desktop.

NEW

>> If you drag a window to fill one edge of the screen, Windows immediately shows thumbnails of your minimized windows. Click the thumbnail of the window you'd like to see fill the screen's other half.

NEW

>> To place four windows onscreen simultaneously, drag the title bar of each window to a different corner of the screen. Each window resizes itself to grab its own quarter of the screen.

>> Right-click on a blank part of the taskbar (even the clock will do) and choose Show Windows Side by Side. The windows align next to each other, like pillars. To align them in horizontal rows, choose Show Windows Stacked. (If you have more than three open windows, Show Windows Stacked tiles them across your desktop, which is handy for seeing just a bit of each one.)

>> If you have more than two windows open, click the Minimize button (the leftmost icon in every window's top-right corner) to minimize the windows you don't want tiled. Then use the Show Windows Side by Side from the preceding bullet to align the two remaining windows.

TIP

>> To make the current window fill the desktop's right half, hold the ⊞ key and press the right-arrow key. To fill the desktop's left half, hold the ⊞ key and press the left-arrow key.

Making windows open to the same darn size

Sometimes a window opens to a small square; other times, it opens to fill the entire desktop. But windows rarely open to the exact size you want. Until you discover this trick, that is: When you *manually* adjust the size and placement of a window, Windows memorizes that size and always reopens the window to that same size. Follow these three steps to see how it works:

1. **Open your window.**

   The window opens to its usual unwanted size.

2. **Drag the window's corners until the window is the exact size and in the exact location you want. Let go of the mouse to drop the corner into its new position.**

   Be sure to resize the window *manually* by dragging its corners or edges with the mouse. Simply clicking the Maximize button won't work.

3. **Immediately close the window.**

   Windows memorizes the size and placement of a window at the time it was last closed. When you open that window again, it should open to the same size you last left it. But the changes you make apply only to the program you made them in. For example, changes made to the Internet Explorer window will be remembered only for *Internet Explorer,* not for other programs you open.

Most windows follow these sizing rules, but a few renegades from other programs may misbehave, unfortunately.

Chapter 5

Storage: Internal, External, and in the Cloud

By leaving their paper-strewn oak desktops and moving to computers, everybody hoped things would be easier. Important papers would no longer slide behind the desk or languish in dusty drawers. Twenty years later, though, we know the truth: Computers come with just as many nooks, crannies, and hiding places as did the desks they replaced. . . . maybe even more.

In Windows, File Explorer serves as your computerized filing cabinet. Insert a flash drive or portable hard drive into your computer, and File Explorer appears, ready for you to start rustling through folders.

You're stuck with File Explorer whenever you need to find folders inside your computer, *outside* your computer on plug-in drives and digital cameras, and even in some storage spots on the Internet.

Whether you're using a touchscreen tablet, a laptop, or a desktop PC, files and folders still rule the computing world. And unless you grasp the Windows folder metaphor, you may not find your information very easily.

This chapter explains how to use the Windows filing program, called *File Explorer.* (You may recognize it as *Windows Explorer,* its name from older Windows versions.) This chapter also explains how to use OneDrive, your Internet storage space, to store files away from your computer.

Along the way, you ingest just enough Windows file management skills for you to save and retrieve your work without too much discomfort.

TIP

MANAGING FILES ON A TOUCHSCREEN

Most touchscreen tablets run in Tablet mode by default. While the Tablet mode includes big buttons and finger-friendly apps, it hides the desktop, which creates a file management problem. Windows 10 doesn't include a touch-friendly file manager, so you're stuck with the desktop's File Explorer.

Chances are good that your fingers won't enjoy poking the File Explorer's tiny buttons and menus. So, start improving things by turning off Tablet mode: Slide a finger inward from the screen's right edge, and when the Action Center appears, tap the pane's Tablet mode button to turn it off, letting you use the desktop more easily. After turning off Tablet mode, you can once again view the desktop and its folders within movable windows.

If you plan to spend a lot of time on the desktop, invest in an inexpensive Bluetooth (wireless) mouse for clicking the controls. And, to remove the tablet's onscreen keyboard that blocks much of your view of the desktop, consider buying a Bluetooth keyboard, as well.

If you want your tablet to double as a desktop PC, buy a *docking station* instead. A docking station lives on your office desk and lets you permanently attach a monitor, wired mouse, and wired keyboard. Then, when you slide your tablet into a docking station, it's nearly indistinguishable from a desktop PC.

Browsing the File Explorer File Cabinets

To keep your programs and files neatly arranged, Windows cleaned up the squeaky old file cabinet metaphor with whisper-quiet Windows icons. Inside File Explorer, the icons represent your computer's storage areas, allowing you to copy, move, rename, or delete your files before the investigators arrive.

 To open File Explorer, shown in Figure 5-1, and begin rummaging around inside your computer, click the Start menu's File Explorer icon. Shown in the margin, it's near the Start menu's lower-left corner.

FIGURE 5-1:
The File Explorer window displays popular storage areas and your most recently opened files.

 You can also open File Explorer with a click on its icon (shown in the margin) on the *taskbar*, that strip along the screen's bottom edge.

In previous versions of Windows, File Explorer opened to show your computer's largest file cabinets, called *drives* or *disks* in computer lingo. Windows 10 goes one step further.

NEW

Instead of dropping you off at the drives and forcing you to dig for your files, the Windows 10 File Explorer tries to be more helpful. It simply lists your most popular folders. For example, it shows Documents, where you store most of your files, and Downloads, the holding tank for everything you download from the Internet. (You also see shortcuts to your Music, Videos, and Pictures folders.)

Below those main folders, File Explorer lists shortcuts to the items you've opened most recently. If you worked on a spreadsheet yesterday, for example, find it again by opening File Explorer: A link to that spreadsheet lives on the front page, ready to be reopened with a double-click.

Seeing your main storage folders and recently opened files may be all you need to start working. But if you need to see *all* of your computer's storage areas, click the words This PC in the pane along the left edge. File Explorer opens to the view you've seen in previous Windows versions, shown in Figure 5-2.

FIGURE 5-2:
Click This PC to see your computer's storage areas, which you can open to find your files.

The File Explorer images shown above will look slightly different from the ones on your PC, but you can still see the same basic sections:

» **Navigation Pane:** The handy Navigation Pane, that strip along every folder's left edge, lists shortcuts to different storage spaces on your PC, on OneDrive, and on any other connected computers. (I cover the Navigation Pane in Chapter 4.)

» **Folders:** When opened, File Explorer lists shortcuts to your main storage folders, as well as your *computing history,* a list of recently accessed folders and files. Unless you're starting a brand-new project, you can probably find your most recent work here.

» **Devices and Drives:** Shown in Figure 5-2, this area lists your PC's storage areas and devices. (The term *devices* usually refers to gadgets plugged into your PC.) Every computer has at least one hard drive. Double-clicking a hard drive icon displays its files and folders, but you can rarely find much useful information when probing that way. No, your most important files live in your Documents, Music, Pictures, and Videos folders, which appear near the top of Figure 5-2.

Notice the hard drive bearing the little Windows icon (shown in the margin)? That means that Windows lives on that drive. And do you see the multicolored line next to the drives' icon? The more colored space you see in the line, the more files you've stuffed onto your drive. When the line turns red, your drive is almost full, and you should think about deleting some unwanted files, uninstalling some unused programs, or upgrading to a larger drive.

You may also see some detachable gadgetry attached to your computer. Here are some of the more common items:

>> **CD, DVD, and Blu-ray drives:** As shown in Figure 5-2, Windows places a short description next to each drive's icon. For example, *CD-RW* means the drive can write to *CDs* but not DVDs. *DVD-RW* means that it can both read and write to DVDs *and* CDs. A *BD-ROM* drive can read Blu-ray discs, but it can write only to CDs and DVDs. And the ever-so-versatile *BD-RE* and *BD-R* drives can read and write to Blu-ray discs, DVDs, *and* CDs.

Writing information to a disc is called *burning*. Copying information from a disc is called *ripping*.

>> **Flash drives:** The icon for some flash drive brands resembles the actual flash drive. Most flash drives simply show a generic icon like the one in the margin.

TIP

Windows doesn't display icons for your computer's memory card readers until you've inserted a card into them. To see icons for your *empty* card readers, open File Explorer, click the View tab, and select the Hidden Items check box in the View tab's Show/Hide section. Repeat to hide them again.

>> **iPads, phones, and MP3 players:** A Windows phone receives a nice icon, but Android phones, iPads, and iPhones usually receive a generic MP3 player icon. If you own an iPhone or iPad, you need the Apple iTunes software (www.apple.com/itunes) that runs on the Windows desktop. Windows can't copy songs to and from an iPod or iPad by itself. (I cover MP3 players in Chapter 16.)

>> **Cameras:** When plugged into your computer's USB port, digital cameras usually appear as camera icons in the File Explorer window. To import your camera's photos, turn on your camera and set it to its View Photos mode rather than its Take Photos mode. Then right-click the camera's icon in File Explorer and choose Import Pictures and Videos from the pop-up menu. After Windows walks you through the process of extracting the images (see Chapter 17), it places the photos in your Pictures folder.

If you plug a digital camcorder, cellphone, or other gadget into your PC, the File Explorer window often sprouts a new icon representing your gadget. If Windows neglects to ask what you'd like to do with your newly plugged-in gadget, right-click the icon to open a list of everything you can do with that item. No icon? Then you need to install a *driver* for your gadget, a precipitous journey detailed in Chapter 13.

If you prefer that File Explorer opens to the traditional This PC view rather than the new Quick Access view, first open any folder. Then click that folder's File tab and choose Change Folder and Search Options. When the Folder Options window appears, open the drop-down menu along the window's top edge and choose This PC instead of the default Quick Access.

To see inside an item listed in File Explorer, perhaps a flash drive or your digital camera, double-click it. To back out of that view, click the left-pointing arrow (shown in the margin) above the Navigation Pane.

Tip for tablets: When you read the word *click*, substitute *tap*. Similarly, *right-click* means *touch and hold*. And the term *drag and drop* means *slide your finger along the screen as if your finger is the mouse pointer and then lift the finger to drop the item*.

Getting the Lowdown on Folders

This stuff is dreadfully boring, but if you don't read it, you'll be just as lost as your files.

A *folder* is a storage area, just like a real folder in a file cabinet. Windows divides your computer's hard drives into many folders to separate your many projects. For example, you store all your music in your Music folder and your pictures in your Pictures folder. That lets both you and your programs find them easily.

Windows gives you six main folders for storing your files. For easy access, they live in the This PC section of the Navigation Pane along the left side of every folder. Shown earlier, Figure 5-2 shows your main storage areas: Desktop, Documents, Downloads, Music, Pictures, and Videos.

Keep these folder facts in mind when shuffling files in Windows:

>> You can ignore folders and dump all your files onto the Windows desktop. But that's like tossing everything into your car's back seat and pawing around to find your sunglasses a month later. Organized stuff is much easier to find.

- >> If you're eager to create a folder or two (and it's pretty easy), page ahead to this chapter's "Creating a New Folder" section.

- >> The new Windows 10 web browser, Microsoft Edge, conveniently drops all of your downloaded files into your Downloads folder. Until you delete it, every file you've downloaded will be in that folder.

- >> File Explorer folders use a tree metaphor as they branch out from one main folder (a drive) that contains folders which contain even more folders.

TECHNICAL STUFF

Peering into Your Drives, Folders, and Other Media

Knowing all this folder stuff not only impresses computer store employees but also helps you find the files you want. (See the preceding section for a lowdown on which folder holds what.) Put on your hard hat and get ready to go spelunking among your computer's drives and folders as well as your CDs, DVDs, and cellphones. The following sections are your guide.

Seeing the files on a drive

Like everything else in Windows, disk drives are represented by buttons, or *icons*. The File Explorer program also shows information stored in other areas, such as phones, MP3 players, digital cameras, or scanners. (I explain these icons in the section "Browsing the File Explorer File Cabinets," earlier in this chapter.)

Opening an icon usually lets you access the device's contents and move files back and forth, just as with any other folders in Windows.

When you double-click a hard drive icon in File Explorer, Windows promptly opens the drive to show you the folders packed inside. But how should Windows react when you insert something new into your computer, such as a CD, DVD, or flash drive?

Earlier versions of Windows tried to second-guess you. When you inserted a music CD, for example, Windows automatically began playing the music. Today's newer, politer Windows, by contrast, asks how you prefer it to handle the situation, as shown by the pop-up notification in the lower-right corner of Figure 5-3.

When that message appears, choose it with a click of the mouse. A second message appears, as shown in Figure 5-4, listing every way your PC and its gang of apps and programs can handle that item.

FIGURE 5-3:
Windows asks
how it should
handle newly
inserted items.

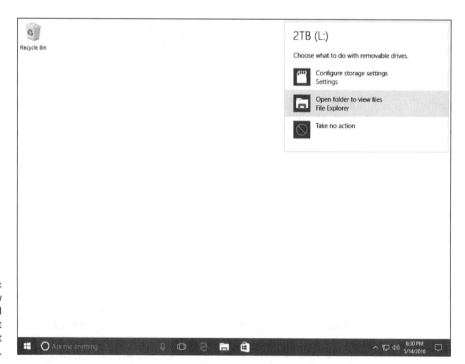

FIGURE 5-4:
Choose how
Windows should
react the next
time you insert
that item.

Choose an option — Open Folder to View Files, for example — and Windows fires up File Explorer to display your newly inserted drive's contents. The next time you plug that drive into your PC, your computer won't bother asking; it will automatically summon File Explorer and display your drive's folders.

But what if you change your mind about how Windows should treat a newly inserted item? Then you need to change how Windows reacts: In File Explorer's This PC section, right-click the inserted item's icon and choose Open AutoPlay. Once again, Windows shows the message from Figure 5-4 and asks you to plot the future course.

Adjusting the AutoPlay settings comes in particularly handy for USB thumbdrives. If your flash drive carries a few songs, Windows may want to play them, slowing your access to your flash drive's other files. To prevent that, select the AutoPlay option, Open Folder to View Files.

>> When in doubt as to what you can do with an icon in File Explorer, right-click it. Windows presents a menu of all the things you can do to that object. (You can choose Open, for example, to see the files on a flash drive, making it simpler to copy them to your computer.)

>> If you double-click an icon for a CD, DVD, or Blu-ray drive when no disk is in the drive, Windows stops you, gently suggesting that you insert a disk before proceeding further.

>> Spot an icon under the heading Network Location? That's a little doorway for peering into other computers linked to your computer — if there are any. You find more network stuff in Chapter 15.

Seeing what's inside a folder

Because folders are really little storage compartments, Windows uses a picture of a little folder to represent a place for storing files.

To see what's inside a folder, either in File Explorer or on the Windows desktop, just double-click that folder's picture. A new window pops up, showing that folder's contents. Spot another folder inside that folder? Double-click that one to see what's inside. Keep clicking until you find what you want or reach a dead end.

Reached a dead end? If you mistakenly end up in the wrong folder, back your way out as if you're browsing the web. Click the tiny Back arrow (shown in the margin) at the window's top-left corner. That closes the wrong folder and shows you the folder you just left. If you keep clicking the Back arrow, you end up right where you started.

WHAT'S ALL THIS PATH STUFF?

TECHNICAL STUFF

A *path* is merely the file's address, similar to your own. When a letter is mailed to your house, for example, it travels to your country, state, city, street, and (with any luck) your apartment or house. A computer path does the same thing. It starts with the letter of the disk drive and ends with the file's name. In between, the path lists all the folders the computer must travel through to reach the file.

For example, look at the Downloads folder. For Windows to find a file stored in my Downloads folder, it starts from the computer's C: drive, travels through the Users folder, and then goes through the Andy folder. From there, it goes into the Andy folder's Downloads folder. (Internet Explorer follows that path when saving your downloaded files.)

Take a deep breath and exhale slowly. Now add in the computer's ugly grammar: In a path, the Windows disk drive letter is referred to as C:\. The disk drive letter and colon make up the first part of the path. All the other folders are inside the big C: folder, so they're listed after the C: part. Windows separates these nested folders with something called a *backslash,* or \. The downloaded file's name — *Tax Form 3890,* for example — comes last.

Put it all together, and you get C:\Users\Andy\Downloads\Tax Form 3890. That's my computer's official path to the Tax Form 3890 file in Andy's Downloads folder. Of course, on your computer, you can substitute your own username for *Andy*. (Microsoft account usernames usually start with the first few letters of the linked Microsoft account email address.)

This stuff can be tricky, so here it is again: The letter for the drive comes first, followed by a colon and a backslash. Then come the names of all the folders leading to the file, separated by backslashes. Last comes the name of the file itself.

Windows automatically puts together the path for you when you click folders — thankfully. But whenever you click the Browse button to look for a file, you're navigating through folders and traversing along the path leading to the file.

The Address bar provides another quick way to jump to different places in your PC. As you move from folder to folder, the folder's Address bar — that wide word-filled box at the folder's top — constantly keeps track of your trek.

Notice the little arrows between the folder names. Those little arrows provide quick shortcuts to other folders and windows. If you try clicking any of the arrows, menus appear, listing the places you can jump to from that point. For example, click the arrow after Music, shown in Figure 5-5, and a menu drops down, letting you jump quickly to your other folders.

FIGURE 5-5:
Click the little
arrow after Music
to jump to any
place that
appears in the
Music folder.

TIP

Here are some more tips for finding your way in and out of folders:

>> Sometimes a folder contains too many files or folders to fit in the window. To see more files, click that window's scroll bars along a window's bottom or right edges. (I cover scroll bars in your field guide, Chapter 4.)

>> While burrowing deeply into folders, the Recent Locations arrow provides yet another quick way to jump immediately to any folder you've plowed through: Click the little downward-pointing arrow next to the Forward arrow in the window's top-left corner. A menu drops down, listing the folders you've plowed past on your journey. Click any name to jump quickly to that folder.

>> Click the Up Arrow button, located just to the right of the Address bar, to move your view up one folder. Keep clicking it, and you'll eventually wind up at someplace recognizable: your desktop.

>> Can't find a particular file or folder? Instead of aimlessly rummaging through folders, check out the Start menu's Search box, which I describe in Chapter 7. Also known as *Cortana*, the Search box can automatically find your lost files, folders, email, and nearly anything else hiding in your PC, as well as on the Internet.

>> When faced with a long list of alphabetically sorted files, click anywhere on the list. Then quickly type the first letter or two of the desired file's name. Windows immediately jumps up or down the list to the first name beginning with those letters.

TECHNICAL STUFF

>> Libraries, a sort of super folder introduced in Windows 7, vanished in Windows 8.1: Microsoft dropped them from the Navigation Pane, and they're still missing from Windows 10. If you miss them, add them back by right-clicking a *blank* portion of the Navigation Pane and choosing Show Libraries from the pop-up menu.

Creating a New Folder

To store new information in a file cabinet, you grab a manila folder, scrawl a name across the top, and start stuffing it with information. To store new information in Windows — notes for your autobiography, for example — you create a new folder, think up a name for the new folder, and start stuffing it with files.

To create a new folder quickly, click Home from the folder's toolbar buttons and choose New Folder from the Ribbon: A folder appears, ready for you to type in its name.

If the menus seem to be hiding, though, here's a quick and foolproof method:

1. **Right-click inside your folder (or on the desktop) and choose New.**

   The all-powerful right-click shoots a menu out the side.

2. **Choose Folder.**

   When you choose Folder, shown in Figure 5-6, a new folder quickly appears, waiting for you to type a new name.

FIGURE 5-6:
Right-click where you want a new folder to appear, choose New, and select Folder from the menu.

3. **Type a new name for the folder.**

   A newly created folder bears the boring name of New Folder. When you begin typing, Windows quickly erases the old name and fills in your new name. Done? Save the new name by either pressing Enter or clicking somewhere away from the name you've just typed.

If you mess up the name and want to try again, right-click the folder, choose Rename, and start over.

>> Certain symbols are banned from folder (and file) names. The "Using legal folder names and filenames" sidebar spells out the details, but you never have trouble when using plain old letters and numbers for names.

>> Shrewd observers notice that in Figure 5-6 Windows offers to create many more things than just a folder when you click the New button. Right-click inside a folder anytime you want to create a new shortcut or other common item.

>> Cautious observers may remark that their right-click menu looks different than the one shown in Figure 5-6. There's nothing wrong; programs often add their own items to the right-click menus, making the menu look different on different PCs.

Renaming a File or Folder

Sick of a filename or folder name? Then change it. Just right-click the offending icon and choose Rename from the menu that pops up. Windows highlights the file's old name, which disappears as you begin typing the new one. Press Enter or click the desktop when you're through, and you're off.

Or you can click the filename or folder name to select it, wait a second, and click the name again to change it. Some people click the name and press F2; Windows automatically lets you rename the file or folder.

TIP

>> When you rename a file, only its name changes. The contents are still the same, the file is still the same size, and the file is still in the same place.

>> To rename large groups of files simultaneously, select them all, right-click the first one, and choose Rename. Type in the new name and press Enter, and Windows renames that file. However, it also renames all your other selected files to the new name, adding a number as it goes: cat, cat(2), cat(3), cat(4), and so on. It's a handy way to rename photographs.

>> Renaming some folders confuses Windows, especially if those folders contain programs. And please don't rename your main folders: Downloads, Documents, Pictures, Music, or Videos.

TECHNICAL
STUFF

>> Windows won't let you rename a file or folder if one of your programs currently uses it. Sometimes closing the program fixes the problem. Other times, you need to restart your PC. That releases the program's clutches so you can rename it.

Selecting Bunches of Files or Folders

Although selecting a file, folder, or other object may seem particularly boring, it swings the doors wide open for further tasks: deleting, renaming, moving, copying, and performing other file–juggling tricks discussed in the rest of this chapter.

To select a single item, just click it. To select several files and folders, hold down the Ctrl key when you click the names or icons. Each name or icon stays high-lighted when you click the next one.

To gather several files or folders sitting next to each other in a list, click the first one. Then hold down the Shift key as you click the last one. Those two items are highlighted, along with every file and folder sitting between them.

TIP

Windows lets you *lasso* desktop files and folders, as well. Point slightly above the first file or folder you want and then, while holding down the mouse button, point at the last file or folder. The mouse creates a colored lasso to surround your files. Let go of the mouse button, and the lasso disappears, leaving all the surrounded files highlighted.

- » You can drag and drop armfuls of files in the same way that you drag a single file.

- » You can also simultaneously cut or copy and paste these armfuls into new locations using any of the methods described in the "Copying or Moving Files and Folders" section, later in this chapter.

- » You can delete these armfuls of goods, too, with a press of the Delete key. (They all drop into the Recycle Bin and are available for emergency retrieval.)

TIP

- » To quickly select all the files in a folder, choose Select All from the folder's Edit menu. (No menu? Then select them by pressing Ctrl+A.) Here's another nifty trick: To grab all but a few files, press Ctrl+A, and while still holding down Ctrl, click the ones you don't want.

Getting Rid of a File or Folder

Sooner or later, you'll want to delete a file that's no longer important — yesterday's lottery picks, for example, or a particularly embarrassing digital photo. To delete a file or folder, right-click its name or icon. Then choose Delete from the pop-up menu. This surprisingly simple trick works for files, folders, shortcuts, and just about anything else in Windows.

To delete in a hurry, click the offending object and press the Delete key. Dragging and dropping a file or folder to the Recycle Bin does the same thing.

WARNING

The Delete option deletes entire folders, including any files or folders stuffed *inside* those folders. Make sure that you select the correct folder before you choose Delete.

NEW

- » Unlike earlier Windows versions, Windows 10 doesn't toss a box in your face, asking whether you're *sure* you want to delete the file. If you prefer being asked, right-click the Recycle Bin, choose Properties, and place a check mark next to Display Delete Confirmation Dialog.

- » Be extra sure that you know what you're doing when deleting any file that depicts a little gear in its icon. These files are usually sensitive hidden files, and the computer wants you to leave them alone. (Other than that, they're not particularly exciting, despite the action-oriented gears.)

- » Icons with little arrows in their corner (like the one in the margin) are shortcuts, which are push buttons that merely load files. (I cover shortcuts in Chapter 6.) Deleting shortcuts deletes only a button that loads a file or program. The file or program itself remains undamaged and still lives inside your computer.

DON'T BOTHER READING THIS HIDDEN TECHNICAL STUFF

TECHNICAL STUFF

You're not the only one creating files on your computer. Programs often store their own information in a *data file*. They may need to store information about the way your computer is set up, for example. To keep people from confusing those files for trash and deleting them, Windows hides them.

However, if you want to play voyeur, you can view the names of these hidden files and folders:

1. **Open any folder and click the View tab from along the top edge.**

   The Ribbon changes to show different ways you can view that folder's files.

2. **Click in the box named Hidden Items.**

   Don't see the Hidden Items box? Make the window a little wider until that option appears.

These steps make the formerly hidden files appear alongside the other filenames. Be sure not to delete them, however: The programs that created them will gag, possibly damaging them or Windows itself. To avoid trouble, click the Hidden Items box again to drape the veil of secrecy back over those important files.

>> As soon as you find out how to delete files, trot off to Chapter 3, which explains several ways to *un*delete them. (**Hint for the desperate:** Open the Recycle Bin, right-click your file's name, and choose Restore.)

Copying or Moving Files and Folders

To copy or move files to different folders on your hard drive, it's sometimes easiest to use your mouse to *drag* them there. For example, here's how to move a file to a different folder on your desktop. In this case, I'm moving the Traveler file from the House folder to the Morocco folder.

1. **Align the two windows next to each other.**

   I explain this in Chapter 4. If you skipped that chapter, try this: Click the first window and then hold the ⊞ key and press the right-arrow key. To fill the screen's left half, click the other window, hold the key, and press the left-arrow key.

2. **Aim the mouse pointer at the file or folder you want to move.**

In my example, I point at the Traveler file.

3. **While holding down the right mouse button, move the mouse until it points at the destination folder.**

As you see in Figure 5-7, I'm dragging Traveler file from the House folder to the Morocco folder.

Moving the mouse drags the file along with it, and Windows explains that you're moving the file, as shown in Figure 5-7. (Be sure to hold down the right mouse button the entire time.)

Always drag icons while holding down the *right* mouse button. Windows is then gracious enough to give you a menu of options when you position the icon, and you can choose to copy, move, or create a shortcut. If you hold down the *left* mouse button, Windows sometimes doesn't know whether you want to copy or move.

REMEMBER

4. **Release the mouse button and choose Copy Here, Move Here, or Create Shortcuts Here from the pop-up menu.**

FIGURE 5-7:
To move a file or folder from one window to another, drag it there while holding down the right mouse button.

When dragging and dropping takes too much work, Windows offers a few other ways to copy or move files. Depending on your screen's current layout, some of the following onscreen tools may work more easily:

>> **Right-click menus:** Right-click a file or folder and choose Cut or Copy, depending on whether you want to move or copy it. Then right-click inside your destination folder and choose Paste. It's simple, it always works, and you needn't bother placing any windows side by side.

>> **Ribbon commands:** In File Explorer, click your file or folder, click the Ribbon's Home tab at the top, and then click the Copy To (or Move To) button. A menu drops down, listing some common locations. Don't spot the right spot? Then click Choose Location and click through the drive and folders to reach the destination folder, and Windows transports the file accordingly. Although a bit cumbersome, this method works if you know the exact location of the destination folder.

I explain more about the Ribbon in Chapter 4.

>> **Navigation Pane:** Described in Chapter 4, this panel along File Explorer's left edge lists popular locations: drives, networks, OneDrive, and oft-used folders. That lets you drag and drop items into a folder on the Navigation Pane, sparing you the hassle of opening a destination folder.

WARNING

After you install a program on your computer, don't ever move that program's folder. Programs wedge themselves deeply into Windows. Moving the program may break it, and you'll have to reinstall it. However, feel free to move a program's *shortcut.* (Shortcut icons contain a little arrow.)

Seeing More Information about Files and Folders

Whenever you create a file or folder, Windows scrawls a bunch of secret hidden information on it, such as the date you created it, its size, and even more trivial stuff. Sometimes Windows even lets you add your own secret information, including reviews for your music files or thumbnail pictures for any of your folders.

You can safely ignore most of the information. Other times, tweaking that information is the only way to solve a problem.

To see what Windows is calling your files and folders behind your back, right-click the item and choose Properties from the pop-up menu. Choosing Properties on a song, for example, brings up bunches of details, as shown in Figure 5-8. Here's what each tab means:

>> **General:** This first tab (far left in Figure 5-8) shows the file's *type* (an MP3 file of the song "Getting Better"), its *size* (6.42MB), the program that *opens* it (in this case, the Groove Music app), and the file's *location.*

FIGURE 5-8:
A file's Properties
dialog box
shows which
program
automatically
opens it, the
file's size, and
other details.

TIP

Want a different program to open your file? Right-click the file, choose Properties, and click the Change button on the General tab, shown in Figure 5-8. A list of your computer's available music players appears, letting you choose your preferred program.

TECHNICAL
STUFF

>> **Security:** On this tab, you control *permissions,* which are rules determining who can access the file and what they can do with it. System administrators earn high wages mostly for understanding this type of stuff.

>> **Details:** True to its name, this tab reveals arcane details about a file. On digital photos, for example, this tab lists EXIF (Exchangeable Image File Format) data: the camera model, f-stop, aperture, focal length, and other items loved by photographers. On songs, this tab displays the song's *ID3 tag* (IDentify MP3), which includes the artist, album title, year, track number, genre, length, and similar information.

>> **Previous Versions:** After you set up the Windows File History backup system, this tab lists all the previously saved versions of this file, ready for retrieval with a click. I cover File History in Chapter 13.

Normally, these tidbits of information remain hidden unless you right-click a file or folder and choose Properties. But what if you want to see details about all the files in a folder, perhaps to find pictures taken on a certain day? For that, switch your folder's view to Details by following these steps:

1. **Click the View tab on the Ribbon along the folder's top edge.**

   A menu appears, listing the umpteen ways a folder can display your files.

2. **In the Layout group, select Details, as shown in Figure 5-9.**

   The screen changes to show your files' names, with details about them stretching to the right in orderly columns.

FIGURE 5-9:
To see details about files in a folder, click the View tab and select Details.

Try all the views to see which view you prefer. (Windows remembers which views you prefer for different folders.)

REMEMBER

» If you can't remember what a folder's toolbar buttons do, rest your mouse pointer over a button. Windows displays a helpful box summing up the button's mission.

» Switch among the different views until you find the one that fits what you're trying to accomplish, be it to see a particular photo's creation date or see thumbnails of every photo in a folder.

» Folders usually display files sorted alphabetically. To sort them differently, right-click a blank spot inside the folder and choose Sort By. A pop-up menu lets you choose to sort items by size, name, type, and other details.

» When the excitement of the Sort By menu wears off, try clicking the words at the top of each sorted column. Click Size, for example, to reverse the order, placing the largest files at the list's top.

» Feel free to add your own columns to Details view: Right-click a column header you don't need, and a drop-down menu appears, letting you choose a different criterion. (I always add a Date Taken column to my photos, so I can sort my photos by the date I snapped them.)

Writing to CDs and DVDs

Most computers today write information to CDs and DVDs by using a flameless approach known as *burning.* To see whether you're stuck with an older drive that can't burn discs, first remove any discs from inside the drive. Then from the desktop, click the taskbar's File Explorer icon and look at the icon for your CD or DVD drive.

Because computers always speak in secret code, here's what you can do with the disc drives in your computer:

» **DVD-RW:** These drives both read and write to CDs *and* DVDs.

» **BD-ROM:** These can read and write to CDs and DVDs, plus they can read Blu-ray discs.

» **BD-RE:** Although these have the same icon as BD-ROM drives, they can read and write to CDs, DVDs, *and* Blu-ray discs.

TECHNICAL
STUFF

If your PC has two CD or DVD burners, tell Windows which drive you want to handle your disc-burning chores: Right-click the drive, choose Properties, and click the Recording tab. Then choose your favorite drive in the top box.

Buying the right kind of blank CDs and DVDs for burning

Stores sell two types of CDs: CD-R (short for CD-Recordable) and CD-RW (short for CD-ReWritable). Here's the difference:

» **CD-R:** Most people buy CD-Rs because they're very cheap and they work fine for storing music or files. You can write to them until they fill up; then you can't write to them anymore. But that's no problem because most people don't want to erase their CDs and start over. They want to stick their burned disc into the car's stereo or stash it as a backup.

>> **CD-RW:** Techies sometimes buy CD-RWs for making temporary backups of data. You can write information to them, just as you can with CD-Rs. But when a CD-RW fills up, you can erase it and start over with a clean slate — something not possible with a CD-R. However, CD-RWs cost more money, so most people stick with the cheaper and faster CD-Rs.

DVDs come in both R and RW formats, just like CDs, so the preceding R and RW rules apply to them, as well. Most DVD burners sold in the past few years can write to any type of blank CD or DVD.

TECHNICAL STUFF

Buying blank DVDs for older drives is chaos: The manufacturers fought over which storage format to use, confusing things for everybody. To buy the right blank DVD, check your computer's receipt to see what formats its DVD burner needs: DVD-R, DVD-RW, DVD+R, or DVD+RW.

>> Discs come rated by their speed. For faster disc burning, buy the largest number "x" speed you can find, usually 52x for CDs and 16x for DVDs.

>> Blank CDs are cheap; borrow one from a neighbor's kid to see whether it works in your drive. If it works fine, buy some of the same type. Blank DVDs, by contrast, are more expensive. Ask the store whether you can return them if your DVD drive doesn't like them.

>> Blank Blu-ray discs cost a lot more than CDs or DVDs. Luckily, Blu-ray drives aren't very picky, and just about any blank Blu-ray disc will work.

>> For some odd reason, Compact Discs and Digital Video Discs are spelled as discs, not disks.

>> Although Windows can handle simple disc-burning tasks, it's extraordinarily awkward at duplicating discs. Most people give up quickly and buy third-party disc-burning software. I explain how Windows creates music CDs in Chapter 16.

>> It's currently illegal to make duplicates of movie DVDs in the United States — even to make a backup copy in case the kids scratch up the new Disney DVD. Windows can't copy DVDs on its own, but some programs on websites from other countries can handle the job.

Copying files to or from a CD or DVD

CDs and DVDs once hailed from the school of simplicity: You simply slid them into your CD player or DVD player, and they played. But as soon as those discs graduated to PCs, the problems started. When you create a CD or DVD, you must tell your PC *what* you're copying and *where* you intend to play it: Music for a CD player? Photo slideshows for a TV's DVD player? Or files to store on your computer?

If you choose the wrong answer, your disc won't work, and you've created yet another coaster.

Here are the Disc Creation rules:

>> **Music:** To create a CD that plays music in your CD player or car stereo, flip ahead to Chapter 16. You need to fire up the Windows Media Player program and burn an *audio CD.*

>> **Photo slide shows:** Windows doesn't include the Windows DVD Maker bundled with Windows Vista and Windows 7. To create photo slideshows, you need a third-party program.

If you just want to copy *files* to a CD or DVD, perhaps to save as a backup or to give to a friend, stick around.

Follow these steps to write files to a new blank CD or DVD. (If you're writing files to a CD or DVD that you've written to before, jump ahead to Step 4.)

1. **Insert the blank disc into your disc burner and push in the tray. Then click or tap the Notification box that appears in the screen's bottom-right corner.**

2. **When the Notification box asks how you'd like to proceed, click the box's Burn Files to a Disc option.**

   Windows displays a Burn a Disc dialog box and asks you to create a title for the disc.

   If the Notification box disappeared before you could click on it, eject your disc, push it back in, and have your hand ready on the mouse. (Alternatively, you can bring back the Notification box by right-clicking the disc drive's icon in File Explorer and choosing the Open Autoplay option.)

3. **Type a name for the disc, describe how you want to use the disc, and click Next.**

   Unfortunately, Windows limits your CD or DVD's title to 16 characters. Instead of typing **Family Picnic atop Orizaba in 2016**, stick to the facts: **Orizaba 2016**. Or, just click Next to use the default name for the disc: the current date.

   Windows can burn the files to the disc two different ways. To decide which method works best for you, it offers you two options:

   • **Like a USB flash drive:** This method lets you read and write files to the disc many times, a handy way to use discs as portable file carriers.

Unfortunately, that method isn't compatible with some CD or DVD players connected to home stereos or TVs.

- **With a CD/DVD player:** If you plan to play your disc on a fairly new home stereo disc player that's smart enough to read files stored in several different formats, select this method.

Armed with the disc's name, Windows prepares the disc for incoming files.

4. **Tell Windows which files to write to disc.**

   Now that your disc is ready to accept the files, tell Windows what information to send its way. You can do this in any of several ways:

   - Drag and drop your files and/or folders into the drive's File Explorer window.

   - Right-click the item you want to copy, be it a single file, folder, or selected files and folders. When the pop-up menu appears, choose Send To and select your disc burner from the menu. (The pop-up menu lists the disc's title you chose in Step 3.)

   - Drag and drop files and/or folders on top of the burner's icon in File Explorer.

   - From your Music, Pictures, or Documents folder, click the Share tab and then click Burn to Disc. This button copies all of that folder's files (or just the files you've selected) to the disc as files.

   - Tell your current program to save the information to the disc rather than to your hard drive.

   No matter which method you choose, Windows dutifully looks over the information and copies it to the disc you inserted in the first step. A progress window appears, showing the disc burner's progress. When the progress window disappears, Windows has finished burning the disc.

5. **Close your disc-burning session by ejecting the disc.**

   When you're through copying files to the disc, push your drive's Eject button (or right-click the drive's icon in File Explorer and choose Eject). Windows closes the session, adding a finishing touch to the disc that lets other PCs read it.

TIP

If you try to copy a large batch of files to a disc — more than will fit — Windows complains immediately. Copy fewer files at a time, perhaps spacing them out over two discs.

TIP

Most programs let you save files directly to disc. Choose Save from the File menu and select your CD burner. Put a disc (preferably one that's not already filled) into your disc drive to start the process.

DUPLICATING A CD OR DVD

Windows doesn't include any way to duplicate a CD, DVD, or Blu-ray disc. It can't even make a copy of a music CD. (That's why so many people buy CD-burning programs.)

But it can copy all of a CD's or DVD's files to a blank disc by using this two-step process:

1. **Copy the files and folders from the CD or DVD to a folder on your PC.**

2. **Copy those same files and folders back to a blank CD or DVD.**

That gives you a duplicate CD or DVD, which is handy when you need a second copy of an essential backup disc.

You can try this process on a music CD or DVD movie, but it won't work. (I tried.) It works only when you're duplicating a disc containing data files.

Working with Flash Drives and Memory Cards

Digital camera owners eventually become acquainted with *memory cards* — those little plastic squares that replaced the awkward rolls of film. Windows can read digital photos directly from the camera after you find its cable and plug it into your PC. But Windows can also grab photos straight off the memory card, a method praised by those who've lost their camera's cables.

The secret is a *memory card reader* — a little slot-filled box that stays plugged into your PC. Slide your memory card into the slot, and your PC can read the card's files, just like reading files from any other folder. Some tablets, laptops, and PCs include built-in memory card readers.

Most office supply and electronics stores sell memory card readers that accept most popular memory card formats: Compact Flash, SecureDigital High Capacity (SDHC), Micro-SecureDigital High Capacity (SDHC), Micro-SecureDigital Extended Capacity (SDXC), and a host of other tongue twisters. Some computers even come with built-in memory card readers on the front of their case.

The beauty of card readers is that there's nothing new to figure out: Windows treats your inserted card just like an ordinary folder. Insert your card, and a folder appears on your screen to show your digital camera photos. The same drag-and-drop and cut-and-paste rules covered earlier in this chapter still apply, letting you move the pictures or other files off the card and into your Pictures folder.

Flash drives — also known as *thumbdrives* — work just like memory card readers. Plug the flash drive into one of your PC's USB ports, and the drive appears as an icon (shown in the margin) in File Explorer, ready to be opened with a double-click.

WARNING

» First, the warning: Formatting a card or flash drive wipes out all its information. Never format a card or flash drive unless you don't care about the information it currently holds.

» Now, the procedure: If Windows complains that a newly inserted card isn't formatted, right-click its drive and choose Format. (This problem happens most often with brand-new or damaged cards.)

» Most smartphones and tablets now contain memory card slots, as well. Their cards work the same as the ones found in digital cameras.

OneDrive: Your Cubbyhole in the Clouds

When you're sitting in front of your computer, you naturally store your files inside your computer. There's really no place else to put them. When you leave your computer, you can bring along important files by stashing them on flash drives, CDs, DVDs, and portable hard drives — if you remember to grab them on the way out.

But how can you access your files from *any* computer, even if you've forgotten to bring along the files? How can you grab your home files from work, and vice versa? How can you view an important document while traveling?

Microsoft's solution to that problem is called *OneDrive*. It's your own private file storage space on the Internet, and it's built into Windows 10. With OneDrive, your files are available from any computer with an Internet connection. You can even grab them from phones or tablets from Apple, Android, Blackberry, or Windows: Microsoft offers a free OneDrive app for all of them.

If you change a file on OneDrive, Microsoft automatically changes that file on *all* of your computers and devices. That way, your OneDrive folder automatically stays up-to-date on every device.

Windows 10 makes OneDrive easily accessible by building it into every folder. However, you still need the following things in order to put OneDrive to work:

» **Microsoft account:** You need a Microsoft account in order to upload, view, or retrieve your files from OneDrive. Chances are good that you created a

Microsoft account when you first created your account on your Windows PC. (I describe Microsoft accounts in Chapter 2.)

>> **An Internet connection:** Without an Internet signal, either wireless or wired, your web-stashed files remain floating in the clouds, away from you and your computer.

>> **Patience:** Uploading files takes longer than downloading files. Although you can upload small files fairly quickly, larger files such as digital photos or movies take much longer to upload.

For some people, OneDrive offers a safe Internet haven, sometimes called the "cloud," where they can always find their most important files. For others, One-Drive brings another layer of complication, as well as another possible hiding place for that missing file.

The following sections explain how to access OneDrive directly from any folder on your computer, as well as by visiting with a web browser. You also find out how to change OneDrive's settings to make sure it doesn't hog all of the storage space on your tiny tablet or file-packed PC.

Setting Up OneDrive on a New PC

Windows 10 places OneDrive in every folder's Navigation Pane, where it's easily accessible. There, OneDrive works like any other folder but with one exception: Files and folders you place inside your OneDrive folder are also copied to your OneDrive storage space on the Internet.

That can create a problem: Today's smaller phones, tablets, and laptops don't include much storage space. OneDrive, by contrast, can hold *lots* of files. Some smaller computers, usually small tablets, don't have enough room to keep a copy of *everything* you've packed away on OneDrive.

Windows 10 offers a solution: You can pick and choose which folders should live only on OneDrive, and which should also be *mirrored* — also known as *synced* — so they live on your computer, as well.

The files that you choose to sync will be automatically updated between your computer and the cloud. On the cloud, your files serve as a backup, as well as a way for you to access them from your phone, tablet, or any PC.

Files that *aren't* synced live only on OneDrive. If you need them, you can access them by visiting OneDrive on the Internet, as I describe later in this section.

When you first click the OneDrive folder on a new PC, Windows makes you choose which files and folders should live *only* on OneDrive, and which should *also* live as copies on your PC. (If you've already set up OneDrive, but want to change its settings, see the next section, "Changing Your OneDrive Settings.")

To set up OneDrive on a new PC and choose which folders should live on both your PC and OneDrive, follow these steps:

1. From the taskbar, click the File Explorer icon and click the OneDrive icon in the folder's left edge.

Since this is the first time you've set up OneDrive on the computer, OneDrive displays an opening screen.

2. If asked, sign in with your Microsoft account and password.

Only Local account holders will need to sign in; Microsoft account holders already sign in when they sign into their user account. (I describe how to convert a Local account into a Microsoft account in Chapter 14.)

A window appears, pointing out the location of your OneDrive folder.

3. If you want to change where to store your OneDrive files, click the Change Location button. Otherwise, click the Next button.

If you're using a desktop PC with plenty of storage space, just click the Next button. OneDrive will store all of your OneDrive files on your C drive, which normally has plenty of room.

Inexpensive tablets, by contrast, contain very limited storage space. To add more storage, many tablet owners buy a memory card and slide it into their tablet's memory slot. If you've bought and inserted a memory card into your tiny tablet, click this window's Change Location button and tell OneDrive to save its files on your tablet's memory card instead of the default C drive.

4. Choose which folders to sync to your PC.

OneDrive lists all of your OneDrive folders, shown in Figure 5-10.

5. Select the files and folders you'd like to keep synced between your PC and OneDrive, then click the Next button.

OneDrive gives you two options:

- **Sync All Files and Folders in my OneDrive:** Unless you have a reason not to, select this option to keep all of your OneDrive files mirrored on your PC's or tablet's memory card. Most desktop PCs won't have a problem with this option, and it's the most trouble-free way to access OneDrive.

- **Sync Only These Folders:** Select this option on tablets or PCs with very little storage. If you select this option, place a check mark next to the folders you consider to be essential enough to warrant storage both on your PC and OneDrive.

FIGURE 5-10:
Place a check
mark next to the
folders you want
to stay on both
your computer
and OneDrive.

6. **Click Next to save your changes.**

OneDrive leaves you with an Open my OneDrive Folder button which you can
click to see the results of your file syncing decisions.

You don't need to sync the same set of folders on each of your computers.
For example, you can choose to sync only the essentials on your small tablet —
perhaps just your photos. On a desktop PC with large storage, you can choose to
sync everything.

If you want to access a OneDrive folder that's not synced on your PC, you have two
options: Change OneDrive's settings to sync that desired folder, or visit OneDrive
on the Internet and access the file there. (I describe how to do this later in this
section.)

Changing your OneDrive settings

As your needs change, you may want to tweak your OneDrive settings, perhaps
changing which OneDrive folders should also live on your PC.

To revisit your OneDrive settings and change them, if necessary, follow these
steps:

1. **From taskbar's notification area, right-click the OneDrive icon and choose
Settings.**

You may need to click the little upward-pointing arrow in the notification area to see the OneDrive icon (shown in the margin). I cover the taskbar's notification area — the tiny icon-filled area to the taskbar's far right — in Chapter 3.

OneDrive's Settings dialog box appears, as shown in Figure 5-11, open to the Account tab.

FIGURE 5-11:
The Microsoft
OneDrive Settings
dialog box lets
you change how
OneDrive
communicates
with your
computer.

2. **To change which files should live both on your PC and on OneDrive, click the Choose Folders button.**

   The Sync Your OneDrive Files to This PC window opens, listing all of your OneDrive folders, as shown earlier in Figure 5-10.

3. **Make any changes, and click the OK button.**

   The Microsoft OneDrive Settings window opens to the Account tab, shown earlier in Figure 5-11, but the other tabs are also worth exploring:

   - **Settings:** A check box here lets you tell OneDrive to start syncing automatically when you log into Windows. Another check box lets you use OneDrive to fetch any files on your PC, a handy option I describe in the "Accessing Your Desktop PC from the Internet" sidebar later in this chapter.

   - **Auto Save:** This tab lets you choose whether all of your new work should automatically be saved on your PC or in the cloud on OneDrive.

   - **Network:** Designed for people without speedy Internet connections, this lets you control how quickly OneDrive should sync. Unless you have good reason, keep this set to Don't Limit.

- **About:** Probably tossed in by the legal department, this offers links to Microsoft's pages of legalese: Terms of Use, and its Privacy and Cookies policy.

When you click the window's OK button, OneDrive begins syncing your files and folders according to your changes.

When rolling out OneDrive, Microsoft gave everybody 15GB of free OneDrive storage space, but Microsoft subsequently reduced the amount to only 5GB. (You can increase that amount by paying a monthly fee.)

TIP

The Accounts tab shown in Figure 5-11 also shows your amount of available One-Drive storage space, as well as offers a Buy More Storage link in case you're running low on space.

Opening and saving files from OneDrive

When you first sign into Windows 10 with a new Microsoft Account, Windows stocks your OneDrive with two empty folders: Documents and Photos.

TECHNICAL
STUFF

OneDrive AND WINDOWS 8.1

In Windows 10, OneDrive works very differently than it does in Windows 8 and 8.1. Unlike Windows 10, those previous Windows versions didn't sync *all* of your OneDrive files to your computer. Instead, they synced something called *smart files* — little stubs that represented your online files and folders.

When you open OneDrive through File Explorer in Windows 8 and 8.1, you see *all* of your files and folders stored on OneDrive, even the ones that are aren't synced to your PC. How? Because you are only seeing *smart files* that represent your offline files and folders. And those smart files work quite well. They let you see the names of your offline files and folders. You can even search some of them.

Some apps can even use smart files like normal files: When you open a smart file, OneDrive quickly downloads it, and seamlessly hands it to your app or program. The only problem? This smart file magic only works if you are online.

As soon as you are offline, smart files can no longer access their real counterparts, leading to error messages. Microsoft found the concept to be too confusing, so it removed smart files from Windows 10. With Windows 10, you can see only the OneDrive files and folders you've chosen to sync on your computer. The rest remain invisible and out-of-reach unless you visit OneDrive online with your web browser.

To see the two folders, open any folder. Don't have a folder open? Then click the File Explorer icon (shown in the margin) on the taskbar. OneDrive is listed in the folder's Navigation Pane along the left edge. Click the word OneDrive, and OneDrive's contents spill out into the folder's right side. You can see the two empty folders, named Documents and Photos. If you already have a OneDrive account, you see *your* OneDrive folders, instead. You have nothing new to learn with OneDrive; its folders work like any other folder on your computer:

>> To view the contents of a OneDrive folder, double-click it. The folder opens to show its contents.

>> To edit a file stored in a OneDrive folder, double-click it. The file opens in the program that created it.

>> To save something new inside a OneDrive folder, save it to a folder inside OneDrive — its Documents folder, for example. Don't just save it to the Documents folder on your PC.

>> To delete something from OneDrive, right-click it and choose Delete. The item moves to your desktop's Recycle Bin, where it can be retrieved later if necessary.

No matter what changes you make to your files and folders in your computer's OneDrive folder, Windows 10 automatically changes the Internet's copies to match.

Later, when you visit OneDrive through anything with a Web browser – your smartphone, tablet, or even another PC – your up-to-date files will be waiting for you to peruse.

TIP

>> By storing a shopping list on OneDrive, you can add needed grocery items while sitting at your PC. Then, when you're at the store, you can view that up-to-date shopping list on your phone. (Microsoft makes OneDrive apps for iPhones and Android phones, as well as phones from Blackberry and Windows.)

>> Want to copy a few favorites to your OneDrive folder? I describe how to copy and move files between folders earlier in this chapter.

TIP

>> Many people keep a few desert island discs on OneDrive. Whenever you have an Internet connection, the Windows 10 Groove Music app, covered in Chapter 16, automatically lists and plays any music you store on OneDrive. (The old school Media Player program, by contrast, plays only the music stored physically on your PC.)

ACCESSING YOUR DESKTOP PC FROM THE INTERNET

OneDrive makes sharing files with all of your gadgets pretty easy. But what if the file you need *isn't* stored on OneDrive? What if it's sitting on the desktop of your Windows 10 PC back home?

Here's a solution: You can make *all* of your PC's files and folders available from the OneDrive website. Look back at Figure 5-11; if you click the Settings tab, you can select the check box labeled Let Me Use OneDrive to Fetch Any of My Files on This PC.

Selecting that check box lets you access *your entire PC* from the OneDrive website. That's right: You can drop by the OneDrive website to grab *any* of your PC's files and folders, even if they're not shared on OneDrive. You can even access files and folders stored on networks accessible from that PC.

Since you're accessing files stored on your *own* PC rather than on Microsoft's cloud service, this doesn't affect your OneDrive storage limit.

Naturally, Microsoft took some security precautions with such a bold move. Before letting you access a new PC for the first time, OneDrive asks you to type in a code.

In the background, Microsoft sends a text message to the cell phone or email associated with your Microsoft account. When you receive the message, you type it into the computer you're using to access the PC. When Microsoft receives the matching code, it adds that PC to your list of accessible PCs.

You can access only a Windows 7, 8, or 10 PC that's turned on, running OneDrive, and connected to the Internet. If you're planning on using this handy OneDrive feature, be sure to enter your cellphone number as a verifier when setting up your Microsoft account.

Accessing OneDrive from the Internet

Sometimes you may need to access OneDrive when you're not sitting in front of your computer. Or, you may need to reach a OneDrive file that's not synced on your PC. To help you in either situation, Microsoft offers OneDrive access from any Internet browser.

When you need your files, drop by any computer, visit the OneDrive website at `http://OneDrive.live.com` and, if asked, sign in with your Microsoft account name and password. The OneDrive website appears, shown in Figure 5-12.

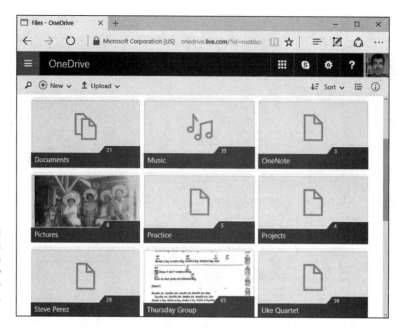

After you sign into the OneDrive website, you can add, delete, move, and rename files, as well as create folders and move files between folders. You can even edit some files directly online. (OneDrive even contains a Recycle Bin for retrieving mistakenly deleted files, whether they were deleted online, on your phone, PC, or other device.)

It's much easier to manage your files directly from the folder on your computer. But if you're away from your computer, the OneDrive website provides a handy fallback zone.

Also, the OneDrive website provides something your OneDrive folder doesn't: It lets you share files by emailing people links to them, making it a handy way to share folders.

REMEMBER

If you find yourself using OneDrive regularly, take note that Microsoft offers free OneDrive apps for Apple, Android, and Windows smartphones and tablets. OneDrive simplifies file sharing among all of your gadgets.

2

Working with Programs, Apps, and Files

Chapter 6

Playing with Programs, Apps, and Documents

I n Windows, *programs* and *apps* are your tools: Load a program or an app, and you can add numbers, arrange words, and shoot spaceships.

Documents, by contrast, are the things you create with apps and programs, such as tax forms, heartfelt apologies, and lists of high scores.

This chapter explains the basics of opening programs and apps from the new Start menu in Windows. It explains how to find and download a new app from the Start menu's Store app. It also shows you where to find an app's menus (Microsoft mysteriously hid them).

As you flip through this chapter's pages, you figure out how to make your *preferred* program open your files. You also create desktop *shortcuts* — buttons that let you quickly load favorite files, folders, and programs.

The chapter ends with the "Absolutely Essential Guide to Cutting, Copying, and Pasting." Put this one trick under your belt, and you'll know how to manipulate words on a word processor, move files between folders, copy files from your camera to your PC, and send files to and from flash drives.

Starting a Program or an App

Windows 10 returns the Start button and menu to their age-old spot in the desktop's bottom-left corner. A click of the Start button brings you the Start menu's latest incarnation, complete with a band of apps clinging to its right side and a string of unlabeled icons along the left. (On touchscreen computers, the Start menu fills the entire screen.)

I explain the new Start menu, shown in Figure 6-1, in Chapter 2; head there for tips on how to customize the menu by adding or removing tiles to ensure you find things more easily.

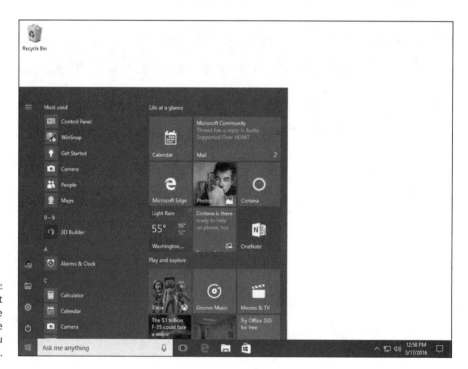

FIGURE 6-1:
On the Start menu, click the tile for the program you want to open.

If you just want to launch a program or app, follow these steps:

1. **Open the Start menu.**

Summon the Start menu by clicking or tapping the Start button in the screen's bottom-left corner. If your hands are already on the keyboard, just press the Windows key (⊞).

The Start menu appears, as shown earlier in Figure 6-1, bringing a list of your apps and programs. In fact, the Start menu automatically updates itself to keep the names of your most recently used programs or apps visible.

If the Start menu fills the entire screen, your computer is running in Tablet mode. To switch to the traditional, corner-sized Start screen, click the Action Center icon (shown in the margin). When the Action Center pane appears, click the Tablet mode toggle in the pane's lower-left corner.

2. **If you spot the tile for your program or app, choose it with a mouse click or, on a touchscreen, a tap of a finger.**

Don't see a tile for your sought-after program on the Start menu's list? Move to the next step.

3. **Scroll down the screen's right side to see more tiles.**

Hidden along the Start menu's far right edge is a scroll bar, similar to scroll bars you see in stocked folders. Sometimes you can't see the scroll bar until your mouse pointer rests directly over it. When you see the scroll bar, drag its scroll box down the screen; then you can see any Start menu tiles that were hiding from view. No scroll bar? Then you're already seeing all that the Start menu has to offer.

On touchscreens, you can view the tiles hidden below the screen's edge by sliding your finger up the screen over the tiles.

TIP

Still don't see your program or app listed? Head for Step 4.

4. **View *all* your apps.**

To keep its list of apps and programs manageable, the Start menu's tile-filled section doesn't list every program or app on your computer.

To reveal them *all,* look at the list of apps along the Start menu's left side. Your most used apps appear along the top; below that appear newly installed apps. And below those, you see all of your apps listed alphabetically by name.

When running in Tablet mode, your computer doesn't show its alphabetized list of apps. To see them, tap the All Apps icon, shown in the margin. All of your installed apps and programs suddenly appear, sorted alphabetically.

If you *still* can't find your program on the admittedly crowded Start menu, follow these tips for other ways to open an app or a program:

>> Click inside the Cortana Search box next to the Start menu. As you type the first letter, the Search box grows taller to present a list of names beginning with that letter. Type a second or third letter, and the list of matches shrinks accordingly. When you spot the app or program you want, open it with a click (or a tap on a touchscreen). As you type letters, the ever-helpful Cortana also finds matching filenames on your PC, as well as matches from the Internet.

 >> Open the File Explorer icon (shown in the margin) from the Start menu's left edge. When File Explorer appears, choose Documents, Music, Pictures, or Videos from the Navigation Pane along the window's left edge, and double-click the file you want to open. The correct program automatically opens with that file in tow. (If the wrong program opens it, head to this chapter's "Choosing Which Program Should Open Which File" section.)

>> Double-click a shortcut to the program. Shortcuts, which often sit on your desktop, are handy, disposable buttons for launching files and folders. (I explain more about shortcuts in this chapter's "Taking the Lazy Way with a Desktop Shortcut" section.)

>> While you're on the desktop, you may spot the program's icon on the taskbar — a handy strip of icons lazily lounging along your desktop's bottom edge. If so, click the taskbar icon, and the program leaps into action. (I cover the desktop's taskbar, including how to customize its row of icons, in Chapter 3.)

>> Right-click on the Windows desktop, choose New, and select the type of document you want to create. Windows loads the correct program for the job. (On a tablet, this trick works only when you turn off Tablet mode, described earlier in this section.)

Windows offers other ways to open a program, but the preceding methods usually get the job done. (I cover the Start menu more extensively in Chapter 2, and the desktop is the star of Chapter 3.)

Opening a Document

Like Tupperware, the Windows desktop is a big fan of standardization. Almost all Windows programs load their documents — often called *files* — exactly the same way:

1. **Click the word File on the program's *menu bar*, that row of staid words along the program's top.**

If your program hides its menu bar, pressing the Alt key often reveals it.

Still no menu bar? Then your program might have a *Ribbon*, a thick strip of multicolored icons along the window's top. If you spot the Ribbon, click the tab or button in its leftmost corner to let the File menu tumble down.

2. **When the File menu drops down, choose Open.**

   Windows gives you a sense of déjà vu with the Open window, shown in Figure 6-2. It looks (and works) just like your Documents folder, which I cover in Chapter 5.

   There's one big difference, however: This time, your folder displays only files that your particular program knows how to open — it filters out all the others.

FIGURE 6-2:
Double-click the filename you want to open.

3. **Point at your desired document (shown in Figure 6-2), click the mouse button, and click the Open button.**

TIP

   On a touchscreen, tap the document to open it. The program opens the file and displays it on the screen.

   Opening a file works this way in most Windows programs, whether written by Microsoft, its corporate partners, or the teenager down the street.

TIP

   » To speed things up, double-click a desired file's name; that opens it immediately, automatically closing the Open window.

>> Humans store things in the garage, but computers store their files in neatly labeled compartments called folders. (Double-click a folder to see what's stored inside. If you spot your file, open it with a double-click.) If browsing folders gives you trouble, the folders section in Chapter 5 offers a refresher.

>> If your file isn't listed by name, start browsing by clicking the buttons or words shown along the left side of Figure 6-2. Click the OneDrive or the This PC folder, for example, to search other folders and their files stored inside.

>> Whenever you open a file and change it, even by accident, Windows usually assumes that you've changed the file for the better. If you try to close the file, Windows cautiously asks whether you want to save your changes. If you updated the file with masterful wit, click Yes. If you made a mess or opened the wrong file, click No or Cancel.

TIP

>> Confused about any icons or commands along the Open window's top or left side? Rest your mouse pointer over the icons, and a little box announces their occupations.

TECHNICAL STUFF

WHEN PROGRAMMERS FIGHT OVER FILE TYPES

When not fighting over fast food, programmers fight over *formats* — ways to pack information into a file. To tiptoe around the format wars, most programs let you open files stored in several different types of formats.

For example, look at the drop-down list box in the bottom-right corner of Figure 6-2. It currently lists all WordPad Documents, the format used by the WordPad text editor built into Windows. To see files stored in *other* formats, click in that box and choose a different format. The Open box quickly updates its list to show files from that new format, instead.

And how can you see a list of *all* your folder's files in that menu, regardless of their format? Select All Documents from the drop-down list box. That switches the view to show all of that particular folder's files. Your program probably can't open them all, though, and it will choke while trying.

For example, WordPad may include some digital photos in its All Documents view. But if you try to open a photo, WordPad dutifully displays the photo as obscure coding symbols. (If you ever mistakenly open a photo in a program and *don't* see the photo, don't try to save what you've opened. If the program is like WordPad, saving the file will ruin the photo. Simply turn tail and exit immediately with a click on the Cancel button.)

Saving a Document

Saving means to send the work you've just created to a hard drive, flash drive, or disc for safekeeping. Unless you specifically save your work, your computer thinks that you've just been fiddling around for the past four hours. You must specifically tell the computer to save your work before it will safely store it.

Thanks to Microsoft snapping leather whips, a Save command appears in nearly every Windows program no matter what programmer wrote it. Here are a few ways to save a file:

» Click File on the top menu and choose Save. (Pressing the Alt key, followed by the F key and the S key, does the same thing.)

» Click the Save icon (shown in the margin).

» Hold down Ctrl and press the S key. (*S* stands for *Save*.)

TIP

WHAT'S THE DIFFERENCE BETWEEN SAVE AND SAVE AS?

Huh? Save as *what*? A chemical compound? Naw, the Save As command just gives you a chance to save your work with a different name and in a different location.

Suppose that you open the *Ode to Tina* file and change a few sentences. You want to save your new changes, but you don't want to lose the original words, either. Preserve *both* versions by selecting Save As and typing the new name, *Tentative Additions to Ode to Tina.*

When you're saving something for the *first* time, the Save and Save As commands are identical: Both make you choose a fresh name and location for your work.

Perhaps more important, the Save As command also lets you save a file in a different *format*. You can save your original copy in your normal format, but you can also save a copy in a different format for a friend clinging to older software that requires a format from yesteryear.

If you're saving something for the first time, Windows asks you to think up a name for your document. Type something descriptive using only letters, numbers, and spaces between the words. (If you try to use one of the illegal characters I describe in Chapter 5, the Windows Police step in, politely requesting that you use a different name.)

>> You can save files to any folder, CD, DVD, or even a flash drive. But files are much easier to find down the road when they stay in one of your four main folders: Documents, Music, Pictures, or Videos. (Those folders are listed on the left edge of every folder, making it easy to place files inside them.)

>> Choose descriptive filenames for your work. Windows gives you 255 characters to work with. A file named *January 2016 Squeegee Sales* is easier to locate than one named *Stuff*.

>> If you want to access your current file from other devices, perhaps your phone or tablet, save it to the Documents folder on OneDrive: Choose OneDrive from the Save window's left edge and then choose the OneDrive Documents folder. Then click the Save button.

>> Most programs can save files directly to a CD or DVD. Choose Save from the File menu and choose your preferred drive from the right pane's This PC section. Put a disc (preferably one that's not already filled) into your disc-writing drive to start the process.

>> A few newer programs spare you the chore of clicking the Save button: They save your work automatically as you type. Microsoft's OneNote note taking program and many Start menu apps save your work automatically, so they lack a Save button.

>> If you're working on something important (and most things are important), click the program's Save command every few minutes. Or use the Ctrl+S keyboard shortcut. (While holding down the Ctrl key, press the S key.) Programs make you choose a name and location for a file when you *first* save it; subsequent saves are much speedier.

Choosing Which Program Should Open Which File

Most of the time, Windows automatically knows which program should open which file. Open a file, and Windows tells the correct program to jump in and let you view its contents.

But sometimes Windows doesn't choose your preferred program, and that holds especially true for Windows 10. For example, the new app-loving Windows tells the Start menu's Groove Music app to play your music. You may prefer that the desktop's Windows Media Player handle the music-playing chores instead.

When the wrong program opens your file, here's how to make the *right* program open it instead:

1. **Right-click your problematic file and choose Open With from the pop-up menu.**

As shown in Figure 6-3, Windows lists a few capable programs, including ones you've used to open that file in the past.

FIGURE 6-3:
Windows lists
some programs
that opened
that type of
file in the past.

2. **Click the Choose Another App option.**

The window that appears, as shown in Figure 6-4, lists more programs, and the currently assigned program appears at the list's top. If you spot your favorite program, double-click to tell it to open your file. (Make sure the Always Use This App to Open Files check box is selected so you don't need to repeat these steps.) Then click OK. You're done!

Don't see the program you want or need to open the file? Move to Step 3.

3. **Click the words Look for An App in the Store, and click the OK button.**

The Store app appears, leaving you at a virtual shelf stocked with apps capable of opening the file.

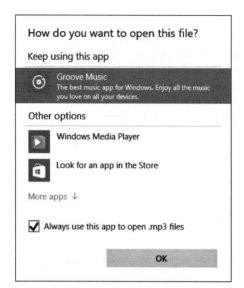

FIGURE 6-4:
Choose the program you want and select the check box at the bottom.

> How do you want to open this file?
>
> Keep using this app
>
> ⊚ **Groove Music**
> The best music app for Windows. Enjoy all the music you love on all your devices.
>
> Other options
>
> ▶ Windows Media Player
>
> 🏬 Look for an app in the Store
>
> More apps ↓
>
> ☑ Always use this app to open .mp3 files
>
> **OK**

If you install a new program or app to open a particular file, the newcomer usually assigns itself the rights to open that type of file in the future. If it doesn't, head back to Step 1. This time, however, your newly installed program or app will appear on the list. Choose it, and you've *finally* finished.

REMEMBER

>> In a bit of revisionist history, Windows 10 uses the term *app* when referring to both traditional desktop programs and Start menu apps. Be mindful of the Windows terminology when on the desktop. If Windows says an action will affect your apps, it will also affect your desktop programs.

>> Windows lets you choose your default programs from the Start menu, as well. From the Start menu, click the Settings icon. When the Windows Setting app appears, click the System icon. From the System window, choose Default Apps from the left pane. On the right, Windows lists the programs currently opening each type of file. Click any program's name, and a list appears for you to hand the reins to a different program.

>> Sometimes you'll want to alternate between different apps or programs when working on the same file. To do so, right-click the file, choose Open With, and select the program you need at that time.

>> Occasionally, you can't make your favorite program open a particular file because it simply doesn't know how. For example, Windows 10 can't play DVD movies. Your only solution is to install a DVD playing program or app from the Microsoft Store.

>> If somebody says something about "file associations," feel free to browse the technical sidebar "The awkward world of file associations," which explains that awful subject.

THE AWKWARD WORLD OF FILE ASSOCIATIONS

Every Windows program slaps a secret code known as a *file extension* onto the name of every file it creates. The file extension works like a cattle brand: When you double-click the file, Windows eyeballs the extension and automatically summons the proper program to open the file. Notepad, for example, tacks on the three-letter extension .txt to every file it creates. So, Windows associates the .txt extension with the Notepad program.

Windows normally doesn't display these extensions, isolating users from such inner mechanisms for safety reasons. If somebody accidentally changes or removes an extension, Windows won't know how to open that file.

If you're curious about what an extension looks like, sneak a peek by following these steps:

1. **Click the View tab from atop any folder.**

   The menu quickly changes across the folder's top, showing different ways to view that folder's contents.

2. **Select the File Name Extensions check box.**

   The files inside the folder immediately change to show their extensions — a handy thing to know in technical emergencies.

Now that you've peeked, hide the extensions again by repeating the steps but deselect the File Name Extensions check box.

Warning: Don't change a file's extension unless you know exactly what you're doing. Windows will forget what program to use for opening the file, leaving you holding an empty bag.

Navigating the Windows Store

Apps, which are mini-programs specialized for single tasks, come from the world of *smartphones* (computerized cellphones). And, like the apps from smartphones, apps come only from an App store. In Windows, they come from the Windows Store, available with a click on the taskbar's Windows Store icon (shown in the margin).

Apps differ from traditional desktop programs in several ways:

>> Windows 10 allows apps to run within desktop windows rather than consuming the entire screen as they did in earlier Windows versions. When running in Tablet mode, though, apps return to their full-screen antics.

>> Apps are tied to your Microsoft account. That means you need a Microsoft account to download a free or paid app from the Store app.

>> When you download an app from the Windows Store app, you can usually run it on up to ten PCs or devices — as long as you're signed in to those PCs or devices with your Windows account. (Some apps may raise or lower that number.)

>> Newly installed apps consume just one Start menu tile. Newly installed programs, by contrast, often sprinkle several tiles onto your Start menu.

Apps and programs can be created and sold both by large companies and basement-dwelling hobbyists working in their spare time. It's hard to tell beforehand which one will give you the most support when things go wrong.

Although desktop programs and Start menu apps look and behave differently, Microsoft unfortunately refers to both as *apps.* You might run across this terminology quirk when dealing with older programs, as well as newer programs created by companies not hip to Microsoft's new lingo.

Adding new apps from the Store app

When you're tired of the apps bundled with Windows or you need a new app to fill a special need, follow these steps to bring one into your computer.

1. **Click the Start button and open the Store app from the Start menu.**

The Store app jumps to the screen, as shown in Figure 6-5. You can also click the Store app (shown in the margin) from the taskbar that always runs along the bottom of your screen.

Although the Store changes its layout frequently, it usually opens to show its Spotlight category along the top edge, where Microsoft highlights a few chosen apps. Beneath that, you may find links to popular apps. The Store usually offers a Picks For You section which suggests apps you may be interested in, based on your past downloads.

To see more, point near the Store app's top edge to see the top few apps in each category: Apps, Games, and Music & TV. (You can also buy or rent movies from the Store app.)

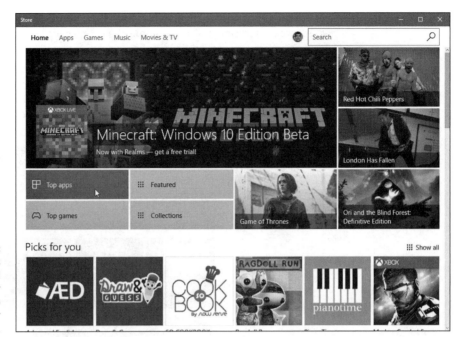

FIGURE 6-5:
The Store app lets
you download
free, trial, or
paid apps to
launch from your
Start menu.

2. To narrow your search, choose a category by clicking its name.

The Store lists its offerings based on your chosen category.

TIP

Save some time by clicking the "Top" button, if you spot one. (The mouse points to it in Figure 6-5.) If you spot an interesting free app, click it. When the Install button appears, click the button to install the app and get the hang of the process. (Similarly, to buy a paid app, click the button that lists its price.)

Didn't find the right app? Head to the next step.

3. Search for a particular app by typing a keyword into the Search box in the upper-right corner and pressing Enter.

The Search box lives in the store's upper-right corner. Shown in Figure 6-6, the Search box narrows down the apps by a keyword.

REMEMBER

Like the Store app, almost all searchable apps include a built-in Search box, which appears in their upper-right corner.

When you press Enter, the Store app lists all matching apps, games, artists, albums, songs, movies, and TV shows.

4. Sort the listed apps.

The Refine pane, listed to the left of your matching apps, lets you fine tune your app search. Click Apps, for example, to further sort your search by types of apps: games, education, entertainment, utilities, and other categories. Or, if you searched for a musical artist's name, the Refine pane lets you sort their music by genre.

5. **Click any app to read a more detailed description.**

   A page opens to show more detailed information, including its price tag, pictures, reviews left by previous customers, and more technical information.

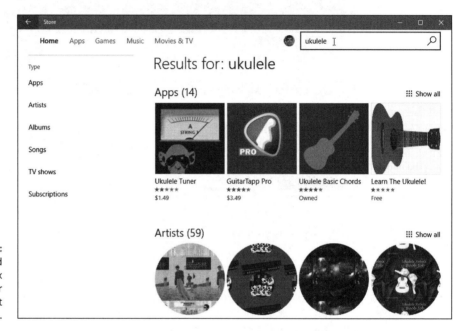

FIGURE 6-6:
Type a keyword in the Search box and press Enter to see relevant apps.

6. **Click the Free or Price button.**

   When you find a free app that you can't live without, click the Free button. To buy a paid app, click the button bearing its price tag. The price will be charged to the credit card linked to your Microsoft account. If you haven't yet entered a card, Microsoft walks you through the process.

   The Store may ask you to choose which drive to use for installing your app. Most people choose their C: drive; owners of small tablets may prefer to choose their memory card, instead. (Tiny tablets traditionally come with tiny C: drives.)

   No matter what you download from the Windows Store, the new item appears on your Start menu's alphabetical All Apps list as quickly as your Internet connection speed allows.

To copy an app from the All Apps list to a front-page Start menu tile, right-click the app's name and choose Pin to Start. I explain how to customize your Start menu further in Chapter 2.

Uninstalling apps

Downloaded a dud app? To uninstall any app from the Start menu, right-click its tile. When the pop-up menu appears, click Uninstall.

Uninstalling an app removes that app only from *your* account's Start menu. Your action won't affect other account holders who may have installed the app.

TIP

UPDATING YOUR APPS

Programmers constantly tweak their apps, smoothing over rough spots, adding new features, and plugging security holes. Whenever you connect with the Internet, Windows examines your installed apps. If any are out of date, Windows automatically downloads any waiting updates and applies the updates.

If you're using a cellular connection, don't worry: Apps don't update when you're using a metered Internet connection like those found on cellphones. Windows resumes updating the apps as soon as you connect to a Wi-Fi or wired Internet connection.

Don't want automatic updates for some reason? You can turn off automatic updating by following these steps:

1. **From the Store app, click your account icon and choose Settings from the drop-down menu.**

   Your account icon is your user account photo, located in the Store app's upper-right corner next to the Search box.

2. **When the Settings screen appears, click to make sure the Update Apps Automatically slider is set to Off.**

   Your changes take place immediately. To make sure your apps update automatically, by contrast, set the slider to On.

When the App Updates control is on, *all* your apps update. You can't keep individual apps from updating, unfortunately. That's why I recommend that you keep your apps set to update automatically. If you try to stop one from updating, you could miss out on security patches as well as improvements to all of your other apps.

Taking the Lazy Way with a Desktop Shortcut

As you work, you'll constantly find yourself traveling between the desktop and the Start menu. When you grow tired of meandering through the woods to find a program, folder, disc drive, document, or even a website, create a desktop *shortcut* — an icon that takes you directly to the object of your desires.

Because a shortcut is a mere icon that launches something else, shortcuts are safe, convenient, and disposable. And they're easy to tell apart from the original because they have a little arrow lodged in their bottom-left corner, as you can see on the folder shortcut shown in the margin.

To skip the Start menu, follow these instructions to create desktop shortcuts to your oft-used items:

» **Folders or Documents:** From the desktop's File Explorer, right-click a favorite folder or document, choose Send To, and select the Desktop (Create Shortcut) option. The shortcut appears on your desktop.

» **Websites:** On Internet Explorer, see the little icon in front of the website's address in Internet Explorer's Address bar? Drag and drop that little icon to your desktop for quick access later. (Windows 10's replacement Microsoft Edge browser doesn't let you create desktop shortcuts.)

» **Control Panel:** The desktop's Control Panel contains eight sections, each with links beneath it. Every icon and link in Control Panel can be dragged onto your desktop to create a shortcut. (An easy way to access the Control Panel from the desktop is to right-click in the screen's bottom-left corner and choose Control Panel from the pop-up menu.)

» **Storage areas:** Open File Explorer with a click of its icon on the desktop's taskbar. From the Navigation Pane along File Explorer's left side, drag and drop any storage area you want to the desktop. Windows immediately places a shortcut to that drive on your desktop. (This works for your main OneDrive folder, This PC, flash drives, disc drives, and even network locations.)

Here are some more tips for desktop shortcuts:

» For quick CD or DVD burning, put a shortcut to your disc drive on your desktop. Burning files to disc becomes as simple as dragging and dropping them onto the disc drive's new shortcut. (Insert a blank disc into the disc drive's tray, confirm the settings, and begin burning your disc.)

WARNING

>> Want to send a desktop shortcut to the Start menu? Right-click the desktop shortcut and choose Pin to Start; the item appears as a tile on the Start menu, as well as in the Start menu's All Apps list.

>> Feel free to move shortcuts from place to place, but *don't* move the items they launch. If you do, the shortcut won't be able to find the item, causing Windows to panic and search (usually in vain) for the relocated goods.

>> Want to see what program a shortcut will launch? Right-click the shortcut and click Open File Location (if available). The shortcut quickly takes you to its leader.

Absolutely Essential Guide to Cutting, Copying, and Pasting

Windows took a tip from the kindergartners and made *cut* and *paste* an integral part of computing life. You can electronically *cut* or *copy* just about anything and then *paste* it just about anyplace else with little fuss and even less mess.

For example, you can copy a photo and paste it onto your party invitation fliers. You can move files by cutting them from one folder and pasting them into another. You can cut and paste your digital camera's photos into a folder inside your Pictures folder. And you can easily cut and paste paragraphs to different locations within a word processor.

The beauty of the Windows desktop is that, with all those windows onscreen at the same time, you can easily grab bits and pieces from any of them and paste all the parts into a brand–new window.

TIP

Don't overlook copying and pasting for the small stuff. Copying a name and an address is much faster and more accurate than typing them into your letter by hand. Or, when somebody emails you a web address, copy and paste it directly into your browser's Address bar. It's easy to copy most items displayed on websites, too (much to the dismay of many professional photographers).

The quick 'n' dirty guide to cut 'n' paste

REMEMBER

In compliance with the Don't Bore Me with Details Department, here's a quick guide to the three basic steps used for cutting, copying, and pasting:

1. **Select the item to cut or copy: a few words, a file, a web address, or any other item.**

2. **Right-click your selection and choose Cut or Copy from the menu, depending on your needs.**

Use *Cut* when you want to *move* something. Use *Copy* when you want to *duplicate* something, leaving the original intact.

Keyboard shortcut: Hold down Ctrl and press X to cut or C to copy.

3. **Right-click the item's destination and choose Paste.**

You can right-click inside a document, folder, or nearly any other place.

Keyboard shortcut: Hold down Ctrl and press V to paste.

The next three sections explain each of these three steps in more detail.

Selecting things to cut or copy

Before you can shuttle pieces of information to new places, you have to tell Windows exactly what you want to grab. The easiest way to tell it is to *select* the information with a mouse. In most cases, selecting involves one swift trick with the mouse, which then highlights whatever you've selected.

>> **To select text in a document, website, or spreadsheet:** Put the mouse arrow or cursor at the beginning of the information you want and hold down the mouse button. Then move the mouse to the end of the information and release the button. That's it! That action selects all the stuff lying between where you clicked and released, as shown in Figure 6-7.

TIP

On a touchscreen, double-tap one word to select it. To extend your selection, touch the highlighted word again, keeping your finger pressed on the glass. Slide your finger along the glass until you've reached the area where the highlighting should stop. Done? Remove your finger to select that portion of text.

WARNING

Be careful after you highlight a bunch of text. If you accidentally press the K key, for example, the program replaces your highlighted text with the letter *k*. To reverse that calamity, choose Undo from the program's Edit menu (or press Ctrl+Z, which is the keyboard shortcut for Undo).

>> **To select any files or folders:** Simply click a file or folder to select it. To select *several* items, try these tricks:

- **If all the files are in a row:** Click the first item in the bunch, hold down the Shift key, and then select the last item. Windows highlights the first and last items as well as everything in between.

- **If the files *aren't* in a row:** Hold down the Ctrl key while clicking each file or folder you want to select.

TIP

SELECTING INDIVIDUAL LETTERS, WORDS, PARAGRAPHS, AND MORE

When dealing with words in Windows, these shortcuts help you quickly select information:

- To select an individual *letter or character,* click in front of the character. Then while holding down the Shift key, press the right-arrow key. Keep holding down these two keys to keep selecting text in a line.

- To select a single *word,* point at it with the mouse and double-click. The word changes color, meaning it's highlighted. (In most word processors, you can hold down the button on its second click, and then by moving the mouse around you can quickly highlight additional text word by word.)

- To select a single *line* of text, simply click next to it in the left margin. To highlight additional text line by line, keep holding down the mouse button and move the mouse up or down. You can also keep selecting additional lines by holding down the Shift key and pressing the left-arrow key or the right-arrow key.

- To select a *paragraph,* just double-click next to it in the left margin. To highlight additional text paragraph by paragraph, keep holding down the mouse button on the second click and move the mouse.

- To select an entire *document,* hold down Ctrl and press A. (Or choose Select All from the program's Edit menu.)

Now that you've selected the item, the next section explains how to cut or copy it.

REMEMBER

>> After you've selected something, cut it or copy it *immediately*. If you absent-mindedly click the mouse someplace else, your highlighted text or file reverts to its boring self, and you're forced to start over.

>> To delete any selected item, be it a file, paragraph, or picture, press the Delete key. Alternatively, right-click the item and choose Delete from the pop-up menu.

Cutting or copying your selected goods

After you select some information (which I describe in the preceding section, in case you just arrived), you're ready to start playing with it. You can cut it or copy it. (Or just press Delete to delete it.)

REMEMBER

This bears repeating. After selecting something, right-click it. (On a touchscreen, touch it and hold down your finger to fetch the pop-up menu.) When the menu appears, choose Cut or Copy, depending on your needs, as shown in Figure 6-8. Then right-click your destination and choose Paste.

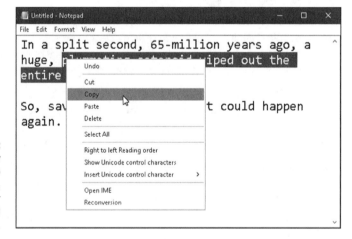

FIGURE 6-8:
To copy information into another window, right-click your selection and choose Copy.

The Cut and Copy options differ drastically. How do you know which one to choose?

>> **Choose Cut to *move* information.** Cutting wipes the selected information off the screen, but you haven't lost anything: Windows stores the cut information

TIP

in a hidden Windows storage tank called the *Clipboard,* waiting for you to paste it.

Feel free to cut and paste entire files to different folders. When you cut a file from a folder, the icon dims until you paste it. (Making the icon disappear would be too scary.) Changed your mind in mid-cut? Press Esc to cancel the cut, and the icon reverts to normal.

» **Choose Copy to make a copy of the information.** Compared with cutting, *copying* information is quite anticlimactic. Whereas cutting removes the item from view, copying the selected item leaves it in the window, seemingly untouched. Copied information also goes to the Clipboard until you paste it.

To save a picture of your entire screen, press ⊞+PrtScr. (Some keyboards call that key *Print Screen* or *PrintScr.*) Windows quickly saves the image in a file called Screenshot inside your Pictures folder. Do it again, and the screenshot is named Screenshot (2). (You get the idea.)

Pasting information to another place

After you cut or copy information to the Windows Clipboard, it's checked in and ready for travel. You can *paste* that information nearly anyplace else.

Pasting is relatively straightforward:

1. **Open the destination window and move the mouse pointer or cursor to the spot where you want the stuff to appear.**

2. **Right-click the mouse and choose Paste from the pop-up menu.**

   Presto! The item you just cut or copied immediately leaps into its new spot.

Or, if you want to paste a file onto the desktop, right-click on the desktop and choose Paste. The cut or copied file appears where you've right-clicked.

TIP

» The Paste command inserts a *copy* of the information that's sitting on the Clipboard. The information stays on the Clipboard, so you can keep pasting the same thing into other places if you want.

» To paste on a touchscreen, hold down your finger where you'd like to paste the information. When the menu pops up, tap Paste.

» Some programs, including File Explorer, have toolbars along their tops, offering one-click access to the versatile Cut, Copy, and Paste buttons, as shown in Figure 6-9. (Hint: Look on File Explorer's Home tab.)

FIGURE 6-9:
The Cut, Copy,
and Paste
commands on
the Ribbon (left)
and traditional
menu (right).

TIP

UNDOING WHAT YOU'VE JUST DONE

Windows offers a way for you to undo your last action, which quickly pours the spilled milk back into the carton:

Hold down the Ctrl key and press the Z key. The last mistake you made is reversed, sparing you from further shame. (Pressing a program's Undo button, if you can find one, does the same thing.)

And, should you mistakenly undo something that really should have stayed in place, press Ctrl+Y. That undoes your last undo, putting it back in place.

Chapter 7

Finding the Lost

S ooner or later, Windows gives you that head-scratching feeling. "Golly," you say as you drum nervous fingers, "that stuff was *right there* a second ago. Where did it go?"

When Windows starts playing hide-and-seek, this chapter tells you where to search and how to make it stop playing foolish games.

Finding Currently Running Apps and Programs

Apps usually hog the entire screen on Windows 10 tablets. Switch to another app, and *it* fills the screen, covering up the previous app. Sure, your current app is easy to read, but at a cost: Your other running apps remain constantly hidden beneath an invisibility cloak.

The Windows desktop, by contrast, lets you run apps and programs in separate windows. But even then, those windows tend to overlap, hiding the ones beneath.

How do you find and return to an app or program you just used? How do you jump between them, perhaps glancing at a report while creating a spreadsheet?

Windows offers a quick solution to the problem: It can clear the screen, shrink all your running apps and programs into miniature windows, and show you the lineup, as displayed in Figure 7-1. Click the app or program you want, and it returns to active duty at its normal size.

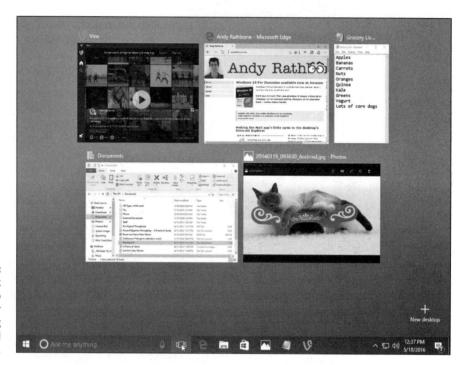

FIGURE 7-1:
Click the Task
View button to
see all your
currently running
apps and
programs.

To see the list of your recently used apps and programs (and to close unwanted ones, if desired), employ any of these tricks:

>> **Mouse:** Click the taskbar's Task View button, just to the right of the taskbar's search box, to see your open apps appear. To switch to an app, click it. To close an app, right-click its thumbnail and choose Close. (You can also click the X in the thumbnail's upper-right corner.)

>> **Keyboard:** Press ⊞+Tab to see the list of your most recently used apps, as shown in Figure 7-1. Press the Left or Right arrows to select different minia-ture windows. When you've selected your desired window, press Enter, and the app fills the screen.

TIP

>> **Touchscreen:** Slide your finger gently inward from the screen's left edge, and your open apps and programs align themselves as miniatures, as shown earlier in Figure 7-1. Tap any app on the strip to make it fill the screen. To close an unwanted app, tap the X in its upper-right corner. (A tap on the Task View icon also brings the thumbnails into view.)

The Windows 10 Task View button shows your currently running apps *and* desktop programs, making it easy to return to work.

Clicking the Task View button also lets you create a *virtual desktop,* an odd, new Windows 10 concept that I cover in Chapter 3.

Finding Lost Windows on the Desktop

The Windows desktop works much like a spike memo holder. Every time you open a new window or program, you toss another piece of information onto the spike. The window on top is easy to spot, but how do you reach the windows lying beneath it?

If you can see any part of a buried window's edge or corner, a well-placed click fetches it, bringing it to the top.

When your window is completely buried, look at the desktop's *taskbar* — that strip along your screen's bottom edge. Spot your missing window's icon on the taskbar? Click it to dredge the window back to the top. (See Chapter 3 for details about the taskbar.)

Still can't get at that missing window? Hold down the Alt key and press Tab. Shown in Figure 7-2, Windows shows thumbnails of all your open windows, programs, and apps in a strip across the screen's center. While holding down the Alt key, repeatedly press Tab, and Windows highlights a different app or window with each press of the Tab key. When your window is highlighted, let go of the Alt key, and that window appears atop your desktop.

WHERE'S THE CHARMS BAR'S SEARCH COMMAND?

TECHNICAL STUFF

In Windows 8, the Charms bar's Search command was integrated throughout Windows. If you wanted to search for something inside an app, you'd fetch the Charms bar, click the Search icon, and type in your keyword.

Windows 10 dropped the Charms bar, instead placing a dedicated Search box into the upper-right corner of every app that allows searching. Type your search into the Search box and press the Enter key to search inside the app.

Desktop programs, by contrast, don't stick to the same rules as apps, so you won't find a standard Search box in their upper-right corner.

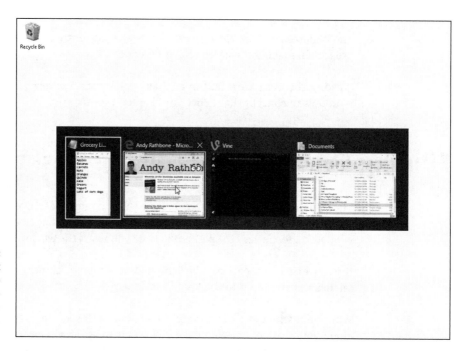

FIGURE 7-2:
Hold down the Alt
key and press Tab
repeatedly to
cycle through
your open
windows.

If you're convinced a window is open but you still can't find it, spread all your open windows across the desktop by right-clicking a blank spot on the taskbar along the desktop's bottom and choosing Show Windows Side By Side from the pop-up menu. It's a last resort, but perhaps you'll spot your missing window in the lineup.

TIP

Locating a Missing App, Program, Setting, or File

The preceding two sections explain how to find *currently running* apps and programs. But what about things that you haven't looked at for a while?

That's the job of the Cortana Search box, which lives next to the Start button. To help you find wandering files, hidden settings, or even things stashed on websites you've never visited, Cortana searches for *everything*.

To search for missing things, follow these steps:

1. **Click or tap in the Cortana Search box and type what you'd like to find.**

The Search box accepts typing as soon as you click or tap inside it. (Don't see a Search box? Then your computer is in Tablet mode; tap the Cortana icon, shown in the margin, to bring Cortana's Search box to the screen.)

As you begin typing, Windows immediately begins searching for matches. (You can also verbally tell your computer what to search for, as described in this chapter's "Searching with Cortana" section.)

For example, here's what happens when searching for pianist Aaron Parks: As you begin typing letters, Windows begins listing files with matching names, shown in Figure 7-3. After just typing in **Aaron** on my computer, for example, Windows found several matches and organized them in the Search pane in these categories:

- **Best Match:** Cortana's Search box lists the best match at the top, in this case, a mini biography of pianist Aaron Parks.

- **Web:** Here, Cortana lists matches from the Internet, including Aaron Brothers art store.

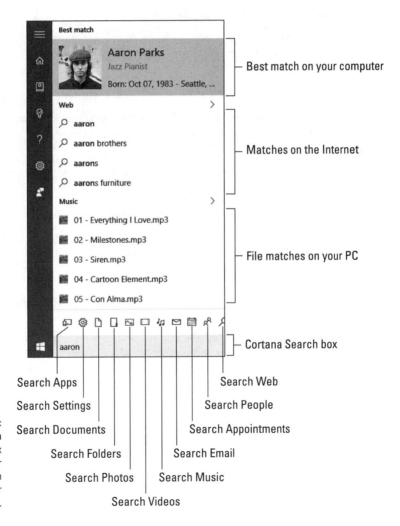

- **Music:** Since Aaron Parks' Live in Japan album is stored on my computer, Cortana lists those songs.

- **Icons:** Click any of these icons along the pane's bottom edge, labelled in Figure 7-3, to route your search to specific areas — your computer's folder names, for example.

As you begin typing, the Search box concentrates on speed, so it searches only for matching filenames stored on your computer and OneDrive, as well as doing a quick Internet search.

If you spot your missing item, jump ahead to Step 3.

If you finish typing your complete search term but *don't* see your sought-after item on the Search list, move on to Step 2. You need to define your search more thoroughly.

2. **Limit your search to a specific category.**

When launched, the Search box searches only for matching filenames. If it doesn't find a match, route your search to one of the icons along the bottom of the Search pane.

Hover your mouse pointer over an icon, and its name appears in a pop-up menu.

Click the Music icon, for example, shown in the bottom of Figure 7-4, and the Search pane only lists music that matches your search.

No matter which category you choose, Windows immediately shows any available matches. Changed your mind about a search category? Click a different icon to route your search there, instead.

3. **Choose a matching item to open it, bringing it to the screen.**

Click a song, for example, and it begins playing. Click a setting, and the Control Panel or Settings app appears, open to your setting's contents. Click a letter, and it opens in your word processor.

These tips can help you wring the most out of the Search feature:

>> In its emphasis on speed, the Cortana Search pane lists only files with names that match your search term. While this strategy sometimes helps you find quick matches, it won't find your shopping list if you search for **oranges**. When you don't spot a sure match, finish typing your search term and then click one of the icons along the pane's bottom to route your search to the appropriate spot.

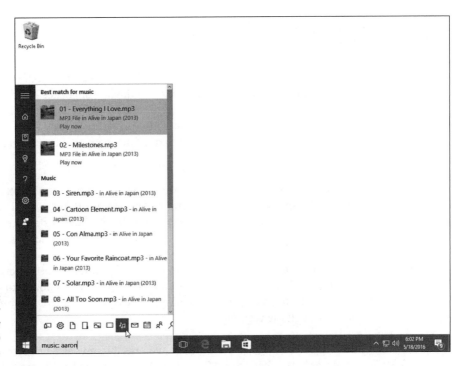

FIGURE 7-4:
Narrow your
search further by
limiting it to
certain areas.

>> Don't press the Enter key after typing in your Search. If you do that, Windows calls up the first match, which may not be what you want. Wait to see what matches turn up and then click the desired match.

>> The Cortana Search box scours every file in your Documents, Music, Pictures, and Videos folders, which makes storing your files in those folders more important than ever.

>> The Cortana Search box also scours every file you store on OneDrive, even if those files aren't also stored on your PC.

>> Windows doesn't search for files stored in removable devices, such as flash drives, CDs, DVDs, or portable hard drives.

>> If you're searching for a common word and Windows turns up too many files, limit your search by typing a short phrase from your sought-after file: **Shortly after the cat nibbled the bamboo**, for example. The more words you type, the better your chances of pinpointing a particular file.

>> The Search box ignores capital letters. It considers **Bee** and **bee** to be the same insect.

Searching with Cortana

Windows 10 includes a friendly personal digital assistant named *Cortana*. Cortana tries to simplify your life by finding not only missing files but also helpful bits of information about you and your surroundings. It finds local weather updates, for example, traffic information about the drive home, and even a list of popular nearby restaurants. A forward thinker, Cortana can even remind you when your favorite band visits your town.

You've already met Cortana: It's the brains behind the Search box next to the Start menu. As Microsoft keeps updating Windows 10, Cortana pitches in with additional tasks. In Chapter 9, for example, I explain how Cortana teams up with the new Microsoft Edge browser to help with your Internet searches.

Cortana can tell you the weather in almost any city, no matter how you phrase the question. When she doesn't understand a question well enough to give a confident answer, she fetches your browser and routes the search to the Internet, letting you sort through the results.

Before Cortana works well, though, you need to give it a few tweaks. This section explains how to set up and fine-tune Cortana, as well as how to turn it off if you're simply not interested in a robotic assistant.

Setting up Cortana for the First Time

In order to serve you better, your servants must know a lot about you, including your habits, interests, and appointments. When your computer plays the role of digital assistant, it must know just as much information in order to be helpful.

To introduce yourself to Cortana and let her know your habits, follow these steps:

1. **Click in the Search box, and the Cortana pane appears.**

   Cortana speaks to you through the Cortana pane, shown in Figure 7-5. These icons along the pane's left edge let you control Cortana's behavior:

   - **Home:** Click this to return to Cortana's main screen, shown in Figure 7-5. Once you set up Cortana, this pane shows information about your day: upcoming appointments, traffic and weather updates, local news, and other helpful tidbits.

   - **Notebook:** Here, you can choose which of your interests Cortana should track, be that finance, health, and fitness; TV shows and movies; or sports, travel, and others. Most are simply on/off toggle switches; others let you enter things like your favorite stocks or sports teams.

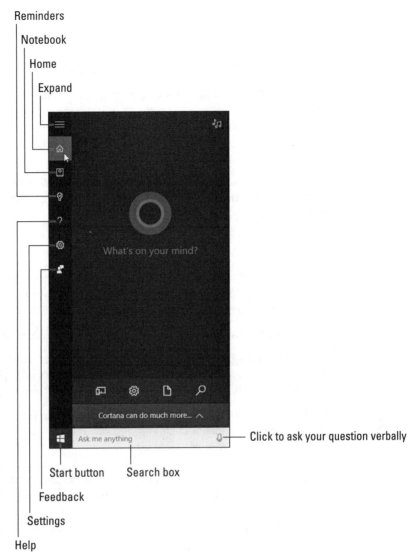

Reminders

Notebook

Home

Expand

What's on your mind?

Cortana can do much more... ∧

Ask me anything — Click to ask your question verbally

Start button   Search box

Feedback

Settings

Help

FIGURE 7-5:
Click the icons along Cortana's left edge to change the program's settings.

- **Reminders:** Drop by here for Cortana to remind you about certain things, as they relate to a person, place, or time. You can simply set a morning alarm clock, for example, or you can make Cortana remind you to call your spouse when you arrive at a new city on a business trip.

- **Help:** If Cortana seems too complex, click here for walkthroughs on how Cortana can make appointments, set reminders, send email, play music, and do other chores.

- **Settings:** You won't find an Off button here, but you can click toggle switches that decide how much of your personal information Cortana may access.

- **Feedback:** Wish Cortana did something a little differently? Here's your chance to tell Microsoft about it.

2. **Choose whether to sign in with a Microsoft account, if asked.**

   Cortana works with a Local account, but not very well. She won't remember things about you, leading to less accurate results. If you sign in with a Microsoft account, Cortana will learn about you, as well as be able to send results to anywhere you've logged in with your Microsoft account, be it another PC, tablet, or phone.

3. **Choose whether to grant Cortana access to your physical location, contacts, appointments, messages, and web browsing history. Then click the Next button.**

   You can say no, of course, but what good is a butler who doesn't know that your coat belongs in the closet?

   Not signing in with a Microsoft account and denying Cortana access to your personal information makes Cortana revert to a fairly standard Search box, as described in the previous section.

4. **Fine-tune Cortana by visiting the Settings and Notebook areas.**

   Drop by the Settings area first. There, you can set up Cortana to understand the nuances of your voice as picked up by your computer's microphone. You can also manage how much of your information Cortana may access.

   Next, visit the Notebook area. Here, let Cortana know your interests — and perhaps more important — the things you don't like. That helps Cortana tailor her information to things you want to hear.

Don't know where to start with Cortana? Begin by typing, **What can you do?** into the Search box and pressing the Enter key. Cortana begins explaining it all.

These tips will help you train Cortana into being the most helpful personal assistant:

>> To bypass the Search box and simply talk to Cortana, click Cortana's Settings icon to turn on the voice-activated search. When the Settings pane appears, choose Microphone to make sure Cortana can hear you. Then turn on the Hey Cortana toggle switch.

>> With Hey Cortana turned on, your PC, tablet, or phone waits anxiously for the term "**Hey Cortana.**" When Cortana hears you say those two words, it listens closely for your search term and begins processing your request.

>> To search the Internet for the singer Lady Gaga, for example, say "**Hey Cortana Lady Gaga.**" Don't pause after saying "Hey, Cortana," or you'll create confusion. Say the phrase in one fairly quick burst.

TIP

RUNNING CORTANA ON YOUR PHONE

Cortana isn't limited to your desktop computer. Microsoft makes Cortana apps for Android, Apple, and Windows phones, as well. This way, Cortana can keep offering you helpful reminders and suggestions while you're on the road.

The latest Android app links Cortana with your Windows PC; you can give Cortana a location-or-time-based note on your PC, and your phone will remind you to buy milk when you pull into the grocery store parking lot.

You can even tell Cortana which phone apps should be able to send their notifications to your PC. That way, you can keep up with your phone's nags even when your phone stays in your pocket. (You can respond to them from your PC, as well.)

WARNING

REMEMBER

» Turning on Hey Cortana will drain the batteries more quickly on your phone or tablets. Try it for a while and track your battery life to see whether the trade-off is worth it.

» Cortana only works when you have an Internet connection.

» Drop by the Notebook area's About Me section. There, you can list your Home and Work addresses so that Cortana can give you traffic reports before you head for your car. The Family Finder section lets you enter your children's Microsoft accounts to keep track of their location. (Or their phone's location, at least.)

Turning Off Cortana

Some people accept their new robotic overlords with great relief. For years, Apple product owners have relied on *Siri* to find the best sushi joint when they travel. Android phone owners fetch *Google Now* for tailored news articles and traffic updates for the drive to work. Amazon's *Alexa* checks the weather and helps you choose the right movie.

Other people cringe at a tail-wagging robot trying to butt into their personal life. Cortana no longer includes the simple On/Off switch found in earlier versions of Windows 10. To turn Cortana back into a simple Search box, follow these steps:

1. **Click in the Search box, and when the Search pane appears, click the Notebook icon (shown in the margin).**

2. **When the Notebook pane appears, click Permissions.**

3. **Turn off all the toggle switches on the Permissions pane.**

4. **Visit the Notebook pane's About Me section.**

5. **Visit Cortana's Settings pane and turn off all the toggle switches.**

6. **At the top of the Settings pane, choose Manage What Cortana Knows About Me In the Cloud.**

   Step 5 erases what Cortana knows about you on your PC; this step lets you erase the information Cortana has stashed away in the cloud, which she shares with your phone, tablets, and other devices.

Finding a Missing File inside a Folder

The Start menu's Search box can be overkill when you're poking around inside a single desktop folder, looking for a missing file. To solve the "sea of files in a folder" problem, Windows includes a Search box in every desktop folder's upper-right corner. That Search box limits your search to files within that *particular* folder.

To find a missing file within a specific folder, click inside that folder's Search box and begin typing a word or short phrase from your missing file. As you type letters and words, Windows begins filtering out files that are missing your sought-after word or phrase. It keeps narrowing down the candidates until the folder displays only a few files, including, I hope, your runaway file.

When a folder's Search box locates too many possible matches, bring in some other helping hands: the headers above each column. For best results, select the Details option in the View tab's Layout group, which lines up your filenames in one column, as shown in Figure 7-6. The first column, Name, lists the name of each file, and the adjacent columns list specific details about each file.

TIP

See the column headers, such as Name, Date Modified, and Type, atop each column? Click any of those headers to sort your files by that term. Here's how to sort by some of the column headers you may see in your Documents folder:

» **Name:** Know the first letter of your file's name? Then click here to sort your files alphabetically. You can then pluck your file from the list. (Click Name again to reverse the sort order.)

» **Date Modified:** When you remember the approximate date you last changed a document, click the Date Modified header. That places your newest files atop the list, making them easy to locate. (Clicking Date Modified again reverses the order, a handy way to weed out old files you may no longer need.)

>> **Type:** This header sorts files by their contents. All your photos group together, for example, as do all your Word documents. It's a handy way to find a few stray photos swimming in a sea of text files.

>> **Size:** Sorting here places your 45-page thesis on one end and your grocery list on the other.

>> **Authors:** Microsoft Word and other programs tack your name onto your work. A click on this label sorts the files alphabetically by their creators' names.

>> **Tags:** Windows often lets you assign tags to your documents and photos, a task I describe later in this chapter. Adding the tag "Moldy Cheese" to that pungent photo session lets you retrieve those pictures by either typing the tag or sorting a folder's files by their tags.

DEEP SORT

A folder's Details view (shown in Figure 7-6) arranges your filenames into a single column, with oodles of detail columns flowing off to the right. You can sort a folder's contents by clicking the word atop any column: Name, Date Modified, Author, and so on. But the sort features in Windows go much deeper, as you'll notice when clicking the little downward-pointing arrow to the right of each column's name.

Click the little arrow by the words *Date Modified,* for example, and a calendar drops down. Click a date, and the folder quickly displays files modified on that particular date, filtering out all the rest. Beneath the calendar, check boxes also let you view files created Today, Yesterday, Last Week, Earlier This Month, Earlier This Year, or simply A Long Time Ago. (The available checkboxes change depending on the age of the files inside your currently viewed folder.)

Similarly, click the arrow next to the Authors column header, and a drop-down menu lists the authors of every document in the folder. Select the check boxes next to the author names you'd like to see, and Windows immediately filters out files created by other people, leaving only the matches. (This feature works best with Microsoft Office documents.)

These hidden filters can be dangerous, however, because you can easily forget that you've turned them on. If you spot a check mark next to any column header, you've left a filter turned on, and the folder is hiding some of its files. To turn off the filter and see *all* that folder's files, deselect the check box next to the column header and examine the drop-down menu. Click any selected check boxes on that drop-down menu to remove their check marks and remove the filter.

TIP

Folders usually display about five columns of details, but you can add more columns. In fact, you can sort files by their word count, song length, photo size, creation date, and dozens of other details. To see a list of available detail columns, right-click an existing label along a column's top. When the drop-down menu appears, select More to see the Choose Details dialog box. Click to put check marks next to the new detail columns you'd like to see and then click OK.

Finding Lost Photos

Windows indexes your email down to the last word, but it can't tell the difference between photos of your cat and photos of your office party. When it comes to photos, the ID work lies in *your* hands, and these tips make the chore as easy as possible:

» **Store shooting sessions in separate folders.** The Windows photo importing program automatically creates a new folder to store each session, named after the current date. But if you're using some other program to dump photos, be sure to create a new folder for each session. Then name the folder with a short description of your session: Dog Walk, Kite Surfing, or Truffle Hunt. (Windows indexes the folder names.)

» **Sort by date.** Have you stumbled onto a massive folder that's a mishmash of digital photos? Try this quick sorting trick: Click the View tab and choose Large Icons to make the photos morph into identifiable thumbnails. Then, from the View tab menu, choose Sort By and select Date Taken. Windows sorts the photos by the date you snapped them, turning chaos into organization.

» **Rename your photos.** Instead of leaving your Tunisian vacation photos with their boring camera-given names like DSC_2421, DSC_2422, and so on, give them meaningful names: Select all the files in your Tunisia folder by clicking the Home tab on the Ribbon and clicking the Select All button. Then right-click the first picture, choose Rename, and type **Tunisia**. Windows names them as Tunisia, Tunisia (2), Tunisia (3), and so on. (If you messed up, press Ctrl+Z to undo the renaming.)

Following those simple rules helps keep your photo collection from becoming a jumble of files.

REMEMBER

Be *sure* to back up your digital photos to a portable hard drive, CDs, DVDs, or another backup method I describe in Chapter 13. If they're not backed up, you'll lose your family history when your PC's hard drive eventually crashes.

Finding Other Computers on a Network

A *network* is simply a group of connected PCs that can share things, such as your Internet connection, files, or a printer. Most people use a public network every day without knowing it: Every time you check your email, your PC connects to another PC on the Internet to grab your waiting messages.

Much of the time, you needn't care about the other PCs on your private network. But when you want to find a connected PC, perhaps to grab files from the PC in your family room, Windows is happy to help.

In fact, Windows has something called a *Homegroup* system that makes it easier than ever to share files with other Windows PCs. Creating a Homegroup is as simple as entering the same password on every connected PC.

To find a PC on your Homegroup or traditional network, open any folder and click the word Network on the Navigation Pane along the folder's left edge, as shown in Figure 7-7.

Clicking Network lists every PC that's connected to your own PC in a traditional network. Clicking Homegroup in the Navigation Pane lists Windows PCs in your Homegroup, a simpler way to share files. To browse files on any of those PCs in either category, just double-click their names.

I walk through the steps of creating both your own Homegroup and home network in Chapter 15.

FIGURE 7-7:
To find computers connected to your PC through a network, click the Navigation Pane's Network category.

Chapter 8

Printing and Scanning Your Work

Occasionally you'll want to take text or an image away from your PC's whirling electrons and place it onto something more permanent: a piece of paper. This chapter tackles that job by explaining all you need to know about printing.

I explain how to print just the relevant portions of a website — without the other pages, the ads, the menus, and the printer-ink-wasting images.

You discover how to print from the Start menu's gang of apps as well as from the desktop's programs.

And should you find yourself near a printer spitting out 17 pages of the wrong thing, flip ahead to this chapter's coverage of the mysterious *print queue*. It's a little-known area that lets you cancel documents *before* they waste all your paper. (I explain how to set up a printer in Chapter 12.)

If you prefer to turn paper into a file on your PC, this chapter closes with a run-down on the Windows Scan app. When combined with a scanner, it transforms maps, receipts, photos, and any other paper items into digital files.

Printing from a Start Menu App

Although Microsoft now tries to pretend that Start menu apps and desktop programs are the same, apps often behave quite differently than traditional desktop programs.

Many of the apps can't print, and those that do allow printing don't offer many ways to tinker with your printer's settings. Nevertheless, when you *must* print something from a Windows app, following these steps ensures the best chance of success:

1. **From the Start menu, load the app containing information you want to print.**

Cross your fingers in the hopes that your app is one of the few that can print.

2. **Click the app's Settings icon or More icon to see the drop-down menus, and click the Print option.**

A click on these three striped lines, known informally as the *hamburger menu,* fetches a drop down menu. (This drop-down menu sometimes replaces the Charms bar's icons found in Windows 8 and Windows 8.1.)

Similarly, a click on an icon of three dots (shown in the margin) found in some apps also fetches a drop-down menu. (The three dots menu is sometimes called a *More* or *Expand* menu, because clicking it expands a menu to display more options.)

When you click Print from the drop-down menu, the app's Print menu appears, shown in Figure 8-1. (If the word Print isn't listed on the drop-down menu or is grayed out, that app isn't able to print.)

3. **Click the printer to receive your work.**

Click the Printer box, and a drop-down menu appears, listing any printers available to your computer. Click the name of printer you want to handle the job.

4. **Make any final adjustments.**

The Printer window offers a preview of what you're printing, with the total number of pages listed above. To browse the pages you're about to print, click the Previous or Next buttons above the preview.

Not enough options? Then click the More Settings link at the bottom of the left pane to see options offered by your particular printer model.

5. **Click the Print button.**

Windows shuffles your work to the printer of your choice, using the settings you chose in Step 4.

FIGURE 8-1:
Choose your
printing options
or click the More
Settings link for
additional
options.

Although you can print from a few apps, you'll eventually run into limitations:

REMEMBER

>> Most apps don't offer many printing options. You can't print a blank monthly calendar from your Calendar app, for example, but you can print a daily or weekly itinerary.

>> The More Settings link, described earlier in Step 4, lets you choose between Portrait and Landscape mode, as well as choose a printer tray. However, you won't find more detailed adjustments, such as choosing margins or adding headers and footers.

In short, although you *can* print from a few apps, your results will be quick and dirty. Desktop programs, described in the rest of this chapter, usually offer much more control over printing jobs.

Printing Your Masterpiece from the Desktop

Built for power and control, the desktop offers many more options when it comes to printing your work. But that power and control often mean wading through a sea of menus.

When working from the desktop, Windows shuttles your work to the printer in any of a half-dozen ways. Chances are good that you'll be using these methods most often:

>> Choose Print from your program's File menu.

>> Click the program's Print icon, usually a tiny printer.

>> Right-click your unopened document's icon and choose Print.

>> Click the Print button on a program's toolbar.

>> Drag and drop a document's icon onto your printer's icon.

If a dialog box appears, click the OK or Print button, and Windows immediately begins sending your pages to the printer. Take a minute or so to refresh your coffee. If the printer is turned on (and still has paper and ink), Windows handles everything automatically, printing in the background while you do other things.

If the printed pages don't look quite right — perhaps the information doesn't fit on the paper correctly or it looks faded — then you need to fiddle around with the print settings or perhaps change the paper quality, as described in the next sections.

>> To print a bunch of documents quickly, select all their icons. Then right-click the selected icons and choose Print. Windows quickly shuttles all of them to the printer, where they emerge on paper, one after the other.

>> When printing with an inkjet printer, faded colors usually mean you need to replace your printer's color inkjet cartridge. You can buy replacement cartridges both online and at most office supply stores.

>> Still haven't installed a printer? Flip to Chapter 12, where I explain how to plug one into your computer and make Windows notice it.

Adjusting how your work fits on the page

In theory, Windows *always* displays your work as if it were printed on paper. Microsoft's marketing department calls it *What You See Is What You Get,* forever disgraced with the awful acronym WYSIWYG and its awkward pronunciation: "wizzy-wig." If what you see onscreen *isn't* what you want to see on paper, a trip to the program's Page Setup dialog box, shown in Figure 8-2, usually sets things straight.

PEEKING AT YOUR PRINTED PAGE *BEFORE* IT HITS PAPER

TIP

Printing often requires a leap of faith: You choose Print from the menu and wait for the paper to emerge from the printer. If you're blessed, the page looks fine. But if you're cursed, you've wasted yet another sheet of paper.

The Print Preview option, found on many print menus, foretells your printing fate *before* the words hit paper. Print Preview compares your current work with your program's page settings and then displays a detailed picture of the printed page. That preview makes it easy to spot off-kilter margins, dangling sentences, and other printing fouls.

Different programs use slightly different Print Preview screens, with some offering more insight than others. But almost any program's Print Preview screen lets you know whether everything will fit onto the page correctly.

If the preview looks fine, choose Print to send the work to the printer. If something looks wrong, however, click Close to return to your work and make any necessary adjustments.

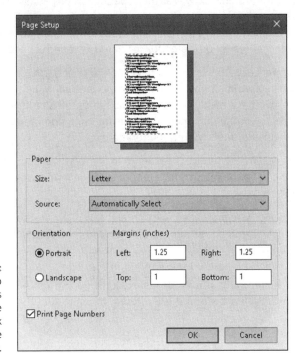

FIGURE 8-2:
The Page Setup dialog box allows you to adjust the way your work fits onto a piece of paper.

On desktop programs, the Page Setup box offers many formatting options; apps, by contrast, offer a more limited version (shown earlier in Figure 8-1). But they both offer several ways to flow your work across a printed page (and subsequently your screen). Page Setup dialog boxes differ among programs and printer models, but the following list describes the options that you'll find most often and the settings that usually work best:

>> **Page Size:** This option lets your program know what size of paper currently lives inside your printer. Leave this option set to Letter for printing on standard, 8.5-x-11-inch sheets of paper. Change this setting only if you're using legal-size paper (8.5 x 14), envelopes, or other paper sizes. (The nearby sidebar, "Printing envelopes without fuss," contains more information about printing envelopes.)

>> **Source:** Choose Automatically Select or Sheet Feeder unless you're using a fancy printer that accepts paper from more than one printer tray. People who have printers with two or more printer trays can select the tray containing the correct paper size. Some printers offer Manual Paper Feed, making the printer wait until you slide in that single sheet of paper.

>> **Header/Footer:** Type secret codes in these boxes to customize what the printer places along the top and bottom of your pages: page numbers, titles, and dates, for example, as well as their spacing. Unfortunately, different programs use different codes for their header and footer. If you spot a little question mark in the Page Setup dialog box's top-right corner, click it and then click inside the Header or Footer box for clues to the secret codes.

>> **Orientation:** Leave this option set to Portrait to print normal pages that read vertically like a letter. Choose Landscape only when you want to print sideways, which is a handy way to print wide spreadsheets. (If you choose Landscape, the printer automatically prints the page sideways; you don't need to slide the paper sideways into your printer.)

>> **Margins:** Feel free to reduce the margins to fit everything on a single sheet of paper. Or *enlarge* the margins to turn your six-page term paper into the required seven pages.

>> **Printer:** If you have more than one printer installed on your computer or network, click this button to choose which one to print your work. Click here to change that printer's settings as well, a job discussed in the next section.

When you're finished adjusting settings, click the OK button to save your changes. (Click the Print Preview button, if it's offered, to make sure that everything looks right.)

TIP

PRINTING ENVELOPES WITHOUT FUSS

Although clicking Envelopes in a program's Page Setup area is fairly easy, printing addresses in the correct spot on the envelope is extraordinarily difficult. Some printer models want you to insert envelopes upside down, but others prefer right side up. Your best bet is to run several tests, placing the envelope into your printer's tray in different ways until you finally stumble on the magic method. (Or you can pull out your printer's manual, if you still have it, and pore over the "proper envelope insertion" pictures.)

After you've figured out the correct method for your particular printer, tape a successfully printed envelope above your printer and add an arrow pointing to the correct way to insert it.

Should you eventually give up on printing envelopes, try using Avery's mailing labels. Buy your preferred size of Avery labels and then download the free Avery Wizard for Microsoft Office software from Avery's website (www.avery.com). Compatible with Microsoft Word, the wizard places little boxes on your screen that precisely match the size of your particular Avery labels. Type the addresses into the little boxes, insert the label sheet into your printer, and Word prints everything onto the little stickers. You don't even need to lick them.

Or do as I did: Buy a little rubber stamp with your return address. It's much faster than stickers or printers.

TIP

To find the Page Setup box in some programs, click the little arrow next to the program's Printer icon and choose Page Setup from the menu that drops down.

Adjusting your printer's settings

When you choose Print from many programs, Windows offers one last chance to spruce up your printed page. The Print dialog box, shown in Figure 8-3, lets you route your work to any printer installed on your computer or network. While there, you can adjust the printer's settings, choose your paper quality, and select the pages (and quantities) you'd like to print.

You're likely to find these settings waiting in the dialog box:

>> **Select Printer:** Ignore this option if you have only one printer, because Windows chooses it automatically. If your computer has access to several printers, click the one that should receive the job. If you have a fax modem on your computer or network, click Fax to send your work as a fax through the Windows Fax and Scan program.

FIGURE 8-3:
The Print dialog
box lets you
choose your
printer and adjust
its settings.

TIP

The printer called Microsoft XPS Document Writer sends your work to a specially formatted file, usually to be printed or distributed professionally. Chances are good that you'll never use it.

» **Page Range:** Select All to print your entire document. To print just a few of its pages, select the Pages option and enter the page numbers you want to print. For example, enter **1-4, 6** to leave out page 5 of a 6-page document. If you've highlighted a paragraph, choose Selection to print that particular paragraph — a great way to print the important part of a web page and leave out the rest.

» **Number of Copies:** Most people leave this set to 1 copy, unless everybody in the boardroom wants their own copy. You can choose Collate only if your printer offers that option. (Most don't, leaving you to sort the pages yourself.)

» **Preferences:** Click this button to see a dialog box like the one in Figure 8-4, where you can choose options specific to your own printer model. The Printing Preferences dialog box typically lets you select different grades of paper, choose between color and black and white, set the printing quality, and make last-minute corrections to the page layout. (This option varies greatly according to your printer model, so yours may look different.)

FIGURE 8-4:
The Printing
Preferences
dialog box lets
you change
settings specific
to your printer
model.

Canceling a print job

Just realized you sent the wrong 26-page document to the printer? So you panic and hit the printer's Off button. Unfortunately, many printers automatically pick up where they left off when you turn them back on, leaving you or your co-workers to deal with the mess.

To purge the mistake from your printer's memory, follow these steps:

1. **From the desktop's taskbar, right-click your printer's icon and choose your printer's name from the pop-up menu.**

   To see your printer's icon, you may need to click the little upward-pointing arrow to the left of the taskbar's icons next to the clock.

   When you choose your printer's name, the handy *print queue* window appears, as shown in Figure 8-5.

2. **Right-click your mistaken document and choose Cancel to end the job. If asked to confirm, click the Yes button. Repeat with any other listed unwanted documents.**

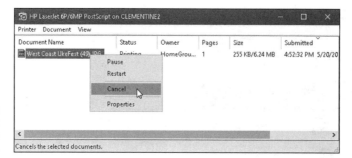

FIGURE 8-5:
Use the print
queue to cancel a
print job.

Your printer queue can take a minute or two to clear itself. (To speed things up, click the View menu and choose Refresh.) When the print queue is clear, turn your printer back on; it won't keep printing that same darn document.

» The print queue, also known as the print spooler, lists every document waiting patiently to reach your printer. Feel free to change the printing order by dragging and dropping documents up or down the list. (You can't move anything in front of the currently printing document, though.)

» Sharing your printer on the network? Print jobs sent from other PCs sometimes end up in your computer's print queue, so you'll need to cancel the botched ones. (And networked folks who share their printer may need to delete your botched print jobs, as well.)

» If your printer runs out of paper during a job and stubbornly halts, add more paper. Then to start things flowing again, open the print queue, right-click your document, and choose Restart. (Some printers have an Online button that you push to begin printing again.)

TIP

» You can send items to the printer even when you're working in the coffee shop with your laptop. Later, when you connect the laptop to your printer, the print queue notices and begins sending your files. (Beware: When they're in the print queue, documents are formatted for your specific printer model. If you subsequently connect your laptop to a *different* printer model, the print queue's waiting documents won't print correctly.)

Printing a web page

Although information-stuffed web pages look awfully tempting, *printing* those web pages is rarely satisfying because they look so awful on paper. When sent to the printer, web pages often run off the page's right side, consume zillions of additional pages, or appear much too small to read.

To make matters worse, all those colorful advertisements can suck your printer's color cartridges dry fairly quickly. Only four things make for successfully printed web pages, and I rank them in order of probable success rate:

» **Use the web page's built-in Print option.** Some websites, but not all, offer a tiny menu option called Print This Page, Text Version, Printer-Friendly Version, or something similar. That option tells the website to strip out its garbage and reformat the page so that it fits neatly onto a sheet of paper. This option is the most reliable way to print a web page.

» **Choose Print Preview from your browser's File or Print menu.** After 15 years, some web page designers noticed that people want to print their pages, so they tweaked the settings, making their pages *automatically* reformat themselves when printed. If you're lucky, a clean look in the Print Preview window confirms that you've stumbled onto one of those printer-friendly sites.

» **Copy the portion you want and paste it into a word processor.** Try selecting the desired text from the web page, copying it, and pasting it into a word processor. Delete any unwanted remnants, adjust the margins, and print the portion you want. I explain how to select, copy, and paste in Chapter 6.

» **Copy the entire page and paste it into a word processor.** Although it's lots of work, it's an option. Right-click a blank portion of the web page and choose Select All. Right-click again and choose Copy. Next, open Microsoft Word or another full-featured word processor and paste the web page inside a new document. By hacking away at the unwanted portions, you can sometimes end up with something printable.

TIP

These tips may also come in handy for moving a web page from screen to paper:

» The Microsoft Edge web browser in Windows 10 is built for speed, not power, but it still prints. To print what you're viewing in Edge, click the browser's More icon (three dots in the top right corner), and choose Print from the drop-down menu.

» For best results, turn on the Reading View mode in Edge by clicking the Reading View icon (shown in the margin). Reading View strips away ads and other detritus, leaving you with a clean page to send to the printer.

» If Microsoft Edge still doesn't print well, try printing from Internet Explorer, instead. (You can still find Internet Explorer by typing its name into the Start menu's Search box.)

>> If you spot an Email option but no Print option, email the page to yourself. Depending on your email program, you may have better success printing it as an email message.

>> To print just a few paragraphs of a web page, use the mouse to select the portion you're after. (I cover the act of *selecting* things in Chapter 6.) Choose Print from Internet Explorer's Tools menu (shown in the margin) to open the Print dialog box, shown earlier in Figure 8-3. Then, in the Page Range box, choose the Selection option.

>> If a web page's table or photo insists on vanishing off the paper's right edge, try printing the page in Landscape mode rather than Portrait. See the "Adjusting how your work fits on the page" section, earlier in this chapter, for details on Landscape mode.

Troubleshooting your printer

When you can't print something, start with the basics: Are you *sure* that the printer is turned on, plugged into the wall, full of paper, and connected securely to your computer with a cable?

If so, try plugging the printer into different outlets, turning it on, and seeing whether its power light comes on. If the light stays off, your printer's power supply is probably blown.

TIP

Printers are almost always cheaper to replace than repair. Printer companies make their money on ink cartridges, so they often sell printers at a loss.

If the printer's power light beams brightly, check these things before giving up:

>> Make sure that a sheet of paper hasn't jammed itself inside the printer. (A steady pull usually extricates jammed paper. Sometimes opening and closing the printer's lid starts things moving again.)

TIP

>> Does your inkjet printer still have ink in its cartridges? Does your laser printer have toner? Try printing a test page: From the desktop, right-click the Start button and choose Control Panel. From the Hardware and Sound category, choose Devices and Printers. Right-click your printer's icon, choose Printer Properties, and click the Print Test Page button to see whether the computer and printer can talk to each other.

>> Try updating the printer's *driver,* the little program that helps it talk with Windows. Visit the printer manufacturer's website, download the newest Windows 10 driver for your particular printer model, and run its installation program. (I cover drivers in Chapter 13.)

Finally, here are a couple of tips to help you protect your printer and cartridges:

WARNING

>> Turn off your printer when you're not using it. Older inkjet printers, especially, should be turned off when they're not in use. The heat tends to dry the cartridges, shortening their life.

>> Don't unplug your inkjet printer to turn it off. Always use the On/Off switch. The switch ensures that the cartridges slide back to their home positions, keeping them from drying out or clogging.

TIP

CHOOSING THE RIGHT PAPER FOR YOUR PRINTER

If you've strolled the aisles at an office-supply store lately, you've noticed a bewildering array of paper choices. Sometimes the paper's packaging lists its application: Premium Inkjet Paper, for example, for high-quality memos. Here's a list of different print jobs and the types of paper they require. Before printing, be sure to click the Printer's Preferences section to select the grade of paper you're using for that job.

- **Junk:** Keep some cheap or scrap paper around for testing the printer, printing quick drafts, leaving desktop notes, and printing other on-the-fly jobs. Botched print jobs work great here; just use the paper's other side.

- **Letter quality:** Bearing the words Premium or Bright White, this paper works fine for letters, reports, memos, and other things designed for showing to others.

- **Photos:** You can print photos on any type of paper, but they look like photos only on actual *photo-quality paper* — the expensive stuff. Slide the paper carefully into your printer tray so that the picture prints on the glossy, shiny side. Some photo paper requires placing a little cardboard sheet beneath it, which helps glide the paper smoothly through the printer.

- **Labels:** They've never sent me a T-shirt, but I still say that Avery's Wizard program (www.avery.com) makes it easy to print Avery labels and cards. The wizard teams up with Microsoft Word to mesh perfectly with Avery's preformatted mailing labels, greeting cards, business cards, CD labels, and many others.

- **Transparencies:** For powerful PowerPoint presentations, buy special transparent plastic sheets designed to be used with your type of printer. Make sure the transparency is compatible with your printer, be it laser or inkjet.

Before plunking down your money, make sure that your paper is designed specifically for your printer type, be it laser or inkjet. Laser printers heat the pages, and some paper and transparencies can't take the heat.

Scanning from the Start Menu

Windows 10 dropped the Scan app that came with Windows 8 and 8.1. However, you can download it for free from the Store app. (It's called Windows Scan in the Store app, which I explain in Chapter 6.)

The new app doesn't work with older scanners, unfortunately. But if your scanner is relatively new, the Scan app is a refreshing change from complicated scanner menus.

Note: Setting up a new scanner for the first time? Be sure to *unlock* it by sliding a lever or turning a dial on the scanner to the unlock position. That lock protects the scanner during shipping, but you must turn it off before use.

After installing the Windows Scan app from the Windows Store and connecting your scanner, follow these steps to scan something into your computer:

1. **From the Start menu, open the Scan app.**

    If you don't spot the Scan app on the Start menu, click the words All Apps in the Start menu's bottom-left corner. The Start menu lists all of its apps alphabetically. *Note:* If you don't find the Scan app on your computer, you can download it for free from the Store app.

     Click the Scan app, shown in the margin, and the Scan app appears on the screen. If it complains that your scanner isn't connected, make sure you've connected the USB cable between your computer's USB port and the scanner and that the scanner is turned on.

    If your scanner's plugged in and turned on, the scan app lists your scanner's name, shown in Figure 8-6, and the *file type* used for saving your files. (The PNG file type is widely accepted by most programs.)

    If the app doesn't recognize your scanner, your scanner is too old. You're stuck with your scanner's bundled software — if it works — or, unfortunately, buying a new scanner.

2. **(Optional) To change the settings, click the Show More link.**

    The app's default settings work fine for most jobs. The Show More link offers these options for specific types of scans:

    *   **File Type:** PNG works fine for most scans. But to create smaller, lower-resolution scans for emailing, choose JPG from this pull-down menu.

    *   **Color mode:** Choose Color for color items, such as photos and glossy magazine pages. Choose Grayscale for nearly everything else and choose Black and White *only* for line drawings or black-and-white clip art.

FIGURE 8-6:
Click the Show
More link for
additional
options or click
Preview to test
a scan.

- **Resolution (DPI):** For most work, the default 300 works fine. Higher resolution scans (larger numbers) bring more detail but consume more space, making them difficult to email. Lower resolution scans show less detail but create smaller file sizes. You may need to experiment to find the settings that meet your needs.

- **Save File To:** The Scan app creates a Scan folder in your PC's Pictures folder, where it stores your newly scanned images. If desired, you can change the Scan folder's name or even create a different folder for each scanning session.

3. **Click the Preview button to make sure your scan appears correct.**

   Click the Preview icon, shown in the margin, and the Scan app makes a first pass, letting you preview a scan made with your chosen settings.

   If the preview doesn't look right, make sure you've made the right choice for your job in Color Mode, described in the preceding step. If the preview shows a blank white page, make sure you've *unlocked* the scanner as described in the scanner's bundled instruction sheets.

   If you're scanning a smaller item that doesn't fill the entire scanner bed, look for the circle markers in each corner of the preview scan. Drag each circle inward to surround the area you want to copy.

4. **Click the Scan button. When the scan finishes, click the View button to see your scan.**

   The Scan app scans your image with the settings you've chosen in the previous steps and then saves your image in your Pictures folder's Scan folder.

The Scan app works well for fast, easy scans. But because it relies on the simple, built-in Windows software, your scanner's built-in control buttons won't work.

If you want your scanner's buttons to work or you need finer control over your scans, skip the Scan app, head for the desktop, and install your scanner's bundled software. (On some scanner models, Windows Update installs the scanner's bundled software automatically as soon as you plug in the scanner.)

TIP

For quick and dirty scans, just take a picture of the document with the camera built into your phone or tablet. That won't work well for photos, but it's an easy way to keep track of receipts and invoices.

If you need more features than the Scan app offers, check out the desktop's Windows Fax and Scan program. It's more complicated and requires special equipment for faxing, but it offers more features than the Scan app.

3
Getting Things Done on the Internet

Chapter 9

Cruising the Web

E ven when being installed, Windows starts reaching for the Internet, hungry for any hint of a connection. After connecting, Windows kindly downloads updates to make your PC run more smoothly. Other motives are less pure: Windows also checks in with Microsoft to make sure that you're not installing a pirated copy.

Windows 10 is so web-dependent that it comes with a savvy new browser named *Microsoft Edge*. Fast and sleek, Microsoft Edge helps you move in and out of today's Internet-dependent world.

In fact, Microsoft Edge is a *universal app,* meaning it looks and behaves the same whether it runs on a Windows 10 phone, tablet, PC, or even on an Xbox game console.

This chapter explains how to find and fire up Microsoft Edge, connect with the Internet, visit websites, and find what you're seeking online.

For ways to keep out the bad stuff, be sure to visit Chapter 11. It's a primer on safe computing that explains how to avoid the web's bad neighborhoods, which harbor viruses, spyware, hijackers, and other Internet parasites.

What's an ISP, and Why Do I Need One?

Everybody needs three things to connect with the Internet and visit websites: a computer, web browser software, and an Internet service provider (ISP).

You already have the computer, be it a tablet, laptop, or desktop PC. And the new Windows 10 browser, Microsoft Edge, handles the software side.

That means most people need to find only an ISP. Most coffee shops, airports, and hotels let you connect wirelessly. At home, though, you must pay an ISP for the privilege of surfing the web. When your computer connects to your ISP's computers, Windows automatically finds the Internet, and you're ready to surf the web.

Choosing an ISP is fairly easy because you're often stuck with whichever ISPs serve your particular geographical area. Ask your friends and neighbors how they connect and whether they recommend their ISP. Call several ISPs serving your area for a rate quote and then compare rates. Most bill on a monthly basis, so if you're not happy, you can always switch.

>> Although ISPs charge for Internet access, you don't always have to pay. More and more public businesses share their Internet access for free, usually through a wireless connection. If your phone, laptop, or tablet includes wireless support, and most do, you can browse the Internet whenever you're within range of a free wireless signal. (I cover wireless in the next section.)

>> Although a handful of ISPs charge for each minute you're connected, most charge from $30 to $100 a month for unlimited service. (Some also offer faster connection speeds for more money.) Make sure that you know your rate before hopping aboard or else you may be unpleasantly surprised at the month's end.

>> ISPs let you connect to the Internet in a variety of ways. The slowest ISPs require a dialup modem and an ordinary phone line; they're still a lifeline for some rural areas. (Satellite access also works well in rural areas.) Faster and the most popular are broadband connections: special DSL or ISDN lines provided by some phone companies, and the even faster cable modems supplied by your cable television company. You're only limited by what's offered in your geographic area.

TIP

>> You need to pay an ISP for only *one* Internet connection. You can share that single connection with any other computers, cellphones, TVs, refrigerators, and other Internet-aware gadgetry in your home, office, or kitchen. (I explain how to share an Internet connection by creating your own wired or wireless network in Chapter 15.)

WHERE'S INTERNET EXPLORER?

After 20 years of service, Internet Explorer finally hit its retirement plan with Windows 10. Built in 1995, Internet Explorer carried plenty of baggage. For example, it needed specialized coding to display websites created with older technology. All that old code slowed down Internet Explorer's performance when viewing modern websites. That old code also made Internet Explorer more vulnerable to viruses and other exploits.

So, Microsoft started anew with Microsoft Edge, its fast, but less-powerful browser. If you prefer Internet Explorer, the old-timer is still around: Click inside the Cortana Search box by the Start button, type **Internet Explorer**, and press Enter to revisit the faithful Windows browser or yesteryear.

If Internet Explorer doesn't appear, you need to visit the Control Panel's Programs and Features section and install it through the Turn Windows Features On and Off area. To install Internet Explorer, follow these steps:

1. **Right-click the Start button, choose Control Panel from the pop-up menu, and click the Control Panel's Programs icon.**

2. **From the Programs and Features category, choose Turn Windows Features On or Off.**

3. **Put a check mark in the box next to Internet Explorer 11, and click the OK button.**

Restart your PC, when asked, by clicking the Restart Now button. When your computer restarts, Internet Explorer appears in the Windows Accessories area of the Start menu. Internet Explorer may not be as sleek and sexy as Microsoft Edge, but some people may find it as comfortable as an old stuffed chair. Microsoft still plans to release security patches for Internet Explorer through Windows Update, but don't expect to see any new features added to the creaky old browser.

Connecting Wirelessly to the Internet

Windows *constantly* searches for a working Internet connection, whether your computer plugs into a cable or scans the airwaves for a Wi-Fi (wireless) connection. If your computer finds a Wi-Fi connection that you've previously connected with, you're set: Windows passes the news along to Microsoft Edge, and you're ready to visit the web.

When you're traveling, however, the wireless networks around are often new, forcing you to find and authorize these new connections.

To connect to a nearby wireless network for the first time (whether it's one in your own home or in a public place), follow these steps:

1. **Click the taskbar's Wi-Fi icon (shown in the margin) near the clock.**

   Windows lists all the nearby wireless networks, shown in Figure 9-1.

   The networks are ranked by signal strength, with the strongest and fastest network listed at the top.

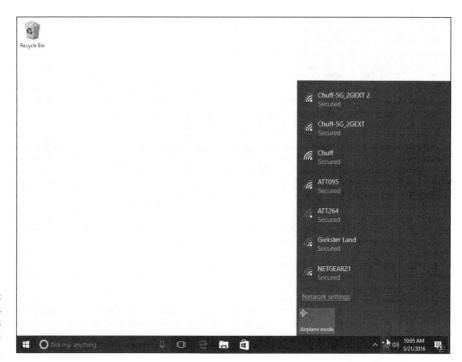

FIGURE 9-1:
Windows lists
every wireless
network within
range.

2. **Choose to connect to the desired network by clicking its name and clicking the Connect button.**

   If you're connecting to an *unsecured network* — a network that doesn't require a password — you're finished. Windows warns you about connecting to an unsecured network, but a click or tap of the Connect button lets you connect anyway. (Don't do any shopping or banking on an unsecured connection.)

   But for a more secure connection, skip the unsecured networks. Instead, ask your hotel staff, coffee shop barista, or airport staff for the password to the secure network. Then head to the next step.

TIP

If you select the adjacent Connect Automatically check box before clicking the Connect button, Windows automatically connects to that network the next time you're within range, sparing you from connecting manually each time.

3. **Enter a password if needed.**

   If you try to connect to a *security-enabled* wireless connection, Windows asks you to enter a *network security key* — technospeak for *password.* If you're at home, here's where you type in the same password you entered into your router when setting up your wireless network.

   If you're connecting to somebody *else's* password-protected wireless network, ask the network's owner for the password. You may need to pull out your credit card at the front counter in some hotels and coffee shops — they may charge for access.

TIP

Windows account owners reap a benefit here: Your Microsoft account remembers your Wi-Fi passwords. When you log onto a Wi-Fi network on a desktop PC, you can automatically log onto it with your tablet without having to retype the password.

4. **Choose whether you want to share your files with other people on the network.**

   If you're connecting on your own home or office network, choose "Yes, turn on sharing and connect to devices." That lets you share files with others and connect to shared devices, such as printers.

   If you're connecting in a public area, by contrast, always choose "No, don't turn on sharing or connect to devices." That helps keep out snoops.

TIP

If you're still having problems connecting, try the following tips:

>> When Windows says that it can't connect to your wireless network, it offers to bring up the Network Troubleshooter. The Network Troubleshooter mulls over the problem and then says something about the signal being weak. It's really telling you this: "Move closer to the wireless transmitter."

>> If you're in a hotel room, moving your computer closer to a window may help you find a stronger wireless signal. (It might even pick up a wider variety of available wireless networks.)

>> If you can't connect to the secured network you want, try connecting to one of the unsecured networks. Unsecured networks work fine for casual browsing on the Internet.

HOW DO MICROSOFT EDGE AND INTERNET EXPLORER INTERACT?

Although Microsoft shines the spotlight on its new Microsoft Edge web browser, Windows 10 still comes with *two* web browsers. Internet Explorer lives on, tucked away in the Start menu's Windows Accessories area.

Microsoft Edge and Internet Explorer live in completely separate worlds. If you add a favorite web page to Microsoft Edge, it doesn't appear in Internet Explorer, and vice versa.

That's a marked contrast from the two browsers in Windows 8 and 8.1. Back then, Windows contained two intertwined versions of Internet Explorer: a simplified app and the standard desktop version. Those two versions of Internet Explorer shared your browsing history, cookies, saved passwords, and temporary files. Deleting those items from one browser also deleted them from the other.

Browsing the Web with Microsoft Edge

Built for speedy browsing of modern websites, Microsoft Edge loads quickly and displays web pages as quickly as your connection allows. Part of its speed and clean look comes from its limitations, though. The browser hides its menus in order to showcase every website's content. That makes navigation challenging.

To open Microsoft Edge, click its icon (shown in the margin) on the taskbar along the bottom of your screen. The browser opens, as shown in Figure 9-2, filling the screen with either your last-viewed site or a launch screen that shows the top news, weather, and links to popular sites.

The browser hides most of its menus behind cryptic icons, so I've called them all out in Figure 9-2 and neatly labeled them here:

>> **Back:** This back-arrow icon in the top-left corner lets you revisit the page you just visited.

>> **Forward:** A click on this icon lets you return to the page you just left.

>> **Refresh:** Handy when viewing sites with breaking news, this icon reloads the currently viewed page, gathering the latest material available.

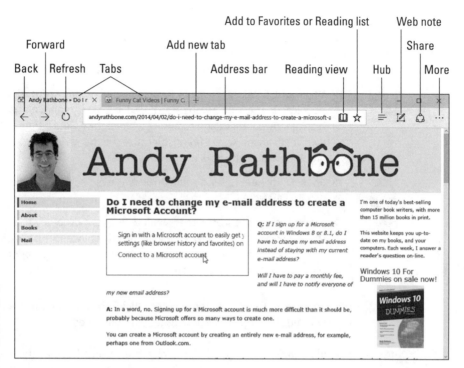

Back   Forward   Refresh   Tabs   Add new tab   Address bar   Reading view   Add to Favorites or Reading list   Hub   Web note   Share   More

FIGURE 9-2:
Microsoft Edge lets you view several websites, each in its own tab.

>> **Tabs:** Your currently open sites appear as tabs along the window's top edge, letting you revisit them with a click. (Or you can close them by clicking the X in their tab's right corner.)

>> **Address bar:** Click the name of the currently displayed site, which usually appears along the site's top edge, and the Address bar appears, letting you type in the address of a website you'd like to visit. Don't know where to go? Type in a few descriptive words, and the browser searches for and displays possible matches. Click any match to visit the site.

>> **Open New Tab:** Clicking the plus sign icon, which lives just to the right of your currently open tab or tabs, fetches a blank window with an Address bar along the top. There, you can type in either the address of a coveted website or a few search terms for the browser to fetch.

>> **Reading view:** This changes the current website's layout so it looks much like a page of a book. How? It ditches a lot of the ads and formatting, leaving only text and pertinent photos.

>> **Add to Favorites or Reading list:** Click the star icon to place your currently viewed page onto your list of *Favorites,* a collection of frequently visited sites. Clicking this offers an option to save a copy of the site to your Reading List for reading later.

» Hub: Despite its non-descriptive name, this icon lets you revisit websites you've marked as Favorites or placed on your Reading List. It also lets you view a history of your visited websites, and find downloaded files.

 » Web note: Coveted mostly by owners of a tablet and stylus, click the Web note icon to mark up a web page and save it as a graphic. It's handy for highlighting passages and scrawling a "Read this!" note before sending a website to an interested friend. (Because the marked-up page is sent as a graphic, none of the links will work.)

 » Share: Click here to send your currently viewed page to another program, usually OneNote.

 » More: Clicking this icon with three dots fetches a drop-down list with options for opening a new window, changing the current website's text size, sharing a site with friends, searching for a word on the current page, printing the page, pinning the page to the Start menu, and viewing other settings.

When you're on the go and looking for quick information, Microsoft Edge's speedy browser and its simple menus might be all you need.

TIP

If you've clicked or tapped the wrong button but haven't yet lifted your finger, stop! Command buttons don't take effect until you *release* your finger or mouse button. Keep holding down your finger or mouse button but slide the pointer or finger away from the wrong button. Move safely away from the button and *then* lift your finger.

Moving from one web page to another

Web pages come with specific addresses, just like homes do. *Any* web browser lets you move among those addresses. You can use Microsoft Edge, Internet Explorer, or even a competing browser such as Firefox (www.getfirefox.com) or Chrome (www.google.com/chrome).

No matter which browser you use, they all let you move from one page to another in any of three ways:

» By pointing and clicking a button or link that automatically whisks you away to another page

» By typing a complicated string of code words (the web address) into the Address bar of the web browser and pressing Enter

» By clicking the navigation buttons on the browser's toolbar, which is usually at the top of the screen

Clicking links

The first way to navigate the web is by far the easiest. Look for *links* — highlighted words or pictures on a page — and click them.

For example, see how the mouse pointer turned into a hand (shown in the margin) as it pointed at the word *Books* in Figure 9-3? That hand means the thing you're pointing at (be it word, button, or picture) is clickable. In this instance, I can click the word *Books* to see a web page with more information about that subject. The mouse pointer morphs into a hand whenever it's over a link. Click any linked word to see pages dealing with that link's particular subject.

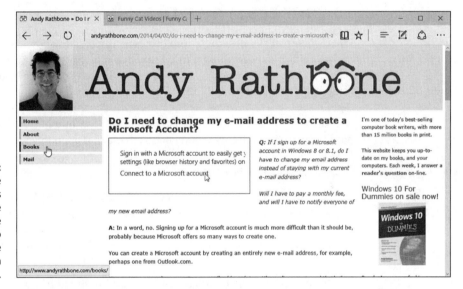

FIGURE 9-3:
When the mouse pointer becomes a hand, click the word or picture to go to a web page with more information about that item.

Typing web addresses in the Address bar

The second method of web surfing is more difficult. If a friend gives you a napkin with a cool website's address written on it, you need to type the website's address into your browser's *Address bar* — the text-filled bar across the top. You'll do fine as long as you don't misspell anything.

See the address for my website along the top of Figure 9-3? I typed **andyrathbone. com** into the Address bar. When I pressed Enter, Microsoft Edge scooted me to my website. (You don't need to type the *http://www* part, thank goodness.)

Using Microsoft Edge's icons

Finally, you can maneuver through the Internet by clicking various buttons on Microsoft Edge's stripped-down menus, as described in the previous section and Figure 9-2. Click the browser's Back arrow button, for example, to return to a page you just visited.

Hover your mouse pointer over a confusing button in any program, and a pop-up usually appears, explaining its purpose in life.

Making Microsoft Edge open to your favorite site

When you open the desktop's web browser, it needs to show you *something* right away. Well, that something can be any website you want. In computer terms, that's called your *home page*, and you can tell Microsoft Edge to use any site you want.

Naturally, Microsoft wants Microsoft Edge to open to a *Microsoft* website, so you need to jump through these many hoops to make it open to your own favorite site:

1. **Visit your favorite website.**

    Choose any web page you like. If you choose Google News (http://news.google.com), for example, Microsoft Edge always opens with the latest headlines. Take note of the web page's name in the Address bar, along the top of Edge; that address must be entered into another box in Step 3. (I describe how to copy and paste things in Windows in Chapter 6.)

2. **Click the More icon in Microsoft Edge and choose Settings from the drop-down menu.**

    The Settings pane appears, listing your options.

3. **Click the Settings pane's Open Microsoft Edge With section; when the drop-down menu appears, choose A Specific Page or Pages.**

    The drop-down menu spills down to offer these options:

    - **Start page:** The default option, this fills your opening screen with Microsoft's carefully curated information: breaking news, local weather, and ads for popular apps sold at the Microsoft store.

    - **New Tab page:** Designed for people who hate distractions, this option opens Edge with an empty box where you can type in a search term or web page address.

- **Previous page:** This option reminds Edge owners of their last web visit by displaying the page they last viewed.

- **A Specific Page or Pages:** Choose this to select your favorite site as the opening screen for Edge; a box called Enter a URL appears beneath it.

4. **Click inside the Enter a URL box, and type in the address of the favorite site you visited in Step 1 (See Figure 9-4). Then click the adjacent Save icon to save your change.**

FIGURE 9-4:
Type in the address of your favorite website, and Microsoft Edge opens to that site.

To open several home pages, each in their own tab, click the Add New Page button below the first web address you enter. A new box appears for you to type in another web address. Repeat until you've stocked Microsoft Edge with all the tabs you'd like to see preloaded whenever you launch Microsoft Edge.

Your changes take place as soon as you click the Save icon. To close the Settings pane, just click on the screen away from the Settings pane. The Settings pane closes, leaving you back at your website.

After Microsoft Edge opens with your chosen home page or pages, you can still browse the Internet, searching for topics by typing them into the Address bar or by simply pointing and clicking different links.

Just as your browser's home page is the site you see when your browser opens, a website's home page is its "cover," like the cover of a magazine. Whenever you navigate to a website, you usually start at the site's home page and begin browsing from there.

Revisiting favorite places

Sooner or later, you'll stumble across a web page that's indescribably delicious. To make sure that you can find it again later, add it to your list of favorite pages. To add the currently viewed page to your Favorites list, follow these steps:

1. **Click the Favorites icon (the little star) near Microsoft Edge's top-right edge. Then choose either Favorites or Reading List from the drop-down menu.**

   The menu offers two places to stash your coveted web page:

   - **Favorites:** Click Favorites to add the site to your list of favorite sites for quick revisiting. Links added here always take you to the current version of the web page.

   - **Reading List:** Choose this option for longer web pages that are packed with information you'd like to read later. Unlike with the Favorites option, web pages added here are saved to Microsoft Edge's *Reading List,* a storage space where you can read them later at your leisure.

2. **Click the Add button.**

   Whether you choose Favorites or Reading List, a box appears, listing the site's name. (Feel free to edit the name to make it more descriptive.)

   Click the Add button, and the name is added to whichever area you chose: your Favorites list or Reading List.

To return to a favorite page, click Microsoft Edge's Hub icon (shown in the margin). When the menu drops down, click the Favorites icon (the little star icon) from the menu's top or the adjacent Reading List icon. Your list of sites appears, letting you return to one with a click on its name.

To remove a disappointing item from your list of Favorites or Reading List, click the Hub button. When the Hub menu appears, click the appropriate icon to see your Favorites or Reading List. Finally, right-click the name of your unwanted item and choose Delete from the pop-up menu.

Finding things on the Internet

When searching for a book in a library, you usually head straight for the computerized index. The same holds true for the Internet because you need an index to ferret out that piece of information you're after.

To help you out, Microsoft Edge lets you consult a *search engine,* a service that contains a vast index of Internet sites. To search for something, head for the Address bar — that space where you normally type in the address of the website you want to visit.

Instead, though, type your search term — **exotic orchids,** for example — directly into the Address bar and press Enter.

Microsoft Edge fires your search off to Bing, Microsoft's own search engine, and spits out names of websites dealing in exotic orchids. Click a website's name to drop by.

Don't like Bing handling your search needs? You can change that search engine to Google (`www.google.com`) or any other search engine you like.

Follow these steps to customize Microsoft Edge's searches to your liking:

1. **Visit the website of your favorite search engine with Edge. Then click Microsoft Edge's More icon (shown in the margin) in Microsoft Edge's top-right corner and choose Settings from the drop-down menu.**

   The Settings pane appears.

2. **Click the View Advanced Settings button, click the Change Search Engine button, and choose or add your desired search engine.**

   Your change takes place immediately. To close the Settings pane, click anywhere on the main page.

Microsoft Edge replaces Bing with your newly selected search provider. Changing the search engine in Microsoft Edge won't change the search engine in Internet Explorer; the two browsers work independently.

However, Cortana won't work as effectively, as Microsoft's assistant is designed to work with Bing's results rather than those from another browser.

Finding More Information with Cortana

Clicking a website's links lets you jump easily to other places online. But what if you want to know more about something that *doesn't* have a clickable link? For example, what if you spot an address for a paleo-diet-friendly donut shop and want to see it on a map? What if you see a term you don't understand, and you simply want more information about it?

That's where Ask Cortana comes in. Cortana, the Windows 10 personal assistant, works inside Microsoft Edge to help you find extra information about things you find online.

Here's how it works:

1. **When visiting a web page in Microsoft Edge, highlight the terms you want to explore.**

   Double-click a word or term, for example, to highlight it. Or, point at the beginning of a phrase, hold down the mouse button, and — while holding down the mouse button — point at the end of a phrase. Release the mouse button, and you've highlighted the entire phrase.

   I provide more detail on how to select items in Chapter 6.

2. **Right-click the highlighted information and choose Ask Cortana from the pop-up menu.**

Cortana appears on the screen's right edge. The little robot searches the Internet for pertinent information for a few seconds and then displays it, as shown in Figure 9-5.

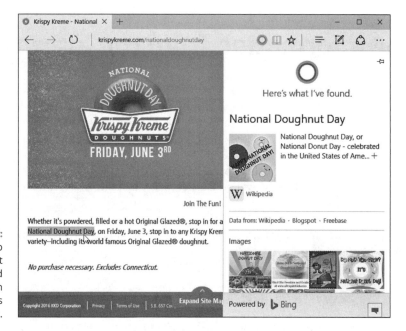

FIGURE 9-5:
Cortana teams up with Microsoft Edge to find information about terms found online.

HAVING SECOND THOUGHTS ABOUT CORTANA?

TIP

Windows 10's built-in personal assistant, Cortana, straddles the worlds between search engine and life coach. Cortana turns off many people because of privacy concerns: Cortana needs to know a *lot* about you before it works effectively. Accordingly, I explain how to turn off Cortana in Chapter 7.

But if you heeded that warning and now wonder what you're missing out on, feel free to give Cortana a new audition: Head for the Turning Off Cortana section in Chapter 7 and reverse the steps. That gives Cortana permission to reacquaint itself with you and your interests.

Cortana may display information from Wikipedia, as well as information and images from Bing, Microsoft's search engine.

If Cortana didn't find enough detailed information, scroll down to the bottom of Cortana's information pane. There, you find a link to search for the term on Bing, which gives you more control over your search.

Saving Information from the Internet

The Internet places a full-service library inside your house, with no long checkout lines. And just as every library comes with a copy machine, Microsoft Edge provides several ways for you to save interesting tidbits of information for your personal use.

This section explains how to copy something from the Internet onto your computer, whether it's an entire web page, a single picture, a sound or movie, or a program.

TIP

I explain how to print a web page (or a snippet of information it contains) in Chapter 8.

Saving a web page

Hankering for a handy Fahrenheit/Centigrade conversion chart? Need that Sushi Identification Chart for dinner? Want to save the itinerary for next month's trip to Norway? When you find a web page with indispensable information, sometimes you can't resist saving a copy onto your computer for further viewing, perusal, or even printing at a later date.

Microsoft Edge lets you save web pages by adding them to your Reading List, described earlier in this chapter's "Revisiting favorite places" section.

Saving text

To save just a little of a web page's text, select the text you want to grab, right-click it, and choose Copy. (I explain how to select, copy, and paste text in Chapter 6.) Open your word processor and paste the text into a new document and save it in your Documents folder with a descriptive name.

Saving a picture

As you browse through web pages and spot a picture that's too good to pass up, save it to your computer: Right-click the picture and choose Save Picture As, as shown in Figure 9-6.

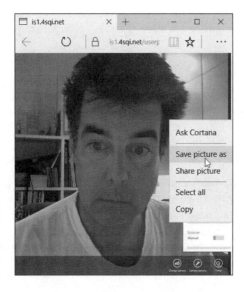

FIGURE 9-6:
Right-click the coveted picture and choose Save Picture As from the pop-up menu.

The Save As window appears, letting you enter a new filename for the picture, if desired. Click Save to place your pilfered picture in your Pictures folder.

The crowded pop-up menu shown in Figure 9-6 offers other handy options, letting you choose to share (email) the picture or copy it to the Windows clipboard for pasting into another program. (To find out more information about the picture, choose Ask Cortana.)

TIP

Remember the little picture by your name on the Windows Start menu? Feel free to use any picture from the Internet. Right-click the new picture and save it to your Pictures folder. Then use the Settings app (see Chapter 2) to transform that picture into your new user account picture.

Downloading a program, song, or other type of file

Microsoft Edge makes it a little easier to download files from the Internet. Best yet, it's easier than ever to *find* the files after you download them.

To download something from a website, click the link to the item or click an adjacent Download button (if one is available). Microsoft Edge downloads the item and automatically places it into your Downloads folder for easy retrieval. The file usually arrives within a few seconds.

WARNING

When choosing the Download button, take some extra time to make sure you're clicking the right button. Many sites deliberately try to confuse you into downloading something else, either spyware, a virus, or something else that gives the website a payback.

You can find your downloaded item in either of two ways:

>> **Downloads folder:** Downloaded items flow into your Downloads folder. To find them, open File Explorer (shown in the margin) from the taskbar. When File Explorer opens, click the Downloads folder listed in the program's left pane. The Downloads folder appears, showing all of your downloaded items.

>> **Microsoft Edge's download queue:** Click the Hub icon (shown in the margin) in Microsoft Edge. When the Hub menu appears, click the Downloads icon. (It's the right-most icon atop the Hub menu.) Microsoft Edge lists all of your downloaded files for one-click access. You can also click the menu's Open Folder link to head straight for the Downloads folder mentioned in the preceding bullet.

Many downloaded files come packaged in a tidy folder with a zipper on it, known as a *Zip file*. Windows treats them like normal folders, so you can just double-click them to see inside them. (The files are actually compressed inside that folder to save download time, if you care about the engineering involved.) To extract copies of the zipped files, right-click the zipped file and choose Extract All.

Chapter 10

Being Social: Mail, People, and Calendar

Thanks to the Internet's never-fading memory, your friends and acquaintances never disappear. Old college chums, business pals, and even those elementary school bullies are all waiting for you online. Toss in a few strangers you may have swapped messages with on websites, and the Internet has created a huge social network.

Windows helps you stay in touch with friends you enjoy and avoid those you don't. To manage your online social life, Windows includes a suite of intertwined social apps: Mail, Calendar, and People. You can pretty much guess which app handles what job.

NEW

If you've used these apps in earlier Windows versions, brace yourself for change: The new People app in Windows 10 no longer integrates your social accounts. Viewing a friend's account shows only basic contact information and no longer shows any Facebook or Twitter updates.

Still, Microsoft has improved the apps since Windows 10's initial release, and they work together quite well, vastly simplifying the chore of tracking your contacts and appointments. This chapter describes the Windows suite of apps and how to set them up.

Adding Your Accounts to Windows

For years, you've heard people say, "Never tell *anybody* your user account name and password." Now, it seems Windows wants you to break that rule.

When you first open your People, Mail, or Calendar apps, Windows may ask you to enter your account names and passwords from your email services, as well as services such as Google or Apple's iCloud.

It's not as scary as you think, though. Microsoft and the other networks have agreed to share your information *only if you approve it.* And should you approve it, Windows connects to your accounts and imports information about your contacts, email, and calendar.

And, frankly, approving the information swap is a huge timesaver. When you link those accounts to Windows, your computer automatically signs in to each service, imports your friends' contact information, and stocks your apps.

To fill in Windows about your life online, follow these steps:

1. **Click the Start button. When the Start menu appears, open the Mail app.**

   Click the Mail tile, found along the Start menu's right edge, and the app opens. Click the Get Started button, if you see one, to move to the Mail app.

2. **Enter your accounts into the Mail app.**

   When you first open the Mail app, it prompts you to add your email account or accounts, as shown in Figure 10-1. If you signed up with a Microsoft account that also serves as a Microsoft email address — one ending in Live, Hotmail, or Outlook, for example — that email address should already be listed and set up.

   To add other accounts, click the Add Account button. Mail then lists the accounts you can add: Outlook.com (which includes mail accounts held at Outlook.com, Live.com, Hotmail, and MSN), Exchange (used mostly by businesses or people using the Office 365 online programs), Google, iCloud (for Apple), Other Account (which means accounts using POP or IMAP for access), or Advanced Setup, which lets you set up Exchange ActiveSync or web-based email.

   To add a Google account, for example, click the word Google. Windows takes you to a secure area on Google's website, where you can authorize the transaction by entering your Gmail email address and password and then clicking Accept or Connect.

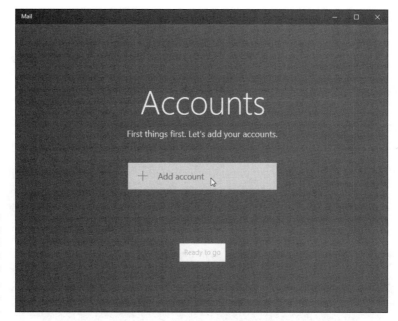

FIGURE 10-1:
The Mail app lets
you enter email
accounts from
services such as
Google, Hotmail,
Outlook, Yahoo!,
and others.

To add new email accounts from inside the Mail app, click the Settings icon (it looks like a gear) and choose Accounts from the Settings pane.

Repeat these steps for any of your other listed accounts, authorizing each of them, if required, to share information with your Windows account.

After you've entered your accounts, Windows automatically fetches your email through your Mail app, fills the People app with your friends' contact information, and adds any appointments in your Calendar app.

Although it might seem frightening to give Windows your coveted usernames and passwords, it enriches Windows in many ways:

>> Instead of typing in your contacts by hand, they're waiting for you automatically, whether they're from your Google, Hotmail, Outlook, Apple, or Windows Live account.

>> Windows apps work well with apps and programs from other companies. Your friends' birthdays from your Google calendar, for example, show up on the Calendar app without your having to enter them.

>> Don't like these new-fangled Windows apps? Then ignore them. You can always spend your time on the Windows desktop instead. There you can visit Facebook and your other accounts from your web browser the same way you've always done.

REMEMBER

>> If you're already accustomed to firing up your browser and reading your mail on Google, Yahoo, or any other online watering hole, you don't have to use the Mail app. You can still send and receive your mail the old-fashioned way.

Understanding the Mail App

Unlike Windows 7, Windows 10 includes a built-in app for sending and receiving email. Considered a *live* app, the Mail app automatically updates its Start menu's tile. A glance at the Start menu's Mail tile quickly shows you the senders' names and subjects of your latest emails.

NEW

Unlike the Mail app in Windows 8 and 8.1, the Windows 10 Mail app finally supports IMAP and POP accounts. That bit of technical jargon means that the Mail app works with a wider variety of email accounts, including those used by many of today's regional Internet service providers. It even works with AOL email addresses.

The following sections explain how to make sense of the Mail app's menus, as well as how to compose, send, and read emails. (If you haven't already imported your email accounts, skip back to this chapter's first section.)

Switching among the Mail app's views, menus, and accounts

To load the Windows Mail app, open the Start menu (by clicking the Start button in the screen's bottom-left corner) and then click the Mail app tile (shown in the margin).

The Mail app appears, shown in Figure 10-2, displaying emails received from your primary email account — the first account you entered when setting up the app.

Figure 10-2, for example, shows the currently viewed Outlook account at the pane's top. To see your mail from a different account, click that account's name along the left pane.

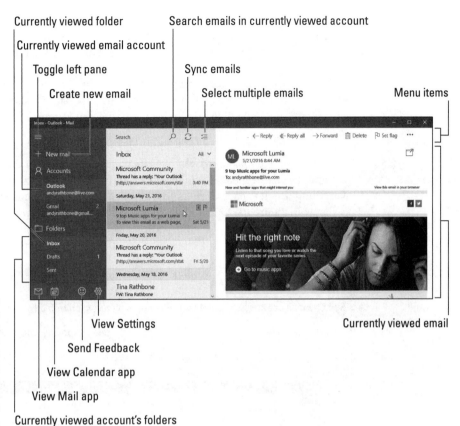

Currently viewed folder

Currently viewed email account

Search emails in currently viewed account

Toggle left pane

Sync emails

Create new email

Select multiple emails

Menu items

FIGURE 10-2:
Email accounts
and folders
appear on the
left, emails
appear in the
center, and an
email's contents
appear on the
right.

View Settings

Send Feedback

View Calendar app

View Mail app

Currently viewed account's folders

Currently viewed email

Beneath the name of your currently viewed email account, the Mail app lists its folders:

>> **Inbox:** Shown when you first load the Mail app, the Inbox folder lists your waiting email, with your newest email at the top. The Mail app automatically checks for new email every few minutes, but if you tire of waiting, click the Sync button (shown in the margin) atop that account's list of received emails. That action immediately grabs any waiting mail.

>> **Sent Items:** Click here to see the messages you've *sent* rather than received from others.

>> **Drafts:** If you write a message but don't send it for some reason, it waits here, ready for your further attention.

>> **More:** If you don't see all of your account's folders, click More to find them. A pop-out menu appears, listing them all. (In particular, peek in here to find your Trash folder, where you can retrieve accidentally deleted emails.)

The icons along the bottom of the left pane let you switch among the Calendar app, the Mail app, the Feedback app, and the Mail app's settings.

Click the Settings icon, for example, and a pane appears along the right, offering all the things you can tweak inside the Mail app. The Feedback app, found in several apps, lets you play armchair critic, advising Microsoft on how to improve its apps.

TIP

The Mail app, like most apps, changes its width depending on the size of your display and the size of the Mail window itself. If the Mail app lacks the width to display everything, the left pane shrinks to a small strip showing icons instead of words, as shown in Figure 10-3. Click the Expand icon in the app's top, left corner, and the tiny left strip expands, showing you the same left pane shown in Figure 10-2, earlier.

View current account's folders

Switch email accounts   Insert file, table, pictures, or web link   Send message

Start new email   Check spelling, zoom, or find

Toggle left pane   Display formatting options   Discard draft

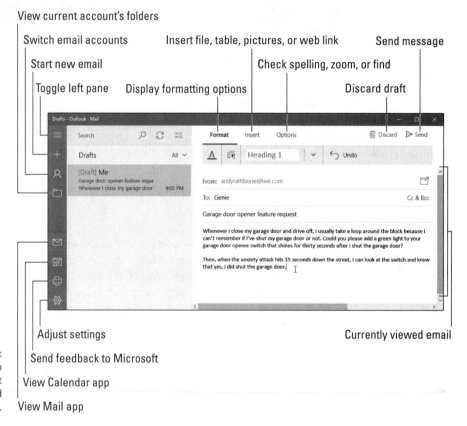

Adjust settings   Currently viewed email

FIGURE 10-3:
The Mail app   Send feedback to Microsoft
resizes to adjust
to different sized   View Calendar app
screens.   View Mail app

TWEAKING THE MAIL APP'S SETTINGS

Click the little gear icon in the Mail app's bottom-left corner, and the Settings pane slides into view along the app's right edge. There, the Mail app lets you adjust its behavior. Here are some of the most useful switches:

- **Manage Accounts:** Head here to tweak the settings of your currently entered email accounts, as well as to add new accounts. Once an email account's settings finally work, though, you rarely need to change them.

- **Personalization:** Interior decorators can visit here to change the Mail app's colors.

- **Options:** Here's where you can adjust how the app responds to your fingers on a touchscreen. You can also change your *signature* — the words appearing beneath every email you send.

- **Automatic Replies:** Head here to create an "I'm sunning myself in Mazatlán for the next week" reply. The Mail app then automatically sends that reply to any email you receive while vacationing.

- **Signature:** Microsoft automatically slips the words "Sent from Mail from Windows 10" to every email you send. Head here to either turn it off or change the wording.

- **Trust Center:** This oddly named and mysterious entry lets you control whether Microsoft can send you information based on your email's content. Presumably, this authorizes Microsoft's robots to send you pertinent ads, as well as for Cortana to read your mail. (When the Trust Center pane appears, click the Learn More link to read Microsoft's online privacy page.)

- **Feedback:** A holdover from when Microsoft let people test Windows 10 before its release, this option lets you send Microsoft comments about the app's performance. Presumably, somebody at Microsoft is still listening.

- **About:** Handy mostly when troubleshooting, this area reveals the app's version number.

You may never need to set foot in the Settings area, but when things go wrong, this is usually the first troubleshooting destination.

Composing and sending an email

When you're ready to send an email, follow these steps to compose your letter and drop it in the electronic mailbox, sending it through virtual space to the recipient's computer:

1. **From the Start menu, open the Mail app's tile (shown in the margin) and click the New Mail icon (it's a plus sign icon) in the app's top-left corner.**

A new and blank email appears, awaiting your words.

If you've added more than one email account to the Mail app, first choose your return address by clicking your desired account name from the Mail app's bottom-right corner. *Then* click the New Mail icon in the program's top-left corner.

2. **Type your friend's email address into the To box.**

As you begin typing, the Mail app scans your contacts for both names and email addresses, listing potential matches below the To box. Spot a match on the list? Click it, and the Mail app automatically fills in the rest of the email address.

To add another person to the list, begin typing their name in the To box, as well. However, the Mail app currently has no way to send an email to a large group without typing in everybody's name.

3. **Click in the Subject line and type a subject.**

Click in the line labeled Subject and type your subject. In Figure 10-3, for example, I've added the subject "Garage Door Opener Feature Request." Although technically optional, the Subject line helps your friends sort their mail.

4. **Type your message into the large box beneath the Subject line.**

Type as many words as you want. As you type, the Mail app automatically corrects any noticed misspellings.

5. **If you want, add any formatting, tables, files, or photos to your email.**

The menu directly above your composed email offers three tabs, each with different options:

- **Format:** This option lets you change your email's formatting by selecting portions of your email and then clicking the bold, italics, underline, or font color icons along the window's top edge, as shown earlier in Figure 10-3. To change the font size, click the tiny downward-pointing arrow next to the underlined *A* icon. A menu drops down, letting you change fonts, font size, as well as clear the formatting from any selected item.

- **Insert:** Click here to attach files, as I describe in this chapter's later section, "Sending and receiving files through email." This tab also lets you insert tables, pictures, and add hyperlinks.

- **Options:** Click here after composing your email to give it a final spellcheck.

Most ISPs don't send attached files totaling more than 25MB. That lets you send a song or two, a few digital photos, and most documents. It's *not* enough room to send any but the smallest videos.

6. **Check your spelling, if desired.**

The Mail app does a pretty good job of correcting your spelling as you type. But to proofread more closely before sending your mail, click the Options button along the Mail app's top edge. Then choose Spelling from the drop-down menu.

The Mail app jumps to each error it finds. When it finds a problem, it highlights the word and places a drop-down menu where you can choose from potential replacements.

If the spellchecker constantly flags a correctly spelled word as being misspelled, choose Add to Dictionary from the drop-down menu. That trick adds the word to the spellchecker's dictionary, preventing it from bugging you about it.

TIP

7. **Click the Send button along the top-right corner.**

Whoosh! The Mail app whisks your message through the Internet to your friend's mailbox. Depending on the speed of your Internet connection, mail can arrive anywhere from 5 seconds later to a few hours later, with a few minutes being the average.

Don't want to send the message? Then delete it with a click of the Discard button in the top-right corner.

Reading a received email

When your computer is connected to the Internet, Windows 10 heralds the arrival of a newly received email in several ways. An announcement appears in the Action Center, the pane that periodically appears along the screen's right edge. Also, the Mail app's tile automatically updates itself to show the sender and subject of your latest unread emails.

To see more information than that — or to respond to the message — follow these steps:

1. **Click the Start menu's Mail tile.**

Mail opens to show the messages in your Inbox, as shown earlier in Figure 10-3. Each subject is listed, one by one, with the newest one at the top.

To find a particular email quickly, click the Magnifying Glass icon at the top of your email column. A search box appears alongside the icon where you can type the sender's name or a keyword into the search box. Press the Enter key to see all the matching emails.

TIP

2. **Click the subject of any message you want to read.**

The Mail app spills that message's contents into the pane along the window's right side.

3. **From here, the Mail app leaves you with several options, each accessed from the buttons along the email's top edge:**

- **Nothing:** Undecided? Don't do anything, and the message simply sets up camp in your Inbox folder.

- **Reply:** Click the Reply button, and a new window appears, ready for you to type in your response. The window is just like the one that appears when you first compose a message but with a handy difference: This window is already addressed with the recipient's name and the subject. Also, the original message usually appears at the bottom of your reply for reference.

- **Reply All:** Some people address emails to several people simultaneously. If you see several other people listed on an email's To line, you can reply to *all* of them by clicking Reply All.

- **Forward:** Received something that a friend simply must see? Click Forward to kick a copy of the email to your friend's Inbox.

- **Delete:** Click the Delete button to toss the message into your Trash or Deleted Items folder. (Different email accounts use different words for that folder.)

- **Set Flag:** Clicking the Set Flag icon places a little flag icon next to an email, reminding you to deal with it at a later date.

- **More:** Clicking this fetches a drop-down menu that lists any menu items above that didn't fit on your particular screen. The menu's Move option, for example, lets you move an item out of your Inbox and into a different folder. (Save and Print options appear on the More drop-down menu, as well.)

The Mail app works well for basic email needs. If you need more, you can find a more full-featured email program to run on the Windows desktop. Or you can open the web browser and manage your email online, such as at Outlook (`www.outlook.com`), Google (`www.google.com/gmail`), or your ISP's own website.

⚠️ **WARNING**

If you ever receive an unexpected email from a bank or any other money related website, don't click any of the email's web links. A criminal industry called *phishing* sends emails that try to trick you into entering your name and password on a phony website. That gives your coveted information to the evil folk, who promptly steal your money. I write more about phishing in Chapter 11.

TIP

Don't want your Mail app's Start menu tile to display your emails' sender and subject? Then right-click its Start menu tile, click More from the pop-up menu, and choose Turn Live Tile Off.

Sending and receiving files through email

Like a pair of movie tickets slipped into the envelope of a thank-you note, an *attachment* is a file that piggybacks onto an email message. You can send or receive any type of file as an attachment.

The following sections describe how to both send and receive a file through the Mail app.

Saving a received attachment

When an attachment arrives in an email, you'll recognize it: A paperclip icon rests next to the email's subject. And when you open the email, you see a generic photo thumbnail or a message saying, "Download Message and Pictures."

Saving the attached file or files takes just a few steps:

1. **Download the attached file.**

The Mail app doesn't download the files until you specifically give it the command. Instead, the Mail app shows generic thumbnails — placeholders for attached folders — along the email's top edge.

You can save the file either of two ways:

- Click the attached file's thumbnail icon. When the thumbnail shows a miniature of the attached file, right-click it and choose Save.

- Right-click the attached file and choose Download from the pop-up menu. When the download completes, the generic thumbnails fill in with images or icons representing the newly downloaded files.

2. **Choose a storage area to receive the saved file.**

File Explorer's Save As window appears, shown in Figure 10-4, ready for you to save the file in your Documents folder. To save it someplace else, choose any folder listed along the Save As window's left edge. Or, click the words This PC, also on the window's left edge, and begin browsing to the folder that should receive the file.

TIP

Saving the file inside one of your four main folders — Documents, Pictures, Videos, or Music — is the easiest way to ensure you'll be able to find it later. (I describe files and folders in Chapter 5.) When you choose a folder, you see a list of existing folders where you can stash your new file.

FIGURE 10-4:
Choose a folder
and click Save.

To create a new folder inside your currently viewed folder, click the New Folder button from the menu along the folder's top and, when the new folder appears, type in a name for the folder.

3. **Click the Save button in the Save As window's bottom-right corner.**

   The Mail app saves the file in the folder of your choosing.

After you've saved the file, the attachment still remains inside the email. That's because saving attachments always saves a *copy* of the sent file. If you accidentally delete or botch an edit on your saved file, you can always return to the original email and save the attached file yet again.

Windows Defender, the built-in virus checker in Windows, automatically scans your incoming email for evil file attachments. I explain more about Windows Defender in Chapter 11. Still, if you feel suspicious about the attachment, or it arrives unexpectedly, don't download it.

Sending a file as an attachment

Sending a file through the Mail app works much like saving an attached file, although in reverse: Instead of grabbing a file from an email and saving it into a folder, you're grabbing a file from a folder and saving it in an email.

To send a file as an attachment in the Mail app, follow these steps:

1. **Open the Mail app and create a new email.**

   I describe creating a new email in this chapter's earlier "Composing and sending an email" section.

2. **Click the Insert tab from the Mail app's top menu and then choose Attach File from the drop-down menu.**

When you choose Attach from the drop-down menu, File Explorer's Open window appears, showing the contents of your Documents folder.

If the Documents folder contains the file you'd like to send, jump to Step 4. To send something from a different folder, move to Step 3.

3. **Navigate to the storage area and file you want to send.**

Click the words This PC along the Open window's left edge, and a menu appears listing all of your storage areas. Most files are stored in your Documents, Pictures, Music, and Videos folders.

 Click a folder's name to open it and see the files lurking inside. Not the right folder? Click the Up Arrow icon (shown in the margin) to move back out of the folder and try again.

4. **Click the file you want to send and click the Open button.**

Click a file to select it. To select several files, hold down the Ctrl key while selecting them. Selected too many files? Deselect unwanted files by clicking their names yet again. When you click the Attach button, the Mail app adds the file or files to your email.

 5. **Click the Send button.**

The Mail app whisks off your mail and its attachment to the recipient.

 When you send an attached file, you're only sending a *copy.* Your original stays safely on your computer. Also, most ISPs limit attachment size to 25MB or less. That's enough to send a few photos, but rarely enough for videos. (Share those on YouTube or Facebook.)

REMEMBER

Managing Your Contacts in the People App

When you enter your email addresses into the Mail app, Windows grabs all of your online contacts it can find. That means you've probably already stocked the People app with your online friends.

 The Windows 10 People app looks quite different than the one in Windows 8 and 8.1. Instead of being a social media hub, it's now a simple address book that lists your contacts and their contact information.

NEW

To launch the People app, click the Start menu's People tile. The People app appears, presenting all of your online friends in an alphabetical list, as shown in Figure 10-5.

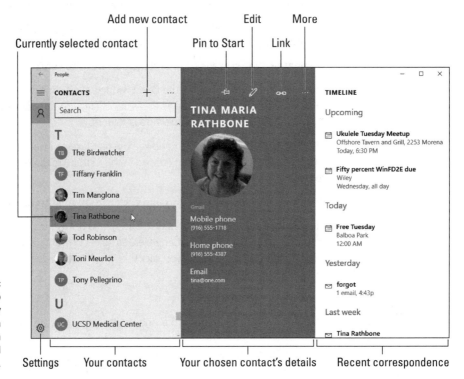

Add new contact   Edit   More

Currently selected contact   Pin to Start   Link

FIGURE 10-5:
The People app automatically stocks itself with contacts from your email accounts.

Settings   Your contacts   Your chosen contact's details   Recent correspondence

The People app contains three main panes:

>> **Contacts:** The app presents an alphabetical list of your friends. When you click a contact's name, their details spill across the two panes to the right.

>> **Details:** This unlabeled pane lists your selected friend's contact information, along with four icons across the top:

• **Pushpin:** When you spot a popular contact, click the pushpin icon atop the pane and choose Pin to Start. That puts their smiling face on a Start menu tile for easy access.

• **Edit:** To edit a contact's details — change a phone number, perhaps — click the pencil icon.

- **Link:** If you spot duplicate entries, click the pencil icon to merge them into one.

- **More:** A catch-all area for items that don't fit elsewhere, this fetches a drop-down menu for sharing a contact through email or deleting them.

» **Timeline:** When you select a contact, the People app races to the Mail and Calendar app, preparing a dossier of your communications. The emails and appointments then appear as clickable links in the Timeline pane to provide quick access.

The People app handles much of its upkeep automatically, updating itself with any changes you make to your iCloud or Google contacts.

Occasionally, though, you need to add or edit some People entries manually. The following sections explain the occasional pruning needed to keep up with your constantly evolving contacts list.

Adding contacts

TIP

Although the People app loves to add contacts automatically, you can easily add people the old-fashioned way, typing them in by hand.

To add somebody to the People app, which makes that person available in your Mail and Calendar apps, follow these steps:

1. **Click the People tile on the Start menu.**

The People app appears onscreen.

2. **Click the Add Contact icon (shown in the margin).**

3. **If asked, choose which account to use for saving new contacts.**

If you've entered more than one email account into Mail, the People app asks you to decide which account should receive the new contact.

The answer hinges mainly on which cellphone you own. Choose your Google account if you use an Android phone, so your newly added contact appears in your Gmail contacts. From there, it also appears in your Android phone's contacts list. Similarly, iPhone owners should choose iCloud.

Choose the Outlook account if you own a Windows phone or you run the Outlook app on your iPhone or Android smartphone.

The People app remembers your choice, and doesn't ask you again.

4. **Fill out the New Contact form.**

   Shown in Figure 10-6, most of the choices are self-explanatory fields such as Name, Phone, Email, Address, and Other. (The Other field lets you add details such as a job title, website, significant other, or notes.)

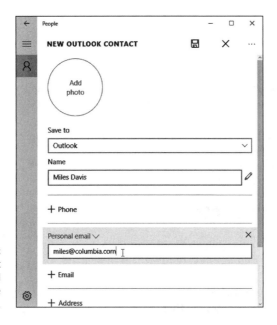

FIGURE 10-6:
Fill in contact
information and
then click the
Save icon.

5. **Click the Save icon, that little disk in the upper-right corner.**

   The People app dutifully saves your new contact. If you spot a mistake, however, you may need to go back and edit the information, described in the next section.

Deleting or editing contacts

Has somebody fallen from your social graces? Or perhaps someone just changed a phone number? Either way, it's easy to delete or edit a contact manually by following these steps:

1. **Click the People tile on the Start menu.**

   The People app appears, as shown earlier in Figure 10-5.

2. **To delete a contact, right-click his name and choose Delete from the pop-up menu.**

   The person disappears from both the People app, and the email account that currently held that contact.

3. **To edit a contact, click the Edit icon (shown in the margin).**

   The person's contact information appears, shown earlier in Figure 10-6, for you to edit.

4. **Click the Save icon.**

   The People app updates your contacts list, both in the app itself and the online account where that contact is stored. Edit a Gmail contact in the People app, for example, and Gmail also reflects the changes.

Managing Appointments in Calendar

After you enter your online accounts such as Gmail, Outlook, Live.com, and others, as described in this chapter's first section, you've already stocked the Calendar app with your existing appointments.

To see your appointments, click the Start menu's Calendar tile, shown in the margin. Or, if you're working in the Mail app, click the Calendar icon from the Mail app's bottom-left corner.

When first opened, the Calendar app asks you to add your email accounts. If you've already entered your accounts into the Mail app, they already show up here.

The Calendar opens to show any appointments associated with your email accounts, like Google or Outlook.com. To see more or less days displayed, click the Day, Work Week, Week, or Month button along the top. If you click Week, for example, the Calendar app appears, as shown in Figure 10-7.

Unless you keep all your appointments online, you'll need to edit some entries, add new ones, or delete those you can no longer attend. This section explains how to keep your appointments up-to-date.

TIP

No matter which view the Calendar app displays, you can flip through the appointments by clicking the little arrows near the listed month in the screen's top-right corner. Click the right arrow to move forward in time; click the left arrow to move backward.

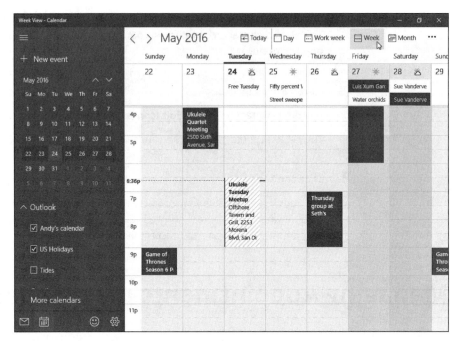

FIGURE 10-7:
The Calendar app displays appointments you add manually or from your online calendars.

To add an appointment to your Calendar app, follow these steps:

1. **Click the Calendar tile on the Start menu.**

   The Calendar app appears, as shown earlier in Figure 10-7.

   If you're in the Mail app, you can also click the Calendar app's icon in the Mail app's lower-left corner (shown in the margin.)

2. **Click the words New Event from the Calendar app's top-right corner.**

   A blank event template appears, ready for you to fill in the time and place, as well as to invite people.

3. **Fill out the Details form.**

   Shown in Figure 10-8, most of the choices are self-explanatory fields.

   The biggest challenge comes with the Details field's drop-down menu, which only appears if you've entered more than one email account into your Mail app. Which email *account* should receive the new calendar appointment?

   Again, the answer depends on your phone. Choose Gmail to send appointments to Gmail's calendar, where they appear on your Android phone. Choose iCloud for your iPhone.

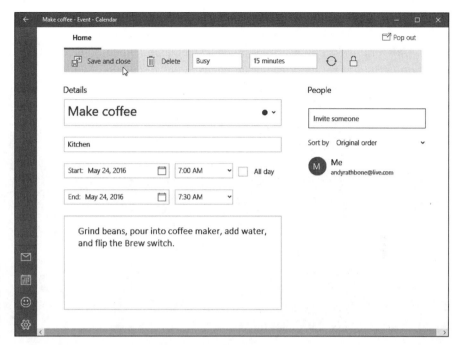

Or, you can choose Outlook: You can then download and install the Outlook app, available on both Android and iPhones. The Outlook app can sync the Windows 10 Calendar app's appointments with your phone.

4. **Click the Save & Close button.**

The Calendar app adds your new appointment to its own calendar, as well as to whichever account you chose in Step 3.

To edit or delete an appointment, open it from the Calendar app. Click the Delete button (shown in the margin) from the top menu. To edit it, open it from the Calendar app, make your changes, and save your changes by clicking the Save & Close button.

Chapter 11

Safe Computing

L ike driving a car, working with Windows is reasonably safe as long as you avoid bad neighborhoods, obey traffic signals, and don't steer with your feet while looking out the sunroof.

But in the world of Windows and the Internet, there's no easy way to recognize a bad neighborhood, find a traffic signal, or know what's *really* official. Something that appears to be fun, innocent, or important — a friend's email, a downloaded program, or a message from a bank — may be a virus that infects your computer.

This chapter helps you recognize the bad streets in virtual neighborhoods and explains the steps you can take to protect yourself from harm and minimize any damage.

Understanding Those Annoying Permission Messages

After more than 20 years of development, Windows is still pretty naive. Sometimes when you run a program or try to change a setting on your PC, Windows can't tell whether *you're* doing the work or a *virus* is trying to move in behind your back.

The Windows solution? When Windows notices anybody (or anything) trying to change something that can potentially harm Windows or your PC, it darkens the screen and flashes a security message asking for permission, like the one shown in Figure 11-1.

FIGURE 11-1:
Click Don't Install,
Cancel, or No if a
message like this
appears
unexpectedly.

If one of these security messages appears out of the blue, Windows may be warning you about a bit of nastiness trying to sneak in. So click Cancel, No, or Don't Install to deny it permission. But if *you're* trying to install a trusted program onto your PC and Windows puts up its boxing gloves, click OK, Yes, or Install instead. Windows drops its guard and lets you in.

If you don't hold an Administrator account, however, you can't simply approve the deed. You must track down an Administrator account holder (usually the PC's owner) and ask her to type her password.

Yes, a rather dimwitted security robot guards the front door to Windows, but it's also an extra challenge for the people who write the viruses.

Avoiding Viruses with Windows Defender

When it comes to viruses, *everything* is suspect. Viruses travel not only through email messages, programs, files, networks, and flash drives, but also in screen savers, themes, toolbars, and other Windows add-ons.

To combat the problem, Windows 10 includes Windows Defender, a free security and antivirus program.

Windows Defender scans everything that enters your computer, whether through downloads, email, networks, messaging programs, flash drives, or discs. Unless you tell it not to, Windows Defender casts a watchful eye on your OneDrive files, as well.

When Windows Defender notices something evil trying to enter your computer, it lets you know with a message, as shown in Figure 11-2. Then Windows Defender quickly quarantines the virus before it has a chance to infect your computer.

FIGURE 11-2:
Windows Defender detects and removes an intruder.

Windows Defender automatically updates itself to recognize new viruses, and it constantly scans your PC for threats in the background. But if your PC acts strangely, tell Windows Defender to scan your PC immediately by following these steps:

1. **Click the taskbar's Windows Defender icon (shown in the margin) near the clock.**

   Windows Defender appears. You can also launch Windows Defender from the Start menu, where the program lives inside the Start menu's Windows System folder.

2. **Click the program's Scan Now button.**

   Windows Defender immediately performs a quick scan of your PC.

TIP

IS WINDOWS DEFENDER GOOD ENOUGH?

Like several Windows versions before it, Windows 10 includes the Windows Defender antivirus program. Windows Defender runs quickly, updates automatically, and catches the most common malware before it invades your computer.

But is it *better* than third-party antivirus programs, including the ones that charge subscription fees? The answer depends on several things.

For example, most third-party antivirus programs will catch more viruses than Windows Defender. However, doing that extra work can slow down your PC. Some powerful security suites throw up false alarms, as well, leaving you the work of sorting out the problem. Many seem complicated and cumbersome.

Windows Defender works best for people who can spot a potential virus as it arrives in the mail, and avoid clicking on suspicious email attachments. People who feel more comfortable with a larger safety net will prefer a paid program. There's no right or wrong answer.

Instead, your answer depends on your personal comfort level. If you find a reasonably priced third-party antivirus program that doesn't slow down your computer too much, then stick with it. But if you feel confident in your ability to weed out most potential attackers before you click on them, Windows Defender might be all you need.

Even with Windows Defender watching your back, follow these rules to reduce your risk of infection:

REMEMBER

>> Open only attachments that you're expecting. If you receive something unexpected from a friend, don't open it. Instead, email or phone that person to ask whether he or she really sent you something. Your friend's computer might be infected and trying to infect your computer, as well.

>> Be wary of items arriving in email that ask for a click. For example, if you receive a message saying somebody wants to be a Facebook friend, don't click it. Instead, visit Facebook from your browser and look to see whether the person is listed on your "waiting to be friended" list. The more emailed links you can avoid, the safer you'll be.

>> If you receive an important-looking email from a financial institution that asks you to click a link and type in your name and password, don't do it. Instead, visit your financial institution's website through your web browser and log in there. Chances are good that there's nothing wrong with your account, and that email was only trying to steal your username and password. (This type of scam is often called phishing, and I describe it further in the next section.)

> ❯❯ Updates for Windows Defender arrive automatically through Windows Update. Windows 10 keeps Windows Update running constantly, so you don't need to worry about keeping Windows Defender updated.

WARNING

> ❯❯ If you prefer running a third-party antivirus programs, you're welcome to do so. It will turn off Windows Defender automatically as part of its install process. But don't install *two* third-party antivirus programs, because they often quarrel.

Avoiding Phishing Scams

Eventually you'll receive an email from your bank, eBay, PayPal, or a similar website announcing a problem with your account. Invariably, the email offers a handy link to click, saying that you must enter your username and password to set things in order.

WARNING

Don't do it, no matter how realistic the email and website may appear. You're seeing an ugly industry called *phishing:* Fraudsters send millions of these messages worldwide, hoping to convince a few frightened souls into typing their precious account name and password.

How do you tell the real emails from the fake ones? It's easy, actually, because *all* these emails are fake. Finance-related sites may send you legitimate history statements, receipts, or confirmation notices, but they will *never, ever* email you a link for you to click and enter your password.

TIP

If you're suspicious, visit the company's *real* website by typing the web address by hand into your web browser's Address bar. Chances are good that the real site won't list anything as being wrong with your account.

Both Internet Explorer and the new Microsoft Edge browser use Microsoft's SmartScreen Filter technology that compares a website's address with a list of known phishing sites. If it finds a match, the SmartScreen filter keeps you from entering, as shown in Figure 11-3. Should you ever spot that screen, close the web page by clicking the words Close This Tab listed on the warning message.

So, why can't the authorities simply arrest those people responsible? Because Internet thieves are notoriously difficult to track down and prosecute. The reach of the Internet lets them work from any place in the world, hidden beneath a maze of networks.

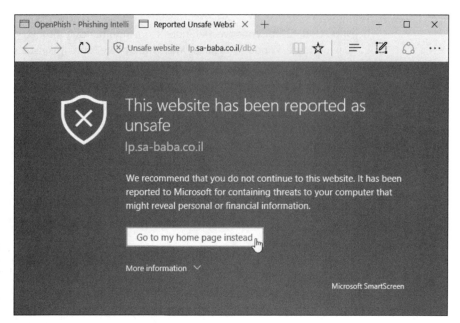

FIGURE 11-3:
Microsoft Edge
warns you when
you visit a
suspected
phishing site.

>> If you've already entered your name and password into a phishing site, take action immediately: Visit the real website and change your password. Then contact the company involved and ask it for help. It may be able to stop the thieves before they wrap their electronic fingers around your account.

>> If you've entered credit card information, call the card's issuer immediately. You can almost always find a toll-free, 24-hour phone number on the back of your credit card.

Setting Up Controls for Children

A feature much-welcomed by parents and much-booed by their children, Microsoft's family controls (formerly called Family Safety), offer several ways to monitor how children can access the computer as well as the Internet.

NEW

Rather than running as a program on your computer, Microsoft's family controls now work online through a Microsoft website. By tracking your children's activity through their Microsoft account usage, you can monitor their online activity wherever they log into a Windows 10 PC or Windows 10 smartphone. The online, password-protected records stay online, where you can access them from any PC, tablet, or smartphone.

Microsoft's family controls only work if both you and your children have Microsoft accounts.

To set up Microsoft's family controls, follow these steps:

1. **Add your children and any adults who want to monitor the children as family members when creating their user accounts.**

   I describe how to add family members when creating user accounts in Chapter 14. When you add family members to your PC's list of user accounts, each member receives an email inviting them to join your family network; when they accept, their accounts automatically appear on your computer.

   Don't want a child to use your particular PC? Then click the Block button beneath that child's name; click the Allow button to let your child regain access.

2. **Visit the Microsoft's family website.**

   Click the Start button, click the Settings icon, and choose Accounts. Click Family & Other People from the left pane; on the right pane, click the Manage Family Settings Online link.

   Alternatively, you can open any browser and visit the website at https:// account.microsoft.com/family#/. The site opens to show your list of family members who have accepted their invitations. Click the name of a family member, and the website, shown in Figure 11-4, lets you set limits on that child's computer behavior, as well as monitor his activity.

3. **Turn on the categories you'd like to enforce, and set the limits.**

   Microsoft's family area contains a variety of categories that let you monitor or control different areas of behavior. Visit any of the categories described below, and each opens a new page with a toggle control at the top. Turn the toggle to either On or Off, then fine-tune the offered settings. (You can also turn categories Off to temporarily suspend monitoring in those areas.)

   Microsoft's family website offers these categories, which apply whenever your child uses his Microsoft account to sign into any computer, phone, or tablet:

   - **Add Money:** Want your child to be able to purchase items from the Windows store? Head here and click the button corresponding to the amount. It's withdrawn from the credit card attached to your Microsoft account, and added to your child's account.

   - **Recent Activity:** A haven for time-stressed parents, this offers a quick rundown of your child's computer activity, along with an option to have the information emailed to you each week.

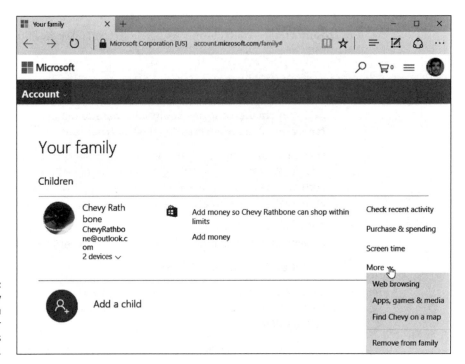

FIGURE 11-4:
Microsoft's family
website lets you
set limits on your
children's
computer activity.

- **Purchase and Spending:** This area lets you see exactly how your child has spent the money you so graciously provided through the Add Money button.

- **Screen Time:** A grid appears here for you to choose the exact hours your child is allowed to access the computer.

Click the More option, and a drop-down menu reveals these options:

- **Web Browsing:** A toggle switch here lets you block adult content, disable browsing in private, and turn on Bing's SafeSearch to protect against viruses. You can also add sites to an Allow or Block list, and toggle whether downloads are allowed.

- **Apps, Games, and Media:** Visit here for a toggle to block inappropriate apps, games, and media.

- **Find Child on a Map:** If your child is one of the few with a Windows smartphone, this flip switch lets you locate the device — and, hopefully, your child — on a map.

- **Remove from Family:** Choosing this removes your child from the Family settings. They still retain their account, but you can no longer monitor their activity.

4. **When you're through, close the Microsoft window in your browser.**

   Your changes take place immediately. When you're through, just close your web browser.

   Although Microsoft's family controls work well, few things in the computer world are foolproof. If you're worried about your children's computer use, cast an occasional eye their way. Also, these controls only monitor your child when he logs in with his Microsoft account and uses either Edge or Internet Explorer. If you spot an unfamiliar account (or a different browser) on the PC, it's time to ask some questions.

4

Customizing and Upgrading Windows 10

Chapter 12

Customizing Windows with the Control Panels

Most science fiction movies include a close-up of a smoking control panel, ready to burst into flames. If that happens in Windows, grab an extra fire extinguisher because Windows contains *two* switch-packed control panels:

NEW

>> **Windows Settings app:** The easily accessible Settings app is full of oversized buttons. Windows 10 expands it quite a bit from the one seen in Windows 8 and 8.1. After Microsoft's latest Windows 10 upgrade, the Settings app now contains so many buttons that you may never need to leave it.

>> **Control Panel:** The Control Panel from earlier Windows version lives on in Windows 10, but its most frequently used switches now live in the Settings app. The Control Panel's remaining switches live on mostly for techies.

Although separate, the two clusters of switches occasionally join forces. Sometimes a click on the Settings app whisks you back to the Control Panel of yesteryear for you to flip the final switch. Likewise, some Control Panel options push you back to the Settings app to complete the job.

But no matter which bank of switches you face, they both let you customize the look, feel, behavior, and vibe of Windows. This chapter explains the switches and sliders you'll want to tweak, and it steers you away from the ones that are prone to causing fires.

One word of caution: Some settings can be changed only by the person holding the almighty Administrator account — usually the computer's owner. If Windows refuses to flip a switch, call the PC's owner for help.

Finding the Right Switch

NEW

Windows 10 adds more controls than ever to the Settings app, but the older Control Panel still holds the reins for a few settings. That makes it difficult to find the switch you need to flip. So, instead of clicking aimlessly at menus, tell Windows to find the switch for you.

Follow these steps to find the setting you need:

1. **Click the Start button, click in the adjacent Search box, and type a word describing your desired setting.**

   When you type the first letter, every setting containing that letter appears in a list above the Search box. If you don't know the exact name of your setting, begin typing a keyword: **display**, **troubleshoot**, **mouse**, **user**, **privacy**, or something that describes your need.

   Don't see the right setting? Press the Backspace key to delete the letters you've typed and then try again with a different word.

   The Search box, described in Chapter 7, also lists other matches for your keyword: files on your computer, apps from Windows Store, and even items found on websites.

TIP

   Don't see the Search box? Right-click the taskbar along the screen's bottom edge and choose Cortana from the pop-up menu. Then choose Show Search Box from the second pop-up menu. (Or, if your computer runs in Tablet mode, click the Cortana icon — the little circle near the Start button — to fetch Cortana and the Search box.)

2. **Click your desired setting on the list.**

   Windows takes you directly to that setting on the appropriate control panel.

When searching for a setting, always try the Search box first. Spending a few minutes at the Search pane yields better results than scouring the hundreds of settings stuffed in the two Windows control panels.

Setting the Stage with the Windows Settings App

NEW

The newly enhanced Settings app in Windows 10 contains many more settings than before. You can find most of your settings there now, sparing you a trip to the old Control Panel from previous Windows versions.

To open the Settings app, click the Start button and click the Settings icon (a little gear) near the bottom of the Start menu's left pane.

The Settings app appears, as shown in Figure 12-1. In fact, the Settings app looks nearly identical whether you're viewing Windows 10 on a PC, tablet, phone, or even on your TV.

The Settings app breaks its settings down into the following categories, each covered later in this chapter:

» **System:** This huge catch-all collects settings that don't fit neatly anywhere else. For instance, you can find ways to adjust your monitor's *resolution* — the amount of information it can pack onto a screen without making everything too tiny to read. You even find settings for how the Maps app should react when disconnected from the Internet.

» **Devices:** In Windows Land, *devices* are physical things such as your mouse, keyboard, printer, and scanner. Accordingly, this area lets you adjust your mouse's scroll wheel, as well as how your computer reacts when you insert a memory card. In short, it's a hodgepodge of settings that you find mostly by searching in the Start menu's Search box, as described in this chapter's previous section.

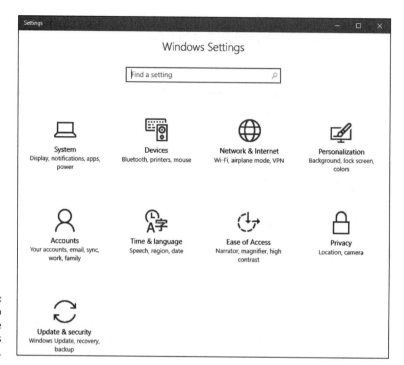

FIGURE 12-1:
The Settings app
lets you change
your computer's
behavior.

>> **Network & Internet:** The Wi-Fi settings listed here are more easily accessed elsewhere. (Click the Wi-Fi icon in the taskbar, as described in Chapter 9.) As a result, this area remains mostly a techie's holdout. Here, geeks can tweak their *VPN* (Virtual Private Network), and old-schoolers can create dial-up Internet connections. Most items listed here simply drop you off in a dusty corner of the desktop's old Control Panel.

>> **Personalization:** Visit here to choose a new photo for your desktop or *lock screen,* the image that greets you when you first turn on your PC. Head here to customize portions of your Start menu, as well, by choosing whether to display recently opened items for convenient return trips.

>> **Accounts:** Head here to create or change accounts for people who can use your computer, a chore I cover in Chapter 14, as well as to delete accounts for those no longer welcome. This area also lets you change your password or account picture. If you work on more than one PC, visit the Sync Your Settings section to control what settings should link to your Microsoft account.

>> **Time & Language:** Visited mostly by frequent fliers, this set-it-once-and-forget-it area lets you change your time zone, adjust the time and date formats to match your region, and tweak other settings relating to your language and geographic location.

>> **Ease of Access:** These settings make Windows more navigable for people with challenges in vision and hearing.

>> **Privacy:** In today's age, there's very little privacy left on the Internet. Nonetheless, this section lets you see the controls that Windows offers to limit the amount of information apps and websites can gather about you. For example, you can control which apps can access your location and control your camera, as well as which apps can see your list of contacts in the People app.

>> **Update & Security:** Drop by here at least once to set up your File History backup, covered in Chapter 18. The Recovery area offers powerful trouble-shooting tools, also covered in Chapter 18.

Bringing out the Big Guns: The Desktop's Control Panel

Although Windows 10 considerably beefs up the Settings app, sometimes you need to bring out the big guns. The desktop's Control Panel lets you while away an entire workweek opening icons and flipping switches to fine-tune Windows. Part of the attraction comes from the Control Panel's magnitude: It houses nearly 50 icons, and some icons summon menus with dozens of settings and tasks. It offers familiarity, too, because many of its settings haven't changed much for 20 years.

REMEMBER

To open the desktop's Control Panel, right-click the Start button and choose Control Panel from the pop-up menu.

To save you from searching aimlessly for the right switch, the Control Panel lumps similar items together in its Category view, as shown in Figure 12-2. Like the Settings app, the Control Panel sports a Search box in its upper-right corner for finding settings dealing with a particular subject. If you hover your mouse pointer over a major category, the Control Panel describes the available settings.

Below each category's name, shortcuts list that category's most popular offerings. The System and Security category icon in Figure 12-2, for example, offers short-cuts to review your computer's maintenance and security status, turn on the File History backup, and access troubleshooting tools.

Some controls don't fall neatly into categories, so they're not listed. To see *every* icon the Control Panel offers, choose either Large Icons or Small Icons from the

View By drop-down list, shown in the top-right corner of Figure 12-2. The window quickly displays *all* umpteen-zillion Control Panel icons, as shown in Figure 12-3. (To return to the Category view in Figure 12-2, select Category from the View By drop-down list.)

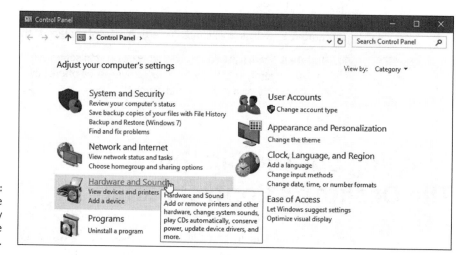

FIGURE 12-2: Rest your mouse pointer over any category to see its settings.

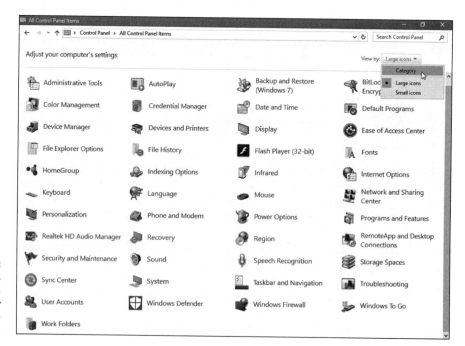

FIGURE 12-3: The Large Icons view displays an icon for *every* setting in the Control Panel.

Don't think that something's astray if your Control Panel differs from the one in Figure 12-3. Different programs, accessories, and computer models often add their own icons to the Control Panel. Different versions of Windows, which I describe in Chapter 1, may also have slightly different icons.

TIP

Rest your mouse pointer over any confusing icon or category in the Control Panel, and Windows thoughtfully explains its meaning in life. (Add this perk to the list of reasons why touchscreen owners will want a mouse when visiting the Windows desktop.)

TIP

The desktop's Control Panel gathers a plethora of switches in Windows into one well-stocked panel, but it's certainly not the only way to change the settings. You can almost always jump to these same settings by right-clicking the item you want to change — be it your desktop, an icon, or a folder — and choosing Properties from the pop-up menu.

The rest of this chapter lists the Control Panel's categories shown earlier in Figure 12-2, the reasons you'd ever want to visit them, and any shortcuts that jump straight to the setting you need. It also explains when a Control Panel setting drops you off at the Settings app, where you make the final changes.

System and Security

Like an old car or a new friendship, Windows needs occasional maintenance. In fact, a little bit of maintenance can make Windows run so much more smoothly that I devote the best of Chapter 13 to that subject. There, you discover how to speed up Windows, free up hard drive space, back up your data, and create a safety net called a *restore point.*

This category's security section contains a full brigade of soldiers, and I've written field manuals for them in Chapter 11. The backup program in Windows, File History, gets its due in Chapter 13.

NEW

Former owners of Windows 7 can find a treat in this section of the Control Panel: Windows 10 brings back the Windows 7 Backup and Restore program. (It was missing from Windows 8 and 8.1.)

User Accounts

You won't visit this area of the Control Panel much. Windows 10 has moved almost all of its switches to the Settings app. I explain in Chapter 14 how to create separate accounts for other people to use your PC. That lets them use your PC but limits the amount of damage they can do to Windows and your files.

If you want to create a user account for a visitor, here's a refresher so you needn't flip ahead to Chapter 14: Click the Start button and click the Settings icon (shown in the margin) from the Start menu. When the Settings app appears, click the Accounts category and then click Family & Other People from the left pane.

Network and Internet

Plug an Internet connection into your PC, and Windows quickly starts slurping information from the web. Connect your PC to a second PC, and Windows wants to connect the two with a Homegroup or another type of network. (I explain Homegroups in Chapter 14.)

But should Windows botch the job, the Control Panel's Network and Internet category offers some troubleshooting tools.

I devote Chapter 15 completely to networking, and the Internet gets its due in Chapter 9.

Changing the Appearance of Windows (Appearance and Personalization)

One of the most popular categories, Appearance and Personalization lets you change the look, feel, and behavior of Windows in a wide variety of ways. Inside the category await these six icons:

>> **Personalization:** Once pay dirt for budding interior designers, this area now contains mostly shortcuts to the Settings app's Personalization section. There, you can change how Windows looks onscreen. A few handy settings still live here, though, including ways to save your window dressing as a theme — a collection of personalization settings. You can also choose a new screen saver. To jump to the Settings app's personalization settings, right-click a blank part of your desktop and choose Personalize.

» Display: Whereas personalization lets you fiddle with colors, the Display area lets you fiddle with your computer's screen. For example, it lets you enlarge the text to soothe tired eyes, adjust the screen resolution, and adjust the connection of an additional computer screen. Again, clicking this takes you to the Settings app's new controls.

 » Taskbar and Navigation: Head here to add program shortcuts to your *taskbar,* the strip living along your desktop's bottom edge. I cover this topic in Chapter 3. (To jump quickly to the taskbar's Settings window, right-click the taskbar and choose Properties. The window that appears also lets you change your Start menu's settings.)

 » Ease of Access Center: This shortcut contains settings to make Windows more navigable for the blind, the deaf, and people with other physical challenges. I describe it in its own section later in this chapter.

 » File Explorer Options: Visited mainly by experienced users, this area lets you tweak how folders look and behave. (To jump quickly to File Explorer Options, open *any* folder, click the View tab and click the Options icon on the far right.)

 » Fonts: Here's where you preview, delete, or examine fonts that spruce up your printed work.

Clicking some of the items listed above takes you to a Control Panel setting. On others, clicking brings you to the appropriate control in the Settings app. In the next few sections, I explain the Appearance and Personalization tasks that you'll reach for most often and how to handle the settings that appear.

Changing the desktop background

A *background,* also known as wallpaper, is simply the picture covering your desktop. To change it, follow these steps:

1. **Right-click your desktop and choose Personalize.**

Windows quickly kicks you over to the Settings app's Personalization section, neatly open to the Background setting shown in Figure 12-4.

 You can't right-click the desktop when in Tablet mode. Instead, press the Start button, tap the Settings icon, and tap the Personalization icon. The Personalization page opens to the Background setting.

TIP

2. **Select Picture from the Background drop-down list.**

The Background section's menu lets you create a background from a picture, a solid color, or a *slideshow* — a combination of photos that automatically changes at preset intervals.

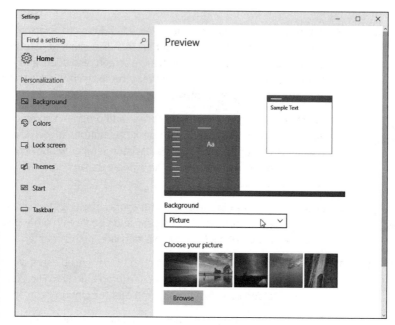

FIGURE 12-4:
Click the
Background
drop-down list to
choose between
different desktop
backgrounds.

3. **Click a new picture for the background.**

   If you don't like Microsoft's picture offerings, click the Browse button, shown along the bottom of Figure 12-4, to search your computer's Pictures folder for potential backgrounds.

TECHNICAL STUFF

   Background files can be stored as BMP, GIF, JPG, JPEG, DIB, TIF, or PNG files. That means you can choose a background from nearly any photo or art found on the Internet, shot from a digital camera, or scanned with a scanner.

   When you click a new picture, Windows immediately places it across your desktop and shows you a preview atop the Personalization window. If you're pleased, jump to Step 4.

4. **Decide whether to fill, fit, stretch, tile, center, or span the picture.**

   Although Windows tries to choose the best-looking setting, very few pictures fit perfectly across the desktop. Small pictures, for example, need to be either stretched to fit the space or spread across the screen in rows like tiles on a floor. When tiling and stretching still look odd or distorted, try the Fill or Fit option to keep the perspective. Or try centering the image and leaving blank space around its edges. Choose the Span option only if you've connected your PC to two monitors and want the image to fill both screens.

5. **Click the Save Changes button to save your new background.**

   Windows saves your new background across your screen.

Did you happen to spot an eye-catching picture while web surfing with Microsoft Edge? Right-click that website's picture and choose Save Picture As to save it in your Pictures folder. Then you can follow the preceding steps to place the picture as your desktop's background.

Choosing a screen saver

In the dinosaur days of computing, computer monitors suffered from *burn-in:* permanent damage when an oft-used program burned its image onto the screen. To prevent burn-in, people installed a screen saver to jump in with a blank screen or moving lines. Today's computer screens no longer suffer from burn-in problems, but people still use screen savers because they look cool and add a small layer of privacy.

Windows comes with several built-in screen savers. To try one out, follow these steps:

1. **Click in the Search box next to the Start menu, type** Screen Saver **and press Enter.**

   The Screen Saver Settings window appears.

2. **Click the downward-pointing arrow in the Screen Saver box and select a screen saver.**

   After choosing a screen saver, click the Preview button for an audition. View as many candidates as you like before making a decision.

   Be sure to click the Settings button because some screen savers offer options, letting you specify the speed of a photo slide show, for example.

3. **If desired, add security by selecting the On Resume, Display Logon Screen check box.**

   This safeguard keeps people from sneaking into your computer while you're fetching coffee. It makes Windows ask for a password after waking up from screen saver mode. (I cover passwords in Chapter 14.)

4. **When you're done setting up your screen saver, click OK.**

   Windows saves your changes.

If you *really* want to extend the life of your display (and save electricity), don't bother with screen savers. Instead, put your computer to Sleep before stepping away: Right-click the Start button, click Shut Down or Sign Out, and choose Sleep from the pop-up menu. To wake your PC, tap any key on the keyboard.

Changing the computer's theme

Themes are simply collections of settings to spruce up your computer's appearance: You can save your favorite screen saver and desktop background as a *theme*, for example. Then, by switching between themes, you can change your computer's clothes more quickly.

To try one of the built-in themes in Windows, click the Start button, type **Change The Theme** into the Search box, and press Enter.

The Control Panel opens to display themes bundled with Windows 10, as shown in Figure 12-5. Click any theme, and Windows tries it on immediately.

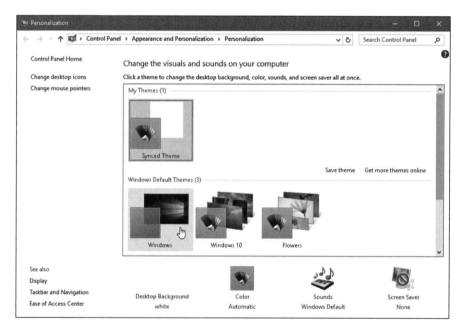

FIGURE 12-5: Choose a preconfigured theme to change how Windows looks and sounds.

The window offers these themes, with options listed along the window's bottom.

>> **My Themes:** Themes you've personally created appear here. If you have a Microsoft account, you see a Synced Theme, meaning the theme is linked to your Microsoft account. Whenever you log onto any PC with that account, the theme tags along to decorate the current PC's screen.

>> **Windows Default Themes:** This category includes the bundled themes in Windows, including its original one, called simply Windows.

>> **High Contrast Themes:** This features high-contrast themes for the visually impaired.

Instead of choosing from the built-in themes, feel free to make your own by clicking the words Save Theme (shown in Figure 12-5) for saving your currently assigned Desktop Background, Window Color, Sounds, and Screen Saver. Type a name for your theme, and it will appear as a choice in this section.

Changing the screen resolution

One of the many change-it-once-and-forget-about-it options in Windows, *screen resolution* determines how much information Windows can cram onto your computer screen. Changing the resolution either shrinks everything to pack more stuff onscreen, or it enlarges everything at the expense of desktop real estate.

To find your most comfortable resolution — or if a program or game mutters something about you having to change your *screen resolution* or *video mode* — follow these steps:

1. **Click the Start button, click the Settings icon, and click the System icon.**

2. **When the System page appears, click the words Advanced Display Settings in the bottom-right corner.**

   The Advanced Display Settings window appears, as shown in Figure 12-6.

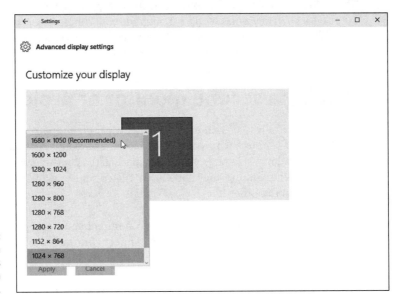

3. **To change the screen resolution, click the Resolution drop-down list and select your desired resolution.**

   The drop-down menu lists a variety of resolutions, all sorted by number. The larger the numbers, the higher the resolution, and the more information Windows can pack onto your computer screen. Unfortunately, packing more information onto your screen shrinks the text and images.

   Unless you have a good reason not to, choose the resolution with the word (Recommended) next to it. That's the highest resolution your computer supports.

   Choosing the Windows-recommended setting makes for the clearest text and images.

4. **View your display changes by clicking the Apply button. Then click the Keep Changes button to authorize the change.**

TIP

   When Windows makes drastic changes to your display, it gives you 15 seconds to approve the change by clicking the Keep Changes button. If a technical glitch renders your screen unreadable, you won't be able to see or click the onscreen button. After a few seconds, Windows notices that you didn't approve, and it reverts to your original, viewable display settings.

5. **Click OK when you're done tweaking the display.**

   After you change your video resolution once, you'll probably never return here unless you buy a new monitor or upgrade your computer's video. You might also need to revisit this window if you plug a second computer screen into your PC, which I describe in the following section.

Adding a second monitor or projector

Have you been blessed with an extra computer screen, perhaps a leftover from a deceased PC? Connect it to your PC or tablet, and you've doubled your Windows desktop: Windows stretches your workspace across both computer screens. That lets you view the online encyclopedia in one computer screen while writing your term paper in the other.

Or, if you've connected a projector, you can mirror your laptop's screen with what you see on the projector. You can even connect your tablet to a widescreen TV for watching movies.

To perform these video gymnastics, your PC needs two *video ports,* and those ports must match the *connectors* on your second monitor or projector. This poses no problem if they're less than two or three years old. Most Windows PCs, laptops, and tablets include an HDMI port for plugging in a second monitor or projector.

You may need to buy an adapter or special cable that matches the ports of both your computer and second display.

After you connect the second monitor or the projector to your computer, follow these steps on your PC:

1. **Click the Start button, and click the Settings icon. When the Settings app appears, click the System icon.**

The Settings app opens to the Display page which shows *two* monitors, side by side, shown in Figure 12-7. (Click the Detect button if the second monitor doesn't appear onscreen. You may need to turn the second monitor off, wait 30 seconds, and turn it back on again.)

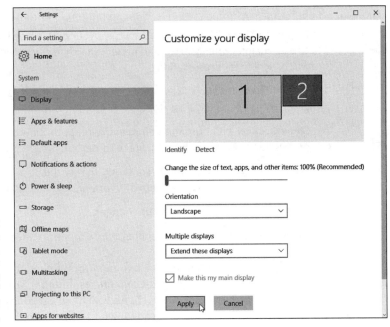

FIGURE 12-7: Drag and drop the onscreen monitors to match the placement of your real monitors.

2. **Drag and drop the onscreen computer screens to the right or left until they match the physical placement of the *real* computer screens on your desk. Then choose your main display.**

The window shows your two monitors as little onscreen squares, as shown in 12-7. Not sure which square represents which monitor? Click the Identify button; Windows displays numbers on the onscreen monitors, as well as your real monitors, so you can tell which is which.

Then, drag and drop the onscreen monitors until they match the placement of your *real* monitors.

Finally, click the onscreen monitor that should display your Start button, and select the Make This My Main Display check box.

3. **Adjust the Orientation setting, if necessary, and the Multiple Displays setting.**

The Orientation drop-down list, useful mostly for swiveling monitors and docked tablets, lets you tell Windows how you want monitors rotated. Stick with the default Landscape mode; choose Portrait mode only if you've turned a monitor or tablet sideways, perhaps to better display a full page of reading material.

The Multiple Displays drop-down list tells Windows how it should display your desktop across the second monitor. It offers these options, each handy for different scenarios:

- **Duplicate These Displays:** This duplicates your desktop on both screens, which is helpful when you want to project an image of your desktop onto a wall or screen for presentations.

- **Extend These Displays:** This stretches Windows to fit across both screens, giving you an extra-wide desktop.

- **Show Only on 1:** Choose this before you're ready to show off your presentation. Then switch to Duplicate These Displays.

- **Show Only on 2:** Choose this to show only the second display, which is useful when hooking up a tablet to a TV for watching movies in a dark room.

4. **Click the Apply button to save your changes.**

If you move the position of your monitors, return to the first step and start over.

To adjust the screen resolution of your two monitors, follow the directions given in the previous section, "Changing the screen resolution." This time, however, the Advanced Display Settings window shows *both* monitors. Click the monitor you want to change, and the Resolution drop-down list applies to that monitor alone.

Hardware and Sound

 The Control Panel's Hardware and Sound category, shown in Figure 12-8, shows some familiar faces. The Display icon, for example, also appears in the Appearance and Personalization category, described in this chapter's previous section, "Changing the Appearance of Windows (Appearance and Personalization)."

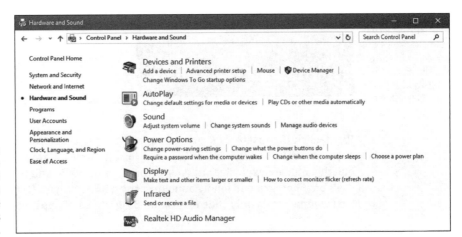

FIGURE 12-8:
The Hardware
and Sound
category lets you
control the
physical aspects
of your PC.

The Hardware and Sound category controls the parts of your PC you can touch or plug in. You can adjust the settings of your display here as well as your mouse, speakers, keyboard, printer, telephone, scanner, digital camera, game controllers, and (for you graphic artists out there) digital pen.

You won't spend much time here, though, especially coming in through the Control Panel's doors. Most settings appear elsewhere, where a click brings you directly to the setting you need.

Whether you arrive at these pages through the Control Panel or a shortcut, the following sections explain the most popular reasons for visiting here.

Adjusting volume and sounds

The Sound area lets you adjust your PC's volume, a handy technique when trying to sneak in a computer game on a Windows tablet during a boring business meeting.

TIP

Most Windows tablets come with toggle-switch volume controls mounted along their left or right edge. The top button turns up the volume; the lower button decreases the volume. Experiment with them a bit before bringing Angry Birds into the board room.

To turn down your PC's volume from the desktop, shown in Figure 12-9, click the little speaker by your clock and slide down the volume.

To mute your PC, click the little speaker icon at the left of the sliding control, as shown in Figure 12-9. Clicking that icon again lets your computer blare music again.

FIGURE 12-9:
Click the speaker
icon and move
the sliding control
to adjust your
PC's volume.

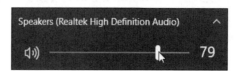

Right-click the taskbar's speaker icon and choose Open Volume Mixer from the pop-up menu to set different volumes for different desktop programs. You can quietly detonate explosives in your favorite game while still allowing your desktop's email program to loudly announce any new messages. (*Note:* The individualized volume levels only control desktop programs, not apps, unfortunately.)

Installing or setting up speakers

Most PCs come with only two speakers. Others come with four, and PCs that double as home theaters or gaming rigs sometimes have up to eight. To accommodate the variety of setups, Windows includes a speaker setup area, complete with a speaker test.

If you're installing new speakers or you're not sure your old ones are working, follow these steps to introduce them properly to Windows:

1. **From the desktop, right-click your taskbar's Speaker icon and choose Playback Devices.**

   The Sound window appears, listing every way your computer can play back sounds.

2. **Right-click your speaker's icon and then choose Configure Speakers from the pop-up menu.**

   Right-click the speaker's icon with the green check mark, because that's the device your computer uses for playing sound. The Speaker Setup window appears.

3. **Click the Test button (as shown in Figure 12-10), adjust your speaker's settings, and click Next.**

   Windows then walks you through selecting your number of speakers and their placement and then plays each one in turn so that you can hear whether they're in the correct locations.

4. **Click Next to adjust any other speakers attached to your PC. When you reach the last screen, click Finish.**

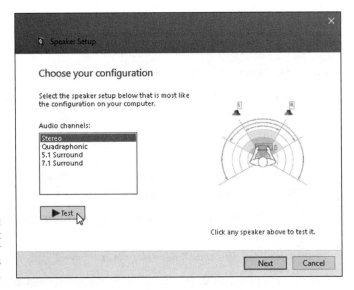

FIGURE 12-10:
Click the Test button to hear your speakers one at a time.

While you're here, check your microphone volume by clicking the Recording tab, as well as tabs for any other sound gadgetry you've been able to afford.

If your speakers and microphone don't show up as devices, Windows doesn't know they're plugged into your computer. That usually means you need to install a new *driver*, an annoying journey I walk you through in Chapter 13.

Adding a Bluetooth gadget

Bluetooth technology lets you connect gadgets wirelessly to your computer, removing clutter from your desktop. On a tablet, Bluetooth lets you add a mouse and keyboard without hogging one of your coveted USB ports.

Bluetooth can also connect your computer, laptop, or tablet with some cellphones for wireless Internet access — if your wireless provider allows it, of course.

To add a Bluetooth item to a computer, laptop, or tablet, follow these steps:

1. **Make sure your Bluetooth device is turned on and ready to pair.**

    Most Bluetooth devices include a simple On/Off switch. Telling the device to begin pairing is a little more difficult. Sometimes you can simply flip a switch. Other devices make you hold down a button until its little light begins flashing.

    When you spot the flashing light, the device is ready to pair with another Bluetooth device including, you hope, your computer.

2. **Click the Start button, click the Settings icon, and click the Settings app's Devices icon.**

   The Settings app opens to the Devices section.

3. **Click the Bluetooth option from the left side of the Devices section.**

   Your computer quickly begins searching for any nearby Bluetooth devices that want to connect, known in Bluetooth parlance as *pair*.

   If your device doesn't appear, head back to Step 1 and make sure your Bluetooth gadget is still turned on and ready to pair. (Many give up and turn off after 30 seconds of waiting to connect.)

4. **When your device's name appears below the Add a Device button, click its name.**

5. **Type in your device's code if necessary and, if asked, click the Pair button.**

   Here's where things get sticky. For security reasons, you need to prove that you're sitting in front of your *own* computer and that you're not a stranger trying to break in. Unfortunately, devices employ slightly different tactics when making you prove your innocence.

   Sometimes you need to type a secret string of numbers called a *passcode* into both the device and your computer. (The secret code is usually hidden somewhere in your device's manual.) But you need to type quickly before the other gadget stops waiting.

   On some gadgets, particularly Bluetooth mice, you hold in a little push button on the mouse's belly at this step.

   Cellphones sometimes make you click a Pair button if you see matching passcodes on both your computer and phone.

TIP

   When in doubt, type **0000** on your keyboard. That's often recognized as a universal passcode for frustrated Bluetooth devices owners who are trying to connect their gadgets.

   After a gadget successfully pairs with your computer, its name and icon appear in the Devices category of the Settings app.

To add a Bluetooth device from the Windows desktop, click the taskbar's Bluetooth icon (shown in the margin), choose Add a Bluetooth Device, and then jump to Step 4 in the preceding list. Don't see the taskbar's Bluetooth icon? Then click the upward-pointing arrow that lives a few icons to the left of the taskbar's clock. The Bluetooth icon appears in the pop-up menu, ready for your click.

Adding a printer

Quarrelling printer manufacturers couldn't agree on how printers should be installed. As a result, you install your printer in one of two ways:

>> Some printer manufacturers say simply to plug in your printer by pushing its rectangular-shaped connector into a little rectangular-shaped USB port on your PC. Windows automatically notices, recognizes, and embraces your new printer. Stock your printer with any needed ink cartridges, toner, or paper, and you're done.

>> Other manufacturers take an uglier approach, saying you must install their bundled software *before* plugging in your printer. And if you don't install the software first, the printer may not work correctly.

Unfortunately, the only way to know how your printer should be installed is to check the printer's manual. (Sometimes this information appears on a colorful, one-page Quick Installation sheet packed in the printer's box.)

If your printer lacks installation software, install the cartridges, add paper to the tray, and follow these instructions to put it to work:

1. **With Windows up and running, plug your printer into your PC and turn on the printer.**

   Windows may send a message saying that your printer is installed successfully, but follow the next step to test it.

2. **Load the Control Panel.**

   Right-click the Start button and choose Control Panel from the pop-up menu.

3. **From the Hardware and Sound category, click the View Devices and Printers link.**

   The Control Panel displays its categories of devices, including your printer if you're lucky. If you spot your USB printer listed by its model or brand name, right-click its icon, choose Printer Properties, and click the Print Test Page button. If it prints correctly, you're finished. Congratulations.

   Test page *didn't* work? Check that all the packaging is removed from inside your printer and that it has ink cartridges. If it still doesn't print, your printer is probably defective. Contact the store where you bought it and ask who to contact for assistance.

To print your documents to a file that you can email to nearly anybody, choose Print As a PDF. That saves your printed, formatted file as a PDF file, a format that's accessible with nearly every type of computer, smartphone, or tablet. (If somebody can't read it, tell them to download Adobe Reader from `https://get.adobe.com/reader`.)

That's it. If you're like most people, your printer will work like a charm. If it doesn't, I've stuffed some tips and fix-it tricks in the printing section in Chapter 8.

If you have two or more printers attached to your computer, right-click the icon of your most oft-used printer and choose Set As Default Printer from the pop-up menu. Windows then prints to *that* printer automatically unless you tell it otherwise.

>> To remove a printer you no longer use, right-click its name in Step 3 and then choose Remove Device from the pop-up menu. That printer's name no longer appears as an option when you try to print from a program. If Windows asks to uninstall the printer's drivers and software, click Yes — unless you think you may install that printer again sometime.

>> You can change printer options from within many programs. Choose File in a program's menu bar (you may need to press Alt to see the menu bar) and then choose Print Setup or choose Print. The window that appears lets you change things such as paper sizes, fonts, and types of graphics.

>> To share a printer quickly over a network, create a Homegroup, which I describe in Chapter 14. Your printer immediately shows up as an installation option for all the computers on your network.

>> If your printer's software confuses you, try clicking the Help buttons in its dialog boxes. Many buttons are customized for your particular printer model, and they offer advice not found in Windows.

Time and Language

Microsoft designed the Settings app's Time and Language area mostly for travelers to different time zones and locations. Desktop computer owners see this information only once — when first setting up the computer. Windows subsequently remembers the time and date even when your PC is turned off.

Portable computers owners will want to drop by here when visiting different time zones. Bilingual computer owners will also appreciate settings allowing characters from different languages.

To visit here, click the Start button, click the Settings icon from the menu, and click the Settings app's Time & Language category. Three sections appear:

» **Date and Time:** This area is fairly self-explanatory. (Clicking your taskbar's clock and choosing Adjust Date/Time lets you visit here, as well.)

» **Region & Language:** If you're bilingual or multilingual, visit this area when you're working on documents that require characters from different languages.

» **Speech:** If Windows doesn't recognize your voice well, visit here to fine-tune its speech recognition settings. (You may need to buy a better microphone to take advantage of Cortana, and other speech-recognition programs.)

Adding or Removing Apps or Programs

Removing an app from your Start menu doesn't take much effort. Right-click the app's tile from the Start menu and choose Unpin from Start from the pop-up menu.

That doesn't physically remove the app, though. The app lives on in the Start menu's alphabetical list and on your computer. To permanently remove an app or program from your PC, follow these steps:

1. **Click Start button and click the Settings icon from the Start menu.**

The Settings app appears.

2. **Click the System icon and then, when the System window appears, click Apps & Features from the window's left pane.**

The Apps & Features window appears, as shown in Figure 12-11, listing your currently installed apps and programs sorted by size.

TIP

To sort the programs by their installation date, click the Sort By box and choose Sort By Install Date from the drop-down menu. You can also view programs installed on certain drives, which comes in handy on small tablets, where you want to store programs on memory cards rather than their main memory.

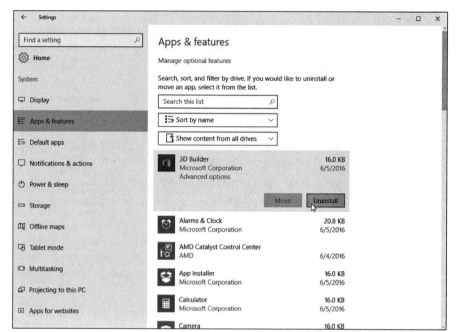

FIGURE 12-11:
Click an
unwanted app or
program and click
the Uninstall
button.

3. **Click the unloved program and then click its Uninstall or Move button.**

   Click a listed program, and two buttons appear below it:

   - **Move:** When you're running out of storage space, choose this option, if available. It lets you move an app or program onto your tablet's memory card, freeing up space for your files.

   - **Uninstall:** Click this button — as well as the confirmation button that follows — to completely remove the app or program from your PC.

   Depending on which button you've clicked, Windows either boots the program off your PC or moves it to another disk drive or memory card.

After you delete a program, it's gone for good unless you kept its installation CD. Unlike other deleted items, deleted programs don't linger inside your Recycle Bin. Mistakenly deleted apps, however, can almost always be relocated and reinstalled from the Windows Store. (The Windows Store also remembers which apps you've purchased, making them easy to reinstall for free.)

WARNING

Always use the Settings app to uninstall unwanted programs. Simply deleting their files or folders doesn't do the trick. In fact, doing so often confuses your computer into sending bothersome error messages.

INSTALLING NEW PROGRAMS

Today, most programs install themselves automatically as soon as you choose them from the Windows Store, double-click their downloaded installation file, or slide their discs into your PC's drive.

If you're not sure whether a program has installed, go to the Start menu and look for its name. If it appears in the All Apps alphabetical list, the program has installed.

But if a program doesn't automatically leap into your computer, here are some tips that can help:

- You need an Administrator account to install programs. (Most computer owners automatically have an Administrator account.) That keeps the kids, with their Standard or Child accounts, from installing programs and messing up the computer. I explain user accounts in Chapter 14.

- Downloaded a program? Windows saves downloaded files in your Downloads folder. To find the Downloads folder, open any folder and click the word Downloads in the folder's Quick Access area atop its left pane. When the Downloads folder appears, double-click the downloaded program's name to install it.

- Many eager, newly installed programs want to add a desktop shortcut, a Start menu tile, *and* a Quick Launch toolbar shortcut. Say "yes" to all. That way you can start the program from the desktop, avoiding a trip to the Start menu. (Changed your mind? Right-click any unwanted shortcuts and choose either Delete or Unpin to remove them.)

- It never hurts to create a restore point before installing a new program. (I describe creating restore points in Chapter 13.) If your newly installed program goes haywire, use System Restore to return your computer to the peaceful state of mind it enjoyed before you installed the troublemaker.

Modifying Windows for the Physically Challenged

Nearly everybody finds Windows to be particularly challenging, but some people face special physical challenges, as well. To assist them, the Control Panel's Ease of Access area offers a variety of welcome changes.

If your eyesight isn't what it used to be, you may appreciate the ways to increase the text size on your computer screen.

Follow these steps to modify the settings in Windows:

1. **Load the Windows Settings app.**

   You can fetch the Settings app any of several ways:

   - **Mouse:** Click the Start button and then click the Settings icon from the Start menu.

   - **Keyboard:** From the desktop, press ⊞+I.

   - **Touchscreen:** Slide your finger inward from the screen's right edge and tap the All Settings icon.

2. **When the Settings app appears, select the Ease of Access icon.**

   The Ease of Access Center appears, as shown in Figure 12-12.

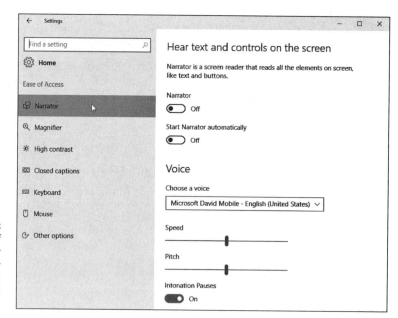

FIGURE 12-12:
The Ease of Access Center provides help for users with physical limitations.

3. **Change the settings according to your needs.**

   The Ease of Access window offers several categories to make your computer easier to control. To turn a feature on or off, click its toggle button in these categories:

- **Narrator:** The awful built-in narrator in Windows reads onscreen text for people who can't view it clearly. It also tells you what button you've pressed. Be prepared to hear a lot of information as you touch a tablet or move a mouse.

- **Magnifier:** Designed for the visually impaired, this option magnifies the mouse pointer's exact location.

- **High Contrast:** This setting eliminates most screen colors but helps vision-impaired people view the screen and cursor more clearly.

- **Closed Captions:** Designed to help the hearing impaired, this option helps you place captions in movies that support Closed Caption technology.

- **Keyboard:** This setting places a clickable keyboard along the screen's bottom, letting you type by pointing and clicking. It also manipulates the keyboard in other ways, making it easier for people with limited typing ability.

- **Mouse:** Head here to enlarge the mouse pointer and make it easier to view.

- **Other options:** This offers a variety of options for the vision impaired, from enlarging cursor width to whether Windows should show animations when opening and closing windows.

Choose any of these options to turn on the feature immediately. If it makes matters worse, choose it again to toggle it off.

If you're still not happy, proceed to Step 4.

4. **Visit the Control Panel's Ease of Access Center.**

Windows 10 still offers the desktop Control Panel's Ease of Access Center, which has been a Windows staple for many years.

To reach it, right-click the Start button, choose Control Panel, and click the Ease of Access Center icon.

Some centers that assist physically challenged people may offer software or assistance for helping you make these changes.

Chapter 13

Keeping Windows from Breaking

I f Windows seems desperately broken, hop ahead to Chapter 18 for the fix; Windows 10 offers more quick fix tricks than ever. But if your computer seems to be running reasonably well, stay right here. This chapter explains how to keep it running that way for the longest time possible.

This chapter is a checklist of sorts, with each section explaining a fairly simple and necessary task to keep Windows running at its best. You discover how to set up and turn on the automatic backup program in Windows called *File History*, for example.

If somebody says your computer has a bad driver, it's not a personal insult. A *driver* is a little program that helps Windows talk to your computer's various parts. This chapter explains how to remove bad drivers by placing an updated driver behind the wheel.

CREATING A RESTORE POINT

Windows is moving away from restore points to its newer Refresh system, covered in Chapter 18. But old-school System Restore fans can still create and use the trusty Windows restore points to return a PC to a time when it was feeling better. Restore points behave a bit like a time capsule, saving your PC's settings at a specific point in time. If those settings become damaged later, returning to an earlier restore point can sometimes solve the problem.

To create a restore point, follow these steps:

1. **Click the Start button, type** System Restore **into the Search box, and click the Create a Restore Point link from the Search results.**

   The System Properties window appears, opened to the System Protection tab, which lists options for System Restore. Look for the *Configure* and the grayed-out *Create* buttons near the window's bottom edge.

2. **In the Available Drives window, click your Local Disk C: (System) drive. Then click the Configure button and, when the System Protection for Local Disk (C:) window appears, click the Turn On System Protection button and click OK.**

   That turns on System Protection for your C: drive, which is required before you can use System Restore. When you click OK, the window closes, returning you to the System Properties window. Note how your handiwork now lets you select the Create button.

3. **Click the Create button to fetch the System Protection window, type a name for your new restore point, and then click the window's Create button to save the restore point.**

   Choose a name that describes your computer's condition, such as "Created just before installing new bowling app," so you'll remember it better. Windows creates a restore point with your chosen name, leaving you some open windows to close.

By creating and labelling your own restore points on good days, you'll know which ones to use on bad days. I describe how to resuscitate your computer from a restore point in the sidebar on System Restore in Chapter 18.

Tuning Up Windows with Built-In Maintenance Tools

Windows contains a slew of tools for keeping itself running smoothly. Several run automatically, limiting your work to checking their On switches. Others help you prepare for coming disasters by automatically backing up your PC's files.

 To check out your computer's survivalist tools, right-click the Start button, choose Control Panel, and select the Control Panel's System and Security category. The Control Panel's troubleshooting tools appear, shown in Figure 13-1.

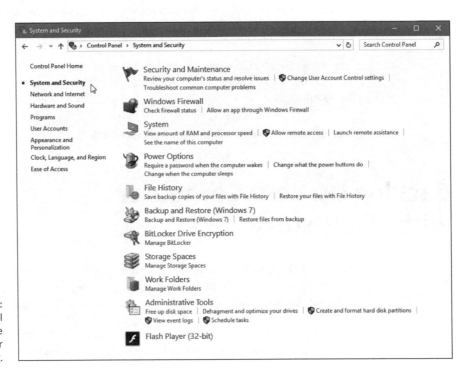

FIGURE 13-1: These Control Panel tools come in most handy for troubleshooting.

Out of the dozen categories, these offer the most help:

 >> **Security and Maintenance:** This lists your computer's main illnesses, and offers one-click fixes that may bring it back to health. It reminds you if your backup drive is unplugged, for example, or if a virus may have turned off important safeguards. (*Tip:* Click the Troubleshooting link to fix problems with older programs, Windows Update, Internet connections, and gadgets attached to your PC.)

>> **System:** Technical support people thrive in this crawlspace. The System area lists your version of Windows, your PC's processor speed and networking status, its amount of memory, and whether it's *activated*, Microsoft's term for legally procured.

>> **Power Options:** Not sure whether your PC is sleeping, hibernating, or just plain turned off? Chapter 3 explains the difference, and this section lets you determine your PC's degree of lethargy when you press its Off button. (Or if you're a laptop owner, when you close its lid.)

>> **File History:** Introduced in Windows 8, this new type of backup program drapes a safety net over every file in your main folders, letting you retrieve backup copies should things go wrong. It's free, leaving you with no excuse not to turn it on. All hard drives eventually die, and you've stored lots of memories on yours. (A File History backup also simplifies moving from an old PC to a new PC.)

>> **Administrative Tools:** One gem lives in this complicated grab bag of tech tools: The Disk Cleanup program deletes your PC's garbage to give you more storage space.

I describe these tasks more fully in the next sections.

Backing Up Your Computer with File History

Your hard drive will eventually die, unfortunately, and it will take everything down with it: years of digital photos, music, letters, financial records, scanned memorabilia, and anything else you've created or stored on your PC.

That's why you must back up your files on a regular basis. When your hard drive finally walks off the stage, your backup copy lets you keep the show on the road.

Windows 8 introduced a backup solution called *File History* that lives on in Windows 10. After you turn it on, File History automatically backs up every file in your main folders every hour. The program is easy to turn on, is simple to figure out, runs automatically, and backs up everything you need.

Before File History can go to work, you need two things:

>> **An external hard drive:** For dependable, automatic backups, you need a portable hard drive, which is a relatively inexpensive hard drive in a little box.

TIP

A cord connects from the box to one of your computer's USB ports, and when the drive is plugged in, Windows recognizes the drive immediately. Keep the drive plugged into your computer, and File History gives you completely automatic backups.

It's hard to keep a portable hard drive constantly plugged into a laptop or tablet because they're constantly being moved around. Instead, consider inserting a flash drive into your laptop's USB port or a memory card into your tablet, and use it for your File History backups. Beware, though: If your device is stolen, you lose your backups. A safer but more expensive option is to buy a *wireless* hard drive that stays at home. Your device will find the drive and back itself up when you walk in the front door.

» **Flip the On Switch:** The File History program comes free in Windows. But the program can't do anything until you tell it to begin running.

Follow these steps to tell your computer to start backing up your work automatically every hour:

1. **Plug your drive or its cable into your USB port. (Alternatively, insert a memory card into your tablet's slot.)**

   The rectangular-shaped plug on the end of the drive or its cable plugs into the rectangular-shaped USB port on your computer. (If the plug doesn't fit in the first time, flip it over.)

   If you're backing up to a memory card, check your tablet's manual to see what size and type of memory card it will accept.

2. **Click the Start button and click the icon for the Settings app.**

   The Settings app appears.

3. **Select the Update & Security category and click Backup from the left pane.**

   The File History settings area jumps to the screen, shown in Figure 13-2.

   If you've never set up a drive for File History, move to Step 4.

   If you've already set up a drive for File History, jump ahead to Step 5.

4. **To select a drive for File History, click Add a Drive, then choose your drive from the drop-down window.**

   The Select a Drive window appears, listing all of the available storage spaces. Click the one you want, and click OK. If your drive isn't listed, then Windows isn't recognizing it. Try unplugging it, restarting your computer, and then plugging it back into a different USB port.

   Since you've added a drive, the Add a Drive button changes to an On/Off toggle switch.

FIGURE 13-2:
Click the Add a
Drive button to
tell Windows
which drive
should store your
backups.

TECHNICAL STUFF

To choose a networked location, visit the Control Panel's File History settings. Networked drives work well as backup locations for portable PCs, such as tablets and laptops. (I explain how to create a home network in Chapter 15.) If you try to save to a networked drive on another PC, Windows asks you to enter a username and password from an Administrator account on the other PC.

5. **Click the On toggle switch.**

   Click the On toggle switch to start the backup process rolling. File History may ask if it should recommend your new File History drive to members of your Homegroup:

   - Click Yes only if you're backing up to a large drive that won't be moving around: a wireless hard drive, for example, or a large shared network drive.

   - Click No if you're running File History on a memory card in your tablet, or on a portable drive that you plan on carrying around with you.

When you turn on File History, Windows immediately starts its backup — even if one isn't scheduled yet. That's because the ever-vigilant Windows wants to make sure that it grabs everything right now, before something goes wrong. After backing up everything, Windows backs up only the changed files every hour. It keeps the original files, as well, giving you plenty of backups to choose from should you need them.

CREATING A SYSTEM IMAGE BACKUP

Windows 7 introduced a popular way to back up a computer. Instead of backing up *files*, it copies *all* of your hard drive's contents into one file and then stores that file on a second hard drive. System images such as this come in handy for two main reasons:

- **Efficiency:** When your computer's hard drive eventually dies, you can replace the hard drive, restore the system image backup, and have all of your files and programs back. It's a quick way to be up and running again.

- **Completeness:** File History backs up only files in your main folders, and the Windows Store backs up only your apps and settings. A system image backs up those things, as well, but it also backs up your Windows *desktop programs* and their information. For example, File History won't back up your email from the desktop version of Microsoft Office. A system image will, though, because it backs up *everything*.

Windows 10 still offers Windows 7's system image backup method, and it still works fine in Windows 10. You can even store a system image on the same portable drive you use for File History. Make sure your portable drive is large enough to hold all of the information on your computer's C: drive.

To create a system image in Windows 10, right-click the Start button and choose Control Panel. Then, in the System and Security section, choose Backup and Restore (Windows 7). When the Backup and Restore Your Files window appears, click the words Create a System Image from the left pane. Follow the steps to tell Windows 10 to create a system image backup of your computer.

You should do this daily, if it's possible; if not, do it weekly or monthly. Then, if you ever need to take your computer to a repair shop, take in your portable hard drive and tell the technician you have a "system image backup." The techie can use that backup to rescue all of your computer's files and programs from the date of your last system image backup.

Although File History does a remarkable job at keeping everything easy to use and automatic, it comes with a few bits of fine print, described here:

- ≫ File History backs up everything in your main folders: Documents, Music, Pictures, Videos, Desktop, Favorites, Downloads, and a few others. To exclude some (perhaps exclude your Videos folder if you already store copies of your videos elsewhere), click the More Options link below the On/Off toggle. All of File History's settings appear, letting you add or exclude folders.

- ≫ Windows normally backs up changed files automatically every hour. To change that schedule, click the More Options link below the On/Off toggle.

Then choose the backup frequency from the Automatically Back Up My Files menu. (You can choose between every 10 minutes to once a day.)

TIP

>> File History also provides a handy way to move your files from an old PC to a new PC, a tiresome chore I describe in Chapter 20.

>> I describe how to restore files from the File History backup in Chapter 18. That section is worth looking at now, though: not only does File History work in emergencies, but it also enables you to compare current files with versions you created hours or days before. It lets you revive better versions of files that you've changed for the worse.

WARNING

>> Windows saves your backup in a folder named FileHistory on your chosen drive. Don't move or delete that folder, or else Windows may not be able to find it again when you choose to restore it.

Finding Technical Information about Your Computer

If you ever need to look under the Windows hood, heaven forbid, head for the desktop's Control Panel by right-clicking your screen's Start button and choosing Control Panel from the pop-up menu.

When the Control Panel appears, select the System and Security category and choose System (shown in the margin). Shown in Figure 13-3, the System window offers an easily digestible technical briefing about your PC's viscera:

>> **Windows Edition:** Windows comes in several versions. In this section, Windows lists the version that's running on your particular computer.

>> **System:** This area lists your PC's type of *processor* (its brains, so to speak) along with its amount of memory. You can upgrade memory fairly easily on a PC or laptop but not on a tablet.

>> **Computer Name, Domain, and Workgroup Settings:** This section identifies your computer's name and *workgroup,* a technical term only needed by highly paid network technicians connecting to other computers in a business network. (I cover networks in Chapter 15; Windows 10 automatically handles the workgroup name stuff on home networks.)

>> **Windows Activation:** To keep people from buying one copy of Windows and installing it on several PCs, Microsoft requires Windows to be *activated,* a process that chains it to a single PC.

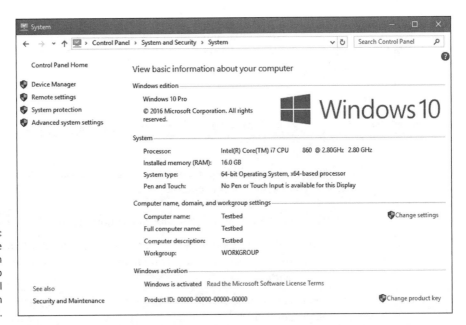

FIGURE 13-3:
Clicking the
System icon
brings up
technical
information
about your PC.

» The pane along the left also lists some more advanced tasks you may find handy during those panic-stricken times when something's going wrong with your PC. Here's the rundown:

- **Device Manager:** This option lists all the parts inside your computer but not in a friendly manner. Parts with exclamation points next to them aren't happy. Double-click them to see an explanation of why they're not working correctly. (Sometimes a Troubleshoot button appears by the explanation, and you can click the button to diagnose the problem.)

- **Remote Settings:** Rarely used, this complicated setup lets other people control your PC through the Internet and, with any luck, fix things. If you can find one of these helpful people, let him or her walk you through this procedure. (However, *never* trust someone who phones you unexpectedly and says she needs to use Remote Settings to "fix your computer." That's an old scam.)

- **System Protection:** This option lets you create restore points (described in this chapter's first section). You can also come here and use a restore point to take your PC back to another point in time when it was in a better mood.

- **Advanced System Settings:** Professional techies spend lots of time in here. Everybody else ignores it.

Most of the stuff listed in the System window is fairly complicated, so don't mess with it unless you're sure of what you're doing or a technical support person tells you to change a specific setting.

TIP

Windows 10 lists similar information in the Settings app's System area, which is easier to access on touchscreens. (Click About, the bottom entry in the System page's left pane.)

Freeing Up Space on Your Hard Drive

If programs begin whining about running out of room on your hard drive, this solution grants you a short reprieve:

1. **Right-click your Start button and choose Control Panel.**

2. **Click the Control Panel's System and Security category. When a long list of categories appears, click Free Up Disk Space in the Administrative Tools section.**

   If your PC has more than one disk drive, Windows asks which drive to clean up. Select your C: drive.

3. **Select your (C:) drive, if necessary, and click OK.**

   The Disk Cleanup program calculates how much disk space you can save and presents the Disk Cleanup dialog box shown in Figure 13-4. (The amount of disk space you can save is shown at the top of the dialog box.)

FIGURE 13-4:
Make sure that all the check boxes are selected.

TIP

If you're really pressed for space, click the window's Clean Up System Files button. Windows takes a second, deeper look and often presents checklists for even more files that can be deleted.

4. **Select the check boxes for all the items and then click OK.**

   Click any entries that puzzle you, and the Description section explains the files that will be deleted. When you click the OK button, Windows asks whether you're *sure* you want to delete the files.

5. **Click the Delete Files button to erase the unneeded files.**

   Windows proceeds to empty your Recycle Bin, destroy leftovers from old websites, and remove other hard drive clutter.

WARNING

If you've upgraded to Windows 10, your old Windows version usually remains on your hard drive in a folder called "Windows.Old." That folder consumes *lots* of space, and you can delete it by choosing the Clean Up System Files button in Step 3, and selecting the check box labeled Previous Windows Installation. Deleting it, of course, means your computer won't be able to return to that older Windows version, a task I cover in Chapter 18.

Empowering Your Power Button

Instead of reaching for your computer's power switch, you should turn off Windows with its *own* power button, as described in Chapter 2. A click of the Start menu's power button offers three options: Sleep, Shut Down, and Restart.

Sleep, the most popular option, puts your computer into a low-power slumber, so it loads quickly when turned back on.

The built-in power switch in Windows takes a few clicks to reach, however. To save time, tell your computer's mechanical *power button* how to react when pressed: Should it Sleep or Shut Down?

The same question applies to laptop owners: Should your computer sleep or shut down when you close the lid?

To answer that question, follow these steps:

1. **Right-click the Start button, choose Control Panel from the pop-up menu, and select the System and Security category.**

2. **Click the Power Options icon.**

   The Power Options window appears, set to the Windows normal setting: Balanced (Recommended).

3. **From the left panel, click the Choose What the Power Buttons Do link.**

   A window appears, as shown in Figure 13-5, offering a menu. The menu differs slightly whether you're viewing it on a desktop PC, a battery powered laptop, or a tablet.

FIGURE 13-5: Choose how your computer should behave when the power button is pressed.

4. **Select your changes.**

   Using the menu, you can tell your PC's power button to Do Nothing, Sleep, Hibernate, or Shut Down. (When in doubt, choose Sleep.)

   Laptops and tablets offer extra options on this window that let them behave differently according to whether they're plugged in or running on batteries. You can let them run at full power when plugged in, for example, but conserve power by putting them to sleep when they're running on batteries.

   Laptop owners also find a menu letting them choose the laptop's behavior when they close its lid or press its sleep button.

   You may need to click the words Change Settings That Are Currently Unavailable to see all your options.

TIP

For extra security, select the Require a Password (Recommended) button so that anybody waking up your PC needs your password to see your information.

5. **Click the Save Changes button.**

Windows saves your changes until you choose to revisit these steps.

Setting Up Devices That Don't Work (Fiddling with Drivers)

Windows comes with an arsenal of *drivers* — software that lets Windows communicate with the gadgets you plug in to your PC. Normally, Windows automatically recognizes your new part, and it simply works. Other times, Windows heads to the Internet and fetches some automated instructions before finishing the job.

But occasionally, you'll plug in something that's either too new for Windows to know about or too old for it to remember. Or perhaps something attached to your PC becomes cranky, and you see odd messages grumble about "needing a new driver."

In these cases, it's up to you to track down and install a Windows driver for that part. The best drivers come with an installation program that automatically places the software in the right place, fixing the problem. The worst drivers leave all the grunt work up to you.

If Windows doesn't automatically recognize and install your newly attached piece of hardware — even after you restart your PC — follow these steps to locate and install a new driver:

1. **Visit the part manufacturer's website and download the latest Windows driver.**

You often find the manufacturer's website stamped somewhere on the part's box. If you can't find it, search for the part manufacturer's name on Google (www.google.com) and locate its website.

Look in the website's Support, Downloads, or Customer Service area. There, you usually need to enter your part's name, its model number, and your computer's operating system (Windows 10) before the website coughs up the driver.

No Windows 10 driver listed? Try downloading a Windows 8.1, 8, or 7 driver, instead — they sometimes work just as well.

2. **Run the driver's installation program.**

   Sometimes clicking your downloaded file makes its installation program jump into action, installing the driver for you. If so, you're through. If not, head to Step 3.

   If the downloaded file has a little zipper on the icon, right-click it and choose Extract All to *unzip* its contents into a new folder that contains the files. (Windows names that new folder after the file you've unzipped, making it easy to locate.)

3. **Right-click the Start button and choose Device Manager from the pop-up menu.**

   The Device Manager appears, listing an inventory of every part inside or attached to your computer. A yellow triangle with an embedded exclamation point icon appears next to the troublemaking part.

4. **Click your problematic device listed in the Device Manager window. Then click Action from the Device Manager's menu bar and choose Add Legacy Hardware from the drop-down menu.**

   The Add Hardware Wizard guides you through the steps of installing your new hardware and, if necessary, installing your new driver. Beware, though: This last-ditch method of reviving problematic parts can frustrate even experienced techies.

Luckily, you need to install drivers only in either of these two cases:

>> You've just bought and installed a new piece of hardware, and it's not working correctly. The drivers packaged with newly bought parts are usually old. Visit the manufacturer's website, download the latest driver, and install it. Chances are good that the new driver fixes problems with the first set of drivers.

>> You've plugged in a new gadget that Windows doesn't recognize. Tracking down and installing the latest driver can often fix the problems.

But if you're not having trouble with a piece of hardware, don't bother updating its driver, even if you find a newer one online. Chances are good that newer driver adds support only for newer models of the gadget you own. And that new driver might throw a glitch into something that was already working fine.

Finally, don't bother signing up for a service that claims to keep your computer up-to-date with the latest drivers. They can do more harm than good.

TIP

If your newly installed driver makes things even worse, there's a solution: Head back to Device Manager, double-click the troublesome part's name, and click the Driver tab on the Properties box. Keep your breathing steady. Then click the Roll Back Driver button. Windows ditches the newly installed driver and returns to the previous driver.

Chapter 14

Sharing One Computer with Several People

Windows allows several people to share one computer, laptop, or tablet without letting anybody peek into anybody else's files.

The secret? Windows grants each person his or her own *user account*, which neatly isolates that person's files. When a person types in his user account name and password, the computer looks tailor-made just for him: It displays his personalized desktop background, menu choices, programs, and files — and it forbids him from seeing items belonging to other users.

This chapter explains how to set up a separate user account for everybody in your home, including the computer's owner, family members, and roommates.

It also explains how to create accounts for children, which allow you to monitor their computer activity and set limits where you feel necessary.

Understanding User Accounts

Windows wants you to set up a *user account* for everybody who uses your PC. A user account works like a cocktail-party name tag that helps Windows recognize who's sitting at the keyboard. Windows offers two types of user accounts: Administrator and Standard. (It also offers a special Standard account for children.)

To begin playing with the PC, people click their account's name when the Windows Sign In screen first appears, as shown in Figure 14-1.

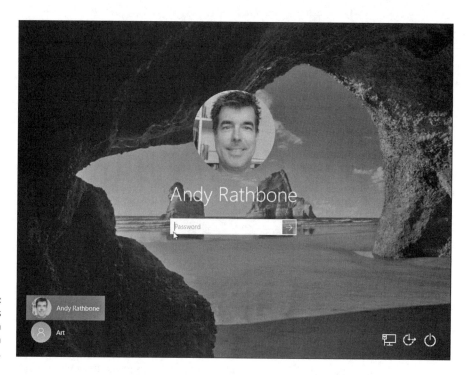

FIGURE 14-1:
Windows lets users sign in under their own accounts.

Who cares? Well, Windows gives each type of account permission to do different things on the computer. If the computer were a hotel, the Administrator account would belong to the desk clerk, and each tenant would have a Standard account. Here's how the different accounts translate into computer lingo:

>> **Administrator:** The administrator controls the entire computer, deciding who gets to play with it and what each user may do on it. On a computer running Windows, the owner usually holds the almighty Administrator account. He or she then sets up accounts for each household member and decides what they can and can't do with the PC.

- >> **Standard:** Standard account holders can access most of the computer, but they can't make any big changes to it. They can't run or install new programs, for example, but they can run existing programs.

- >> **Child:** The Child account setting is actually just a Standard account with the Microsoft Family settings automatically turned on. I cover Microsoft Family controls in Chapter 11.

- >> **Guest:** Windows 10 no longer offers guest accounts. These days, most visitors arrive toting their own smartphones, tablets, or both.

Here are some ways accounts are typically assigned when you're sharing the same computer under one roof:

- >> In a family, the parents usually hold Administrator accounts, and the kids usually have Standard accounts.

- >> In a dorm or shared apartment, the computer's owner holds the Administrator account, and the roommates have Standard accounts, depending on their trustworthiness level (and perhaps how clean they've left the kitchen that week).

To keep others from signing in under your user account, you must protect it with a password. (I describe how to choose a password for your account in this chapter's later "Setting Up Passwords and Security" section.)

TIP

Sometimes somebody will be signed in to her account, but the computer will go to sleep if she hasn't touched the keyboard for a while. When the computer wakes back up, only that person's user account and photo will show up onscreen. Windows 10 lists the other account holders' names in the screen's bottom-left corner, though, letting them sign in with a click on their names.

Changing or Adding User Accounts

Windows 10 offers two slightly different ways to add user accounts. It separates them into the two types of people you're most likely to add to your computer:

- >> **Family members:** By choosing this, you can automatically set up controls on your children's accounts. Any adults you add here will automatically be able to monitor your children's computer usage. All family members must have Microsoft accounts; if they don't already have them, the process helps you create them.

> » **Other members:** This type of account works best for roommates or other long-term guests who will be using your computer, but don't need monitoring or the ability to monitor children.

The next two sections describe how to create both types of accounts, as well as how to change existing accounts.

Only Administrator accounts can add new user accounts to a computer. If you don't have an Administrator account, ask the computer's owner to upgrade your account from Standard to Administrator.

Adding an account for a family member or friend

Adding a family member adds an important distinction to the account. If you add a child, the child's activity will be curtailed according to the limits you set. And if you add an adult, that person will also have the ability to monitor the activity of any added children.

If you want to add an account that's not involved in these family matters, choose the other option, called Adding an Account for Someone Else. There, you can create an account for a roommate or long-term guest.

Administrator account holders can create either type of account by following these steps:

1. **Click the Start button and click the Settings icon.**

2. **When the Settings app appears, click the Accounts icon.**

   The Accounts screen appears, as shown in Figure 14-2, offering ways to change your own account, as well as how to add accounts for other people.

3. **Click the words Family & Other People from the left pane. (If you're adding somebody who's *not* a family member, jump to Step 5.)**

   The right pane of the Family & Other People screen, shown in Figure 14-3, lets you create either of two accounts: One for a family member, or one for someone else. If you're creating an account for a family member, move to Step 4. If you're *not* adding a relative, jump ahead to Step 5.

4. **Choose Add a Family Member, and follow the steps to send the person an invitation.**

   A window appears, shown in Figure 14-4, asking if you're adding a child or an adult. Click the appropriate check box, then decide which email address to use for that person. You have several options:

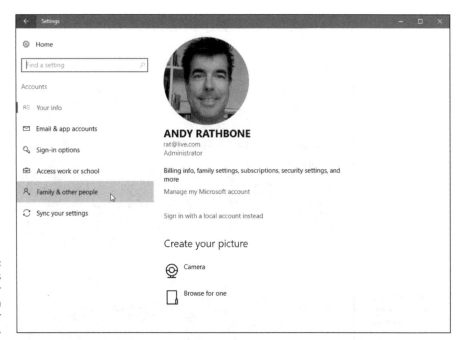

FIGURE 14-2:
Click the words
Family & Other
People to create a
new user
account.

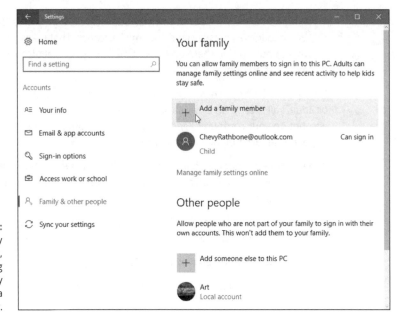

FIGURE 14-3:
Add family
members,
including
children, by
clicking Add a
Family Member.

- If you already know the person's email address, type it into the Enter Their E-mail Address box and click the Next button. (If the email address isn't already a Microsoft account, it will be turned into one.)

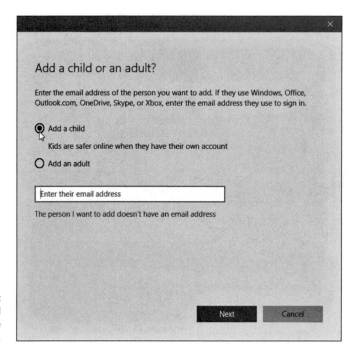

FIGURE 14-4:
Type in the email
address of the
family member.

- If you don't know the person's email address, click the words, The Person I Want to Invite Doesn't Have an E-mail Address. That takes you to a page where you can sign them up for an email address that also serves as a Microsoft account.

No matter which option you choose, your invited family member, either a child or adult, will receive an email saying they've been invited to have a family account on your computer. Once they accept the offer, they automatically appear as an account on your computer.

If they ignore the offer, or don't respond within two weeks, the offer becomes invalid. (If they still want an account after two weeks, you need to send them another invitation.)

At this point, you've finished adding a family member. To add somebody who's not a relative, move to Step 5.

5. **Choose Add Someone Else to Your PC.**

   Microsoft immediately complicates matters, as shown in the How Will This Person Sign In window in Figure 14-5, by asking for the new account holder's email address.

   Microsoft is trying to say that you can choose either of two types of accounts for your new account holder:

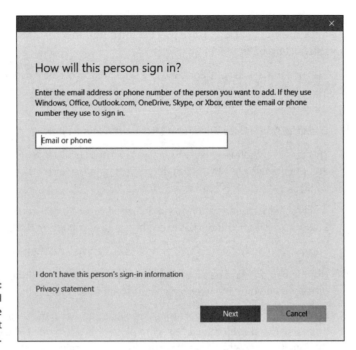

FIGURE 14-5:
Enter the email
address of the
person you want
to add.

- **Microsoft account:** A Microsoft account is required for many Windows 10 features. Described in Chapter 2, a Microsoft account is simply an email address that links to Microsoft, its computers, and its billing department. Only Microsoft account holders can download apps from the Windows Store app, store and retrieve files on an Internet storage space called OneDrive, and access other perks offered by a Microsoft account. To create a Microsoft account, go to Step 6.

- **Local account:** Select this option for people not interested in Microsoft accounts and their privileges. It lets the person use your computer with an account specific to your computer. To create a Local account, jump to Step 7.

TIP

Can't decide which type of account to create? Creating a Local account is always a safe bet. (Local account holders who want or need the advantages of a Microsoft account can upgrade to one at any time.)

6. **Type the email address of the new account holder's Microsoft account into the Email Address text box, click Next, and then click Finish.**

    The account will be waiting on the Sign In screen shown back in Figure 14-1.

    When the person wants to use the computer, he chooses the account bearing his email address and then types in his Microsoft account password. Windows visits the Internet, and if the email address and password match, the account is ready for action. You've finished.

7. **Click the words I Don't Have this Person's Sign-In Information, shown at the bottom of Figure 14-5.**

    Alarmed that you'd consider choosing a lowly Local account over the wondrous Microsoft account, Microsoft tries to make you create a Microsoft account for the new account.

8. **Click the Add a User Without a Microsoft Account link.**

    This tells Microsoft that yes, you really do want a Local account. (After all, Local account holders can always turn their account into a Microsoft account at any time.)

    A new screen appears, asking for a name for the account (username), the account's password, and a password hint in case you forget the password.

9. **Enter a username, password, and password hint and then click Next.**

    Use the person's first name or nickname for the username. Choose a simple password and hint; the user can change them after he signs in.

    Before you forget, tell the person his new username and password. (Or write them down and keep them in a secure place.) His username will be waiting at the Sign In screen's bottom-left corner for him to begin using the computer.

TIP

Windows normally creates Standard accounts for all new users whether or not they've signed in with a Microsoft or Local account. You can upgrade that later to an Administrator account if you want by changing the account, described in the next section.

Changing existing accounts

The Windows 10 Settings app lets you create a new account for a friend or family member, as described in the previous section. And it lets you tweak your own account, changing your account password or switching between a Microsoft or a Local account.

Administrators can even modify other accounts, changing them to either Standard or Administrator accounts, or even deleting them completely.

But if you want to have more control than that — the ability to change an existing account's name or password — you need the power of the desktop's Control Panel.

You can't change Microsoft accounts with these steps — those account holders must go online to do that — but you *can* change a Local account.

To change an existing user's Local account, follow these steps:

1. Right-click the Start button in the screen's bottom-left corner and choose Control Panel from the pop-up menu.

If you're a touchscreen user, hold down your finger on the Start button and tap the words Control Panel from the pop-up menu.

2. Click to open the Control Panel's User Accounts category.

3. Click the User Accounts link and then click the Manage Another Account link.

The Manage Accounts window appears, as shown in Figure 14-6, listing all the accounts on your computer.

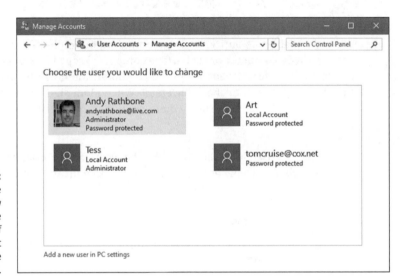

FIGURE 14-6: The Manage Accounts window lets you change the settings of other account holders on the computer.

4. Click the account you'd like to change.

Windows displays a page with the account's photo and lets you tweak the account's settings in any of these ways:

- **Change the Account Name:** Here's your chance to correct a misspelled name on an account. Or feel free to jazz up your own account name, changing Jane to Crystal Powers.

- **Create/Change a Password:** Every account should have a password to keep out other users. Here's your chance to add one or change the existing one.

- **Change the Account Type:** Head here to promote a Standard user of high moral character to an Administrator account or bump a naughty administrator down to Standard.

WARNING

- **Delete the Account:** Don't choose this option hastily, because deleting somebody's account also deletes all her files. If you *do* choose it, also choose the subsequent option that appears: Keep Files. That option places all of that person's files in a folder on your desktop for safekeeping.

- **Manage Another Account:** Save your current crop of changes and begin tweaking somebody else's account.

5. **When you're through, close the window by clicking the red X in its top-right corner.**

   Any changes made to a user's account take place immediately.

Switching Quickly between Users

Windows enables an entire family, roommates, or employees in a small office to share a single computer or tablet. The computer keeps track of everybody's programs while different people use the computer. Mom can be playing chess and then let Jerry sign in to check his email. When Mom signs back in a few minutes later, her chess match is right where she left it, pondering the sacrifice of her rook.

Known as *Fast User Switching*, switching between users works quickly and easily. When somebody else wants to sign in to his account for a moment, perhaps to check email, follow these steps:

1. **Open the Start menu.**

   To open the Start menu, click (or tap) the Start button or press the keyboard's Windows key ( ).

2. **Click your user account photo from along the screen's left edge.**

   A menu drops down, as shown in Figure 14-7.

3. **Choose the name of the user account holder who wants to sign in.**

   Windows leaves you signed in but immediately fetches the other person's account, letting him type in his password.

When that person finishes with the computer, he can sign out just as you did in Step 2 — by clicking his user account photo in the Start menu's left pane. This time, however, he'll choose Sign Out. Windows closes down his session, letting you sign back in with your own password. And when Windows reappears, so will your work, just as you left it.

FIGURE 14-7:
The menu lists
the names of all
user accounts
authorized to use
the computer.

TIP

Keep these tips in mind when juggling several people's accounts on a single PC:

» With all this user switching, you may forget whose account you're actually using. To check, open the Start menu. The current account holder's picture appear in the menu's left pane. (Hover your mouse over the picture to see the name.)

» To see other accounts currently signed in, open the Start menu and click the current account holder's name. A drop-down menu lists the other user accounts but places the words Signed In beneath the name of each account holder who's currently signed in.

WARNING

» Don't restart the PC while another person is still signed in, or that person will lose any work he hasn't saved. (Windows warns you before restarting the PC, giving you a chance to ask the other person to sign back in and save his work.)

» If a Standard account owner tries to change an important setting or install software, a window will appear, asking for Administrator permission. If you want to approve the action, just step over to the PC and type your password into the approval window. Windows lets you approve the change, just as if you'd done it while signed in with your own account.

Changing a User Account's Picture

Okay, now the important stuff: changing the boring picture that Windows automatically assigns to your user account. For every newly created user account, Windows chooses a generic silhouette. Feel free to change the picture to something more reflective of the Real You: You can snap a photo with your computer's webcam or choose any photo in your Pictures folder.

To change your user account's picture, head for the Start menu and click your picture along the menu's left edge. When the menu drops down, choose Change Account Settings. Windows presents the screen shown in Figure 14-8.

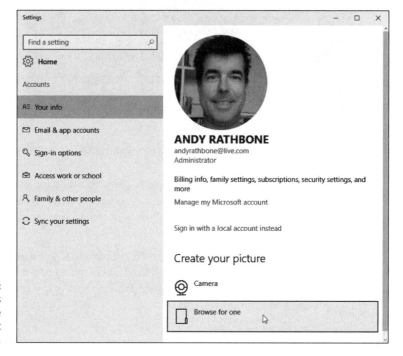

FIGURE 14-8:
Windows lets
each user choose
an account
picture.

The Accounts page lets you change your picture two main ways:

>> **Browse:** To assign a picture already on your computer, click the Browse button. A new window appears, showing photos in your Pictures folder. Click a desired picture and click the Choose Image button. Windows quickly slaps that picture atop your Start menu.

>> **Camera:** This option, available only for people with a camera attached to their computers, lets you take a quick selfie for your account photo.

TIP

Here are a few more tips for choosing your all-important account photo:

» After you've chosen an account photo, it attaches to your Microsoft account and anything you sign in to with that account: Your Microsoft phone, for example, Microsoft websites and programs, and any Windows computer you sign in to with your Microsoft account.

» You can grab any picture off the Internet and save it to your Pictures folder. Then click the Browse button mentioned earlier in this section to locate the picture and assign it as your account photo. (Right-click the Internet picture and, depending on your web browser, choose Save Picture As or a similar menu option.)

» Whenever you choose a new photo, Windows 10 saves the old one. In fact, it saves three photos, letting you return to them easily with a quick click.

» Don't worry about choosing a picture that's too large or too small. Windows automatically shrinks or expands the image to fit the space.

TIP

WHAT DOES MY MICROSOFT ACCOUNT KNOW ABOUT ME?

Like just about any other company in the world, Microsoft collects information about you. It really shouldn't be a surprise. Google, Facebook, and most websites gather information about you, as well. Your bank, Internet Service Provider, credit card, and insurance companies also stockpile information about you.

To combat your erosion of privacy, Microsoft lets you see what information it has stored about you, and it lets you delete portions you aren't comfortable seeing listed.

To do that, visit the Microsoft Privacy Center at https://account.microsoft.com/about and log in with your Microsoft account. There, you can view information about your billing and payments; renew, cancel, or subscribe to Microsoft services like OneDrive and Xbox Live; find your lost devices on a map; clear your Bing search history; and change your marketing preferences. Plus, you can check your kids' computer activity, provided you've set them up with a Microsoft account.

It's worth taking a look just to see what sort of information Microsoft stores, and make sure there aren't any surprises.

Setting Up Passwords and Security

There's not much point to having a user account if you don't have a password. Without one, Charles from the next cubicle can click your account on the Sign In screen, which gives him free reign to snoop through your files.

Administrators, especially, should have passwords. If they don't, they're automatically letting anybody wreak havoc with the PC: When a permission's screen appears, anybody can just press Enter at the password screen to gain entrance.

Microsoft account holders can change their passwords online by visiting www.live.com. Local account holders can create or change a password by following these steps:

1. **Click the Start button and click the Settings icon from the Start menu.**

2. **When the Settings app appears, click the Accounts icon.**

   The familiar Accounts window appears, shown earlier in Figure 14-2, showing ways to change your own account and change your account photo.

3. **Choose the Sign-in Options link from the Accounts window's left edge.**

   The Sign-In Options screen appears.

4. **In the Password section on the window's right side, click the Change button.**

   People who haven't created a password should instead click the Create a Password button.

5. **Make up an easy-to-remember password and type it into the New Password text box. Then retype the same characters into the Retype Password text box below it, and click Next.**

   Retyping the password eliminates the chance of typos.

Changing an existing password works slightly differently: The screen shows a Current Password text box where you must first type your existing password. (That keeps pranksters from sneaking over and changing your password during lunch hours.)

You can find out more about passwords in Chapter 2.

TIP

CREATING A PASSWORD RESET DISK

A Password Reset Disk serves as a key, letting you back into your computer in the event you've forgotten the password to your Local account. (You can't create a Password Reset Disk for a Microsoft account.) To create a Password Reset Disk, follow these simple steps:

1. **Insert a flash drive into a USB port and wait for Windows 10 to recognize it.**

2. **Click in the Search box by the Start button, type** Password Reset Disk, **and press Enter.**

3. **Click the Create a Password Reset Disk option that appears below the Search box.**

   The Forgotten Password Wizard appears and walks you through the process of creating a Password Reset Disk from a memory card or a USB flash drive.

When you forget your password, you can insert your Password Reset Disk as a key. Windows lets you in to choose a new password, and all will be joyous. Hide your Password Reset Disk in a safe place because it lets *anybody* into your account.

No matter how many times you change your password, your original Password Reset Disk still works, always providing a backup key to get into your account.

Signing in with Windows Hello

Password-protected accounts help keep your account secure, both from strangers on the Internet and people nearby. But very few people like to stop and type in a password — if they can even remember it.

Windows 10 tries to solve that problem with its new Windows Hello technology. Windows Hello lets you skip bothersome passwords and log in securely in less than a second. By attaching either a compatible camera or a fingerprint reader to your computer, you can log in with the swipe of a finger or a glance at the camera.

Some new laptops and PCs include built-in Windows Hello compatible readers and cameras; if yours doesn't, you can buy one that plugs into your computer's USB port.

To set up Windows Hello, follow these steps:

1. **Click the Start button, click the Settings icon (shown in the margin), and choose Accounts.**

   The Settings app's Accounts page appears.

2. **Click Sign-In Options from the left pane.**

   The screen shows your options for signing into your account, shown in Figure 14-9. If you don't see an option to set up Windows Hello, make sure your compatible fingerprint reader or camera is plugged into your computer and fully installed.

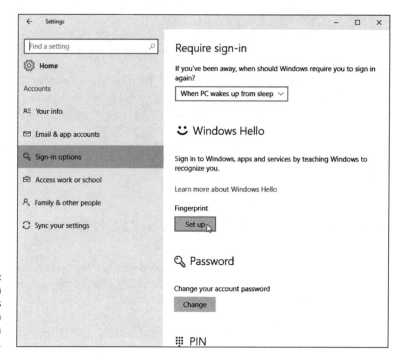

FIGURE 14-9: Choose an option from Windows Hello to sign in without a password.

3. **Click the Set Up button for either the fingerprint reader, or camera, and follow the instructions.**

   Windows walks you through scanning either your fingerprint (any finger will do, as long as you use that finger consistently when you want to sign in to your account), iris, or face. You may need to create a PIN, a four-digit number that adds an additional layer of security for special circumstances.

Windows Hello may seem more like science fiction than reality, but don't write it off too quickly. You'll appreciate Windows Hello for several reasons:

» Fingerprint readers are fairly inexpensive and easy to install. I bought mine on Amazon for $15, and it works amazingly well.

» Many new laptops come with fingerprint readers already installed near the keyboard area. Some tablets, too, include fingerprint readers built-into their clip-on keyboards.

» Windows 10 recognizes most compatible fingerprint readers as soon as they're plugged into your computer's USB port. You rarely need to install any bundled software.

» Whenever you face a Windows 10 sign-in screen, just slide your finger across the reader. The screen quickly clears, and you're ready for work. You don't need to remember or type in a complicated password. There's nothing to forget.

» Windows Hello not only lets you sign into your device, but buy things in the Windows Store, all without typing in a password.

» As the Windows Hello technology grows, Windows Hello may eventually let you enter your favorite password-protected websites, as well.

Chapter 15

Connecting Computers with a Network

B uying yet another PC can bring yet another computing problem: How can two or more PCs share the same Internet connection and printer? And how do you share your files between your two PCs?

The solution involves a *network*. When you connect two or more computers, Windows introduces them to each other, automatically letting them swap information, share an Internet connection, and print through the same printer.

Today, most computers can connect without anybody tripping over cables. Known as *Wi-Fi* or *wireless*, this option lets your computers chatter through the airwaves like radio stations that broadcast and take requests.

This chapter explains how to link a houseful of computers so that they can share things. After you've created a wireless network, you can share your Internet connection with not only your Windows PCs but also smartphones, tablets, and other computerized gadgets. And, if you choose to give the password to your visitors, even they can connect to the Internet.

Be forewarned, however: This chapter contains some pretty advanced stuff. Don't tread here unless you're running an Administrator account and you don't mind doing a little head-scratching as you wade from conceptualization to actualization to, "Hey, it works!"

Understanding a Network's Parts

A *network* is simply two or more computers that have been connected so that they can share things. Although computer networks range from pleasingly simple to agonizingly complex, they all have three things in common:

>> **A router:** This little box works as an electronic traffic cop, controlling the flow of information between each computer, as well as between your network and the Internet. Almost all modern routers support both wired and wireless networks.

>> **A network adapter:** Every computer needs its own network adapter — an electronic mouthpiece of sorts. A wired network adapter lets you plug in a cable; the cable's other end plugs into your router. A wireless network adapter translates your computer's information into radio signals and broadcasts them to the router.

>> **Network cables:** Computers connecting wirelessly don't need cables, of course. But computers without wireless adapters need cables to connect them to the router.

When you plug a modem into the router, the router quickly distributes the Internet signal to every computer on your network. (Some modems come with built-in routers, sparing you from having to connect the two.)

Most home networks resemble a spider, as shown in Figure 15-1, with some computers' cables connecting to the router in the center. Other computers, laptops, tablets, and gadgets connect wirelessly to the same router.

The router divides its attention among networked computers efficiently, letting every computer simultaneously share a single Internet connection.

Windows lets every computer share a single printer, as well. If two people try to print something simultaneously, Windows stashes one person's files until the printer is free and then sends them automatically when the printer is ready for more work.

TIP

CHOOSING BETWEEN WIRED AND WIRELESS NETWORKS

You can easily string cables between computers that sit on the same desk or live within one room. Beyond that, though, cables quickly become messy. To cut the clutter, most computers today include *wireless (Wi-Fi)* adapters, which let the computers chatter through the air.

But just as radio broadcasts fade as you drive out of the city, wireless signals also fade. The more they fade, the slower the connection becomes. If your wireless signals pass through more than two or three walls, your computers may not be able to communicate. Wireless networks are also more difficult to set up than wired networks.

Although wireless connections are popular, wired connections work more quickly, efficiently, securely, and inexpensively than wireless. But if your spouse wants the cables removed from the hallways, wireless may be your best option. For best results, combine the two: Connect adjacent computers with cables and use wireless for the rest.

REMEMBER

Wireless routers deliver an Internet signal to *all* connected wireless gadgets, not just Windows computers. After you set up your router, it also delivers your Internet signal to iPads and other tablets, Apple computers, smartphones, and even some home theater devices (such as Blu-ray players, game consoles, televisions, and streaming video gadgets such as a Chromecast or Roku box).

Setting Up a Small Network

If you're trying to set up a lot of computers — more than ten — you probably need a more advanced book. Networks are fairly easy to set up, but sharing their resources can be scary stuff, especially if the computers contain sensitive material. But if you're just trying to set up a few computers in your home or home office, this information may be all you need.

So without further blabbing, here's a low-carb, step-by-step list of how to set up a small and inexpensive network. The following sections show how to buy the three parts of a network, install the parts, and make Windows create a network out of your handiwork.

Buying parts for a network

Visit the computer store across town or online, buy this stuff, and you're well on your way to setting up your network:

>> **Network adapters (optional):** Because most new computers and laptops include both wired *and* wireless adapters, you can probably cross this off your shopping list. But if you need to add an adapter, pick up an inexpensive wired or wireless adapter that plugs into the computer's USB port. (Mobile devices like laptops, tablets, and smartphones *all* include built-in wireless adapters.)

>> **Network cable (optional):** Not using wireless? Then buy *Ethernet* cables, which resemble phone cables but with slightly thicker jacks. Buy a cable for each computer you want to connect. The cables must be long enough to reach from the computer to the router, described next.

>> **Router:** This little box does all the magic. Most routers today include built-in wireless; many also include a broadband modem for Internet access. Wireless routers usually include four jacks to accommodate up to four nearby computers relying on cables.

TIP

Some Internet service providers (ISPs) supply you with a wireless router/modem, and they even send a techie to your home to set up your network for you. It never hurts to ask.

Setting up a wireless router

Wireless connections bring a convenience felt by every cellphone owner. But with computers, a wireless connection also brings complication. You're basically setting up a radio transmitter that broadcasts to little radios inside your computers. You need to worry about signal strength, finding the right signal, and even entering passwords to keep outsiders from eavesdropping.

Unfortunately, different brands of wireless routers come with different setup software, so there's no way I can provide step-by-step instructions for setting up your particular router.

However, every router requires you to set up these three things:

>> **Network name (SSID):** Enter a short, easy-to-remember name here to identify your particular wireless network. Later, when connecting to the wireless network with your computer, smartphone, or tablet, you'll select this same name to avoid accidentally connecting with your neighbor's wireless network.

>> **Infrastructure:** Of the two choices, choose Infrastructure instead of the rarely used alternative, Ad Hoc.

>> **Security:** To keep out snoops, this option uses a password to encrypt your data as it flies through the air. Most routers offer at least three types of password options: WEP is barely better than no password, WPA is better, and WPA2 is better still. Choose the strongest security option available and create a memorable password with mixed characters, such as **One+One=2!**.

Some routers include an installation program to help you change these settings; other routers contain built-in software that you access with your web browser in Windows.

REMEMBER

As you set each of the preceding three settings, write them on a piece of paper: You must enter these same three settings when setting up the wireless connection on each of your computers and other wireless gadgets, a job tackled in the next section. You also need to pass out that information to any houseguests who want to piggyback on your Internet connection while they visit.

Setting up Windows computers to connect to a network

First, a word to the wired crowd: If you've chosen to connect a computer to your router with a cable, plug one end of the cable into your computer's network port. Plug the cable's other end into one of your router's network ports. (The ports are usually numbered; any number will do.) To connect other computers to the same router, connect cables between those computers' network ports and the router's other empty network ports.

If your Internet company didn't do it for you, plug a cable from your broadband modem's LAN or Ethernet port into your router's WAN port. (If your router and modem live together in one box, you can skip this step.)

Turn on your router, and you've finished: You've discovered how easy it is to create a wired network. (Be sure to set up a Homegroup, described later in this chapter, so your computers can begin sharing their files.)

Wireless is a different story. After you set up your router to broadcast your network wirelessly, you must tell Windows how to receive it. Chapter 9 offers the full course in connecting to wireless networks, both your own and those you'll find in public, but here's an abbreviated version for connecting to your own network:

1. **Click the Start button and choose the Settings icon from the Start menu.**

2. **When the Settings screen appears, click the Network & Internet icon, then click the Show Available Networks link.**

    The Network & Internet page lists whether you're connected to the Internet, and offers a Troubleshoot button for fixing common connection problems.

    Click the Show Available Networks link, and Windows quickly sniffs the airwaves for nearby wireless networks. The taskbar's Wireless Networking icon, shown in Figure 15-2, quickly pops up with a list of all the wireless networks within range of your computer, including, with any luck, your own. (Your network will be the name — the *SSID* — that you chose when setting up your router, described in the previous section.)

3. **Choose the desired wireless network by clicking its name and then clicking the Connect button.**

    The closest wireless network is usually the strongest, so you'll probably spot your own wireless network at the top of the list.

TIP

    If you select the adjacent Connect Automatically check box before clicking the Connect button, Windows automatically connects to that network the next time you're within range, sparing you from following all these steps again.

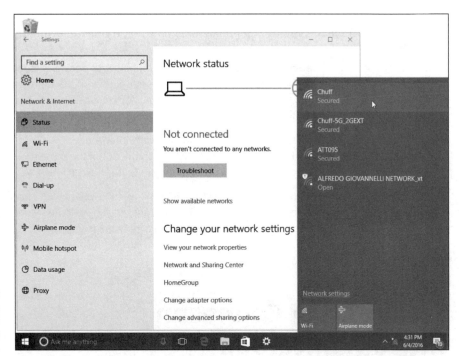

4. **Enter a password and click Next.**

   Here's where you type in the same password you entered into your router when setting up your wireless network. (To confuse things, Windows 10 refers to your password as a "Network Security Key.")

   If your router has a little button labelled *WPS* (Wi-Fi Protected Setup), you can press it at this point. The router then slips the password to your PC through the airwaves, sparing you from having to type it in.

   TIP

   When first released, Windows 10 offered to let you share a wireless network's password with all of your contacts. That feature didn't go over well, and Microsoft removed it a few months later.

   NEW

At this point, Windows 10 treats your newly joined wireless network as a *public* network, the same as one you'd find in a coffee shop or airport. You won't be able to find or access your other networked computers until you create a Homegroup, covered in the next section.

If Windows asks to make your computer discoverable, choose Yes: You're in your own home, and you want your other computers to be able to swap files. But if you're connecting to somebody else's network — a public network, for example, click No. You only want your PC to be discoverable when on your *own* network.

TIP

If you're still having problems connecting, try the following tips:

>> Head back to Step 2 and click the Troubleshoot button. Windows 10 performs some basic diagnostics, and resets your networking equipment. If the troubleshooter can't fix the problem, it offers clues as to the connection-robbing culprit.

>> Cordless phones and microwave ovens interfere with wireless networks, oddly enough. Try to keep your cordless phone out of the same room as your wireless computer, and don't heat up that sandwich when web browsing.

 >> From the Windows desktop, the taskbar's wireless network icon (shown in the margin) provides a one-click way to see available wirelessly networks. If your desktop's taskbar contains a wireless network icon, click it and jump to Step 3 above.

Setting Up or Connecting with a Homegroup

Creating a network between your computers makes it easier for them to share resources, such as an Internet connection, printers, and even your files. But how can you share some files while keeping others private?

Microsoft's solution is called a *Homegroup.* A simpler way of networking, a Homegroup lets every Windows PC in the house share the things nearly everybody wants to share: music, photos, movies, and the household printer. Set up a Homegroup, and Windows automatically begins sharing those items. The Homegroup strategically leaves out the folder you probably *don't* want to share: your Documents folder.

Homegroups work with any Windows 7, 8, and 8.1 computers on your network, as well. (Homegroups *don't* work with Windows Vista or Windows XP, unfortunately.)

Depending on your network, you may be invited to join a Homegroup as soon as your computer connects with your router. If so, jump to Step 2.

Here's how to set up a new Homegroup on your Windows PC as well as how to let Windows join a Homegroup you may have already set up with your other networked computers:

1. **Right-click the Start button and choose Control Panel from the pop-up menu.**

2. **When the Control Panel appears, click the Network and Internet icon. When the Network and Internet page appears, click HomeGroup from the right pane.**

   Can't find the Homegroup setting? Then type **homegroup** into the Settings' window's Search box, located in the window's upper-right corner. When the word HomeGroup appears in the Search Results, click it to open the Homegroup window.

3. **In the Homegroup window, click the Change Network Location link, and click the Yes button in the pane that appears on the right.**

   When you first connect to a wireless network, Windows assumes it's a public network, perhaps at a coffee shop. Naturally, Windows also assumes you don't want anybody to snoop through your computer, so it leaves your PC "undiscoverable." That means nobody can find it on the network, and, you won't be able to find anybody else's computer.

   Choosing Yes, shown in Figure 15-3, tells Windows that you're on a private network where you *want* to share things like files and printers.

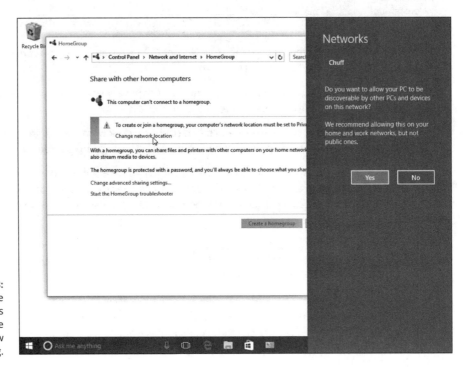

FIGURE 15-3:
Click Yes to make
your wireless
network private
and allow
sharing.

4. Click either the Create a Homegroup or Join Now button.

If you see a Create a Homegroup button, click it to create a new Homegroup.

If you see a Join Now button (as shown in Figure 15-4), somebody has already created a Homegroup on your network. To join it, click the Join Now button.

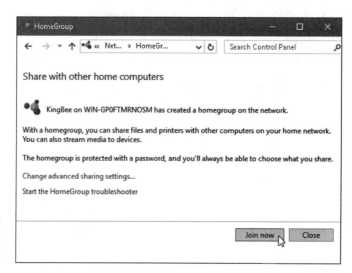

FIGURE 15-4: Click Join Now to join an existing Homegroup.

Whether you click the Join Now or Create a Homegroup button, Windows asks what items you'd like to share.

If you're asked to change the network privacy settings on your computer, be sure to choose Private rather than Public.

5. Choose the items you'd like to share, click Next, and, if joining an existing Homegroup, type in your network's Homegroup password.

Shown in Figure 15-5, the window lets you select the folders and other items you want to share with your Homegroup family. To share an item, choose Share from its adjacent drop-down menu. To keep items private, choose Not Shared.

Most people want to share *everything* listed except for their Documents folder. Unlike the Music and Videos folders, the Documents folder usually contains more private material.

REMEMBER

Sharing a folder simply lets other people access that folder's files to view the pictures or watch a video, for example. They can neither change nor delete those files, nor can they create or place any files in your folder. They can, however, make copies of those files for themselves.

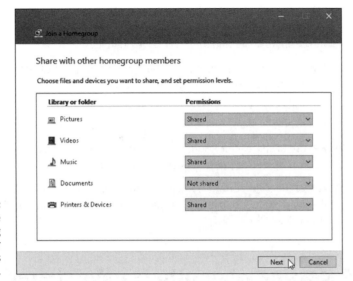

Share with other homegroup members

Choose files and devices you want to share, and set permission levels.

Library or folder	Permissions
Pictures	Shared ⌄
Videos	Shared ⌄
Music	Shared ⌄
Documents	Not shared ⌄
Printers & Devices	Shared ⌄

Next | Cancel

FIGURE 15-5:
Most people share everything but their Documents folder.

TIP

If you're joining an existing Homegroup, type in the Homegroup's existing password. Don't know the password? On a Windows 7, 8, or 8.1 computer, find the password by opening any folder, right-clicking the word HomeGroup in the folder's left pane, and choosing View the Homegroup Password. (The password is case sensitive, so make sure you capitalize the correct letters.)

If you're joining an existing Homegroup, you're finished.

6. **If you clicked the Create a Homegroup button, take note of the password listed at the closing screen.**

You must enter that same password into each computer you want to include in your Homegroup. Leave your computer turned on and follow these steps on your other computers to join the Homegroup you've just created.

When you're through with these steps, you've created or joined a Homegroup that's accessible from every Windows 10, 8.1, 8, and 7 PC on your network. You've also set up your PC to allow its Music, Photos, and Videos folders to be shared, something I describe in the next section.

Hailing strictly from the world of Windows, Homegroups won't allow you to share items with iPads, or smartphones. For sharing files between those devices, download their OneDrive app, which I cover in Chapter 5.

>> When you create or join a Homegroup, you're choosing which folders to share only from your own account. If other account holders on that PC also want to share their folders, they should do this while logged on with their account: Open any folder, right-click Homegroup in the Navigation Pane, and choose

Change HomeGroup Settings. There they can add check marks to the items they want to share and then click Save Changes.

>> Changed your mind about your Homegroup settings? Follow the preceding steps to change which items you'd like to share.

>> After choosing to join a Homegroup, you may need to wait a few minutes until you're able to share files or printers with your networked computers.

>> Be sure to share your Printers & Devices in Step 5. That lets anybody on your network share the printer attached to your computer.

>> Forgot the all-important Homegroup password? Open any folder, right-click the word Homegroup in the Navigation Pane, and then choose View the HomeGroup Password.

Accessing what others have shared

To see the shared folders of other people on your PC and network, click the File Explorer icon (shown in the margin), found on the taskbar that runs along the bottom of every screen.

When File Explorer appears, click the word Homegroup, found in the Navigation Pane along File Explorer's left edge. The right side of the window, shown in Figure 15-6, promptly lists the names and icons of every account holder on your PC who has chosen to share files.

You may also spot names of account holders on *networked* Windows PCs — PCs connected to your own PC either wirelessly or with cables — who've chosen to share their files.

To browse the files shared by another person within the Homegroup, double-click that person's name from the Homegroup window. The window promptly displays that person's shared folders, as shown in Figure 15-7, ready to be browsed as if they were your own.

You can do more than browse those files, as described here:

>> **Opening:** To open a file on a shared folder, double-click its icon, just as you would any other file. The appropriate program opens it. If you see an error message, the sharing person created the file using a program you don't own. Your solution? Buy or download the program from the Internet or ask the person to save the file in a format that one of your programs can open.

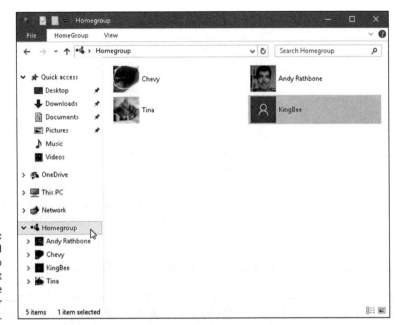

FIGURE 15-6:
Click the word
Homegroup to
see any account
holders who've
shared their
folders.

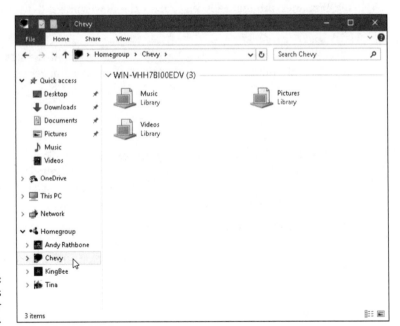

FIGURE 15-7:
Click a person's
name to see her
shared files.

>> **Copying:** To copy a file from one person's Homegroup, drag it into your own folder: Point at the file you want and, while holding down the mouse button, point at your own folder. Let go of the mouse button, and Windows copies the file into your folder. Alternatively, right-click the file's icon and choose Copy from the pop-up menu; then right-click inside the destination folder and choose Paste from the pop-up menu.

>> **Deleting or changing:** You can't delete or change the items in another person's Homegroup folder. If you need to change something, copy it to your own computer's folder and then make your changes on that copy.

Homegroups simplify sharing files among computers, but Homegroups work only with PCs and tablets running Windows 7, 8, 8.1, or 10, unfortunately.

Sharing a printer on the network

If you've created a Homegroup, covered earlier in this chapter, Windows makes sharing a printer extraordinarily easy. After you plug a USB printer — the kind with the connector shown in the margin — into one of your Windows PCs, you're set: Windows automatically recognizes the newly plugged-in printer as soon as it's turned on.

Plus, your Windows PC quickly spreads the news to all the PCs in your Homegroup. Within minutes, that printer's name and icon appear on all those PCs and in all their programs' print menus.

Here's how to see that printer on your other networked Windows PCs:

>> **Windows 10:** Click the Start button and click Settings. When the Settings app appears, click the Devices icon (shown in the margin). When the Devices page appears, click the word Printers along the left edge to see all of the printers available to your computer, including the shared printer.

>> **Windows 8 or 8.1:** Right-click in the screen's bottom-left corner and choose Control Panel from the pop-up menu. From the Control Panel's Hardware and Sound category, click View Devices and Printers. The networked printer appears in the Printers section.

>> **Windows 7:** Click the Start button and choose Devices and Printers. The networked printer appears in the Printers and Faxes section.

5

Music, Photos, and Movies

Chapter 16

Playing and Copying Music

B uilt for minimalists, the Windows 10 Music Groove app sticks to the essentials. With a few clicks, it plays music stored both on your computer and OneDrive. If you pay a monthly fee for Microsoft's Groove Music Pass, you can listen to Internet radio stations based around your favorite artist.

For some, that's plenty. But the Groove Music app lacks more robust features. Stuck in a world of digital files, the Groove Music app can't copy music CDs onto your computer. It can't create CDs from your music files. It can't even *play* a music CD you've slipped into your PC's disc drive.

That's fine for Windows tablets and many new laptops; they lack disc drives, so their owners naturally embrace digital music.

On a desktop PC, however, you probably want to stick with the program from yesteryear, Windows Media Player. Windows Media Player works much like it did in earlier Windows versions with one big exception: It can no longer play DVDs.

This chapter explains how and when to jump between the Groove Music app and Windows Media Player. It also explains when you might want to jump ship with the standard Windows options and download a more full-featured app to meet your music needs.

Playing Music with the Groove Music app

In keeping with the music of today's youth, the Windows Groove Music app recognizes music files only if they're stored on either your PC, OneDrive, or, when told, a flash drive you've placed into your computer's USB port. The Groove Music app turns up its nose at playing those old-fashioned CDs or DVDs, so don't even try.

But if you simply want to play or buy digital music, the Groove Music app handles the job fairly simply and easily. When first opened, as shown in Figure 16-1, the program shows the music stored both on your own PC and — if you have a Microsoft account — in your OneDrive account's Music folder.

To launch the Groove Music app and begin listening to music, follow these steps:

1. **Click the Start menu's Groove Music tile.**

   Fetch the Start menu with a click of the Start button in the screen's lower-left corner. When the Start menu appears, click the Groove Music app's tile, shown in the margin.

   If you don't spot the Groove Music app's tile, choose Groove Music from the Start menu's list of alphabetically sorted apps.

   Don't see the Start menu's alphabetically sorted list of apps? Then your computer is running in Tablet mode. Reveal the apps list by clicking the Start menu's All Apps icon (shown in the margin).

   When launched, the Groove Music app fills the screen, as shown earlier in Figure 16-1, with automatically showing tiles representing your albums, artists, or songs. (When opened for the first time, you may need to click through some welcome screens.)

2. **View your music by album, song, or artist.**

   The Navigation pane along the left edge of the Groove Music app offers these options for viewing your music:

NEW

   - **Your Groove:** Click here to see playlists created by the Groove app itself. The app creates a playlist based on recently played items, for example, as well as playlists based on music in your collection. For example, the app looked at my music and then created new playlists called Post-Bob, Blue Jazz, Focus While You Work, and Morning Blend.

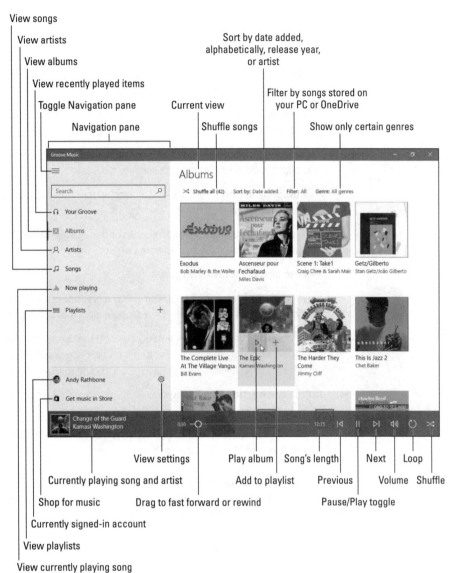

View songs

View artists

View albums

View recently played items

Toggle Navigation pane

Navigation pane

Sort by date added,
alphabetically, release year,
or artist

Current view

Filter by songs stored on
your PC or OneDrive

Shuffle songs

Show only certain genres

View settings

Play album

Song's length

Next

Loop

Currently playing song and artist

Add to playlist

Previous

Volume   Shuffle

Shop for music

Drag to fast forward or rewind

Pause/Play toggle

Currently signed-in account

View playlists

View currently playing song

FIGURE 16-1:
The Groove Music
app plays music
stored on your
PC, as well as on
OneDrive.

- **Albums:** Click Albums from the Navigation pane, and the Groove Music app displays a tile for each of your albums, complete with the album cover on the tile.

- **Artists:** Choose this and the tiles switch to show artists' names, with a picture of a different artist on each tile. It's a handy way to binge listen to your favorite artist.

- **Songs:** This lets you view your entire list of songs, handy when creating a custom playlist for a night's entertainment.

- **Now Playing:** Choose this to see your currently played song, as well as a list of songs that are queued to play next.

- **Playlists:** Playlists *you* create appear here, ready to be played again with a click of their names.

Two additional options appear only to subscribers of the Groove Music Pass, Microsoft's paid music streaming service:

- **Radio:** Head here to create customized streaming music based around favorite albums or artists.

- **Explore:** This leads to a curated area of the Groove Music Pass, letting you check out newly added or featured artists.

3. **Tell the app what music to play.**

Hover your mouse over any tile, and a Play icon appears. Click it to start playing everything contained in the tile, be it a single album or an artist's entire work.

An adjacent Plus sign icon lets you quickly add that item to the current playlist or a new playlist. By hovering over items and clicking the Plus sign, you can quickly create a playlist that will keep you listening to music for hours.

4. **Adjust the music while it plays.**

The App bar, shown along the bottom of Figure 16-1, offers you several icons to control your music: Shuffle, Repeat, Previous (to move to the previous song), Play/Pause, and Next (to move to the next song).

To adjust the volume, click the little speaker on the App bar in the screen's bottom corner. Or, from the desktop, click the little speaker icon next to the clock on the taskbar, that strip along the desktop's bottom edge.

Most touchscreen tablets include a volume toggle switch built in to one of their edges.

The Groove Music app keeps playing music even if you begin working with other apps or switch to the desktop. To pause or move between tracks, you must return to the Groove Music app. (A tap on the taskbar's Task View icon lets you relocate it easily.)

Handing Music-Playing Chores Back to Windows Media Player

Microsoft hopes that the Groove Music app and its easy-to-reach link to the Store app's music marketplace will be a big moneymaker. Accordingly, Windows tries to shoehorn you into using the Groove Music app. Open a music file from your desktop's Music folder, for example, and the Start menu's Groove Music app butts in to play the file.

With its large and simple controls, the Groove Music app works fine on touch-screen tablets. However, when you switch to the desktop, you may prefer a more full-featured music program. Luckily, Windows 10 still includes Windows Media Player, a Windows desktop staple for a decade.

You can hand your computer's music-playing chores back to the tried-and-true Windows Media player, but it's not easy: Windows 10 hides the program's name on the Start menu.

Follow the steps in this section to hand your music-playing chores back to Windows Media Player and to make the program easier to find.

1. **Click the Start button, and when the Start menu appears, click the words All Apps in the menu's bottom-left corner.**

   The Start menu presents an alphabetical list of *all* your installed apps and programs.

    Don't see the Start menu's alphabetically sorted list of apps? Then your computer is running in Tablet mode, which requires you to click the Start menu's All Apps icon (shown in the margin).

2. **Scroll down the Start menu's list of apps, and click the Windows Accessories entry. When the menu drops down, right-click the Windows Media Player tile (shown in the margin) and choose Pin to Start from the bottom menu.**

   That places Windows Media Player's icon as a tile on your Start menu for easy access. (The same right-click menu lets you choose More and select Pin to Taskbar; that places a second link to Windows Media Player on your taskbar, the strip that runs along the bottom of the screen.)

    If you're using a touchscreen, hold down your finger on the Start menu's Windows Media Player entry for a moment and then lift your finger. When the pop-up menu appears, choose Pin to Taskbar.

   TIP

3. **Click the Start menu's Settings icon to fetch the Settings app.**

   The Settings icon, shown in the margin, brings the Settings app to the screen.

4. **When the Settings app appears, click the System icon and then click Default Apps.**

   The right pane lists the apps and programs currently assigned to handle your email, music, videos, and other items.

5. **In the right pane's Music Player section, click the Groove Music app. When the pop-up menu appears, click Windows Media Player, as shown in Figure 16-2.**

   This step tells Windows Media Player to play your music instead of the Start menu's Groove Music app.

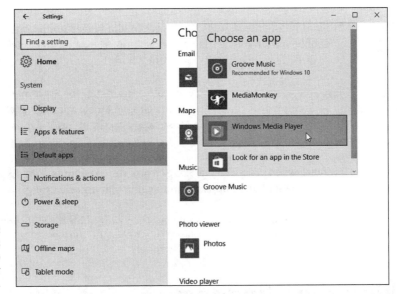

FIGURE 16-2:
Choose Windows
Media Player to
let it play your
music.

TIP

RUNNING WINDOWS MEDIA PLAYER FOR THE FIRST TIME

The first time you open the desktop's Windows Media Player, an opening screen asks how to deal with the player's settings for privacy, storage, and the music store. The screen offers two options:

- **Recommended Settings:** Designed for the impatient, this option loads Windows Media Player with Microsoft's chosen settings in place. Windows Media Player sets itself up as the default player for most of your music and video, but *not* your MP3 files. (The Groove Music app still holds title to those, the most common digital music format.) Windows Media Player will sweep the Internet to update your songs' title information, and it tells Microsoft what you're listening to and watching. Choose Express if you're in a hurry; you can always customize the settings some other time.

- **Custom Settings:** Aimed at the fine-tuners and the privacy-conscious folks, this choice lets you micromanage Windows Media Player's behavior. A series of screens lets you choose the types of music and video that the player can play, and you can control how much of your listening habits should be sent to Microsoft. Choose this option only if you have time to wade through several minutes of boring option screens.

If you later want to customize any Windows Media Player settings — either those chosen for you in Express setup or the ones you've chosen in Custom setup — click Windows Media Player's Organize button in the top-left corner and choose Options.

After you follow these steps, Windows Media Player jumps into action whenever you double-click a music file on the desktop. You can also launch Windows Media Player directly by clicking its icon (shown in the margin) on your taskbar.

REMEMBER

These steps don't permanently disable or uninstall the Start menu's Groove Music app — it still works fine. To open the Groove Music app, just click its tile from the Start menu. When the Groove Music app appears, it still displays and plays all of your music.

However, when you click a song from the desktop's File Explorer program, Windows Media Player pops up and begins playing your song.

Follow these same steps to choose other programs to open your favorite files. You're not limited to the choices Microsoft set up with Windows 10.

Stocking the Windows Media Player Library

You can load Windows Media Player by double-clicking its icon in the Start menu or taskbar, that strip along the desktop's bottom edge. No icon in the Start menu or taskbar? The previous section explains how to put it there.

When you run Windows Media Player, the program automatically sorts through your computer's stash of digital music, pictures, and videos, automatically cataloging everything it finds.

But if you've noticed that some of your PC's media is missing from the Windows Media Player Library, you can tell the player where to find those items by following these steps:

Note: Unlike the Groove Music app, Windows Media Player can play OneDrive files only if they are synced to your PC. It can't play music files that are available on OneDrive only through the Internet.

1. **Click Windows Media Player's Organize button (in the program's top, left corner) and choose Manage Libraries from the drop-down menu to reveal a pop-out menu.**

   The pop-out menu lists the four types of media that Windows Media Player can handle: Music, Videos, Pictures, and Recorded TV.

2. **From the pop-out menu, choose the name of the type of files you're missing.**

A window appears, as shown in Figure 16-3, listing your monitored folders. For example, the player normally monitors the contents of your Music folder, so anything you add to your Music folder automatically appears in the Media Player Library, as well.

FIGURE 16-3:
Click the Add button and browse to a new folder you want Windows Media Player to monitor.

But if you're storing items elsewhere — perhaps on a portable hard drive, flash drive, network location, or your Public folder — here's your chance to give the player directions to that other media stash.

3. **Click the Add button, select the folder or drive containing your files, click the Include Folder button, and click OK.**

Clicking the Add button brings the Include Folder in Music window to the screen. Navigate to the folder you'd like to add — the folder on your portable hard drive, for example — and click the Include Folder button. Windows Media Player immediately begins monitoring that folder, adding the folder's music to its library.

To add music from even more folders or drives — perhaps a folder on another networked PC or a flash drive — repeat these steps until you've added all the places Windows Media Player should search for media.

To stop the player from monitoring a folder, follow these steps, but in Step 3, click the folder you no longer want monitored and then click the Remove button shown in Figure 16-3.

When you run Windows Media Player, the program shows the media it has collected (shown in Figure 16-4) and it continues to stock its library in the following ways:

FIGURE 16-4:
Click an item
from the left to
see its contents
on the right.

>> **Monitoring your folders:** Windows Media Player constantly monitors your Music, Pictures, and Videos folders, as well as any other locations you've added. Windows Media Player automatically updates its library whenever you add or remove files from your folders. (You can change what folders Windows Media Player monitors by following the three preceding steps.)

>> **Adding played items:** Anytime you play a music file on your PC or from the Internet, Windows Media Player adds the song or its Internet location to its library so that you can find it to play again later. Unless specifically told to, Windows Media Player doesn't add recently played items residing on other people's PCs, USB flash drives, or memory cards. (It can't play any music from OneDrive unless you've chosen to keep that music in sync with your PC, which I cover in Chapter 5.)

>> **Ripped music from CD:** When you insert a music CD into your CD drive, Windows may offer to rip it. That's computereze for copying the CD's music to your PC, a task described in the "Ripping (Copying) CDs to Your PC" section,

later in this chapter. Any ripped music automatically appears in your Windows Media Player Library. (Windows Media Player won't copy DVD movies to your library, unfortunately, nor does it play the discs.)

>> **Downloaded music from online stores:** When you buy a song and place it in your Music folder, Windows Media Player automatically stocks its library with your latest purchase.

Feel free to repeat the steps in this section to search for files whenever you want. Windows Media Player ignores the files it has already cataloged and adds any new ones.

Windows Media Player doesn't offer an advanced editor for changing a song's *tags*, which are described in the nearby sidebar. Instead, the player edits them for you automatically from an online database.

WHAT ARE A SONG'S TAGS?

Inside every music file lives a small form called a *tag* that contains the song's title, artist, album, and other related information. When deciding how to sort, display, and categorize your music, Windows Media Player reads those tags — *not* the songs' filenames. Nearly every digital music player, including the iPod, also relies on tags.

Tags are so important, in fact, that Windows Media Player visits the Internet, grabs song information, and automatically fills in the tags when it adds files to its library.

Many people don't bother filling out their songs' tags, but other people update them meticulously. If your tags are already filled out the way you prefer, stop Windows Media Player from messing with them: Click the Organize button, choose Options, click the Library tab, and deselect the check box next to Retrieve Additional Information From The Internet. If your tags are a mess, leave that check box selected so that the player will clean up the tags for you.

If Windows Media Player makes a mistake, fix the tags yourself: Right-click the song (or, in the case of an album, the selected songs) and choose Find Album Info. When a window appears listing the player's guess as to the song or album, choose the Edit link. In the new window that appears, you can fill in the album, artist, genre, tracks, title, contributing artist, and composer. Click Done when you're through tidying up the information.

Browsing Windows Media Player's Libraries

The Windows Media Player Library is where the behind-the-scenes action takes place. There, you organize files, create playlists, burn or copy CDs, and choose what to play.

When first loaded, Windows Media Player displays your Music folder's contents, appropriately enough. But Windows Media Player actually holds several libraries, designed to showcase not only your music but also photographs, video, and recorded TV shows.

All your playable items appear in the Navigation Pane along the window's left edge, shown in Figure 16-5, where they can be accessed with a click. The pane's top half shows your own media collection, appropriately listed with your name at the top.

FIGURE 16-5:
Click the type of media you're interested in browsing from the Navigation Pane along the left.

The bottom half, called Other Libraries, lets you browse the collections of other people with accounts on your PC. You can also access the music shared by *Homegroups* — multiple PCs linked together through a special network. (I describe Homegroups in Chapter 15.)

Windows Media Player organizes your media into these categories:

>> **Playlists:** Do you enjoy playing albums or songs in a certain order? Click the Save List button atop your list of songs to save it as a playlist that shows up in this category. (I cover playlists in this chapter's later "Creating, Saving, and Editing Playlists" section.)

>> **Music:** All your digital music appears here. Windows Media Player recognizes most major music formats, including MP3, WMA, WAV, and even 3GP files used by some cellphones. (It recognizes non-copy-protected AAC files, sold by iTunes.) And Windows 10 finally adds support for the lossless FLAC, a format that compresses the music without losing any sound quality.)

>> **Videos:** Look here for videos you've saved from a camcorder or digital camera or for videos you've downloaded from the Internet. Windows Media Player recognizes AVI, MPG, WMV, ASF, DivX, some MOV files, and a few other formats. Windows 10 also adds support for MKV files, a relatively new video format for high-definition videos.

>> **Pictures:** Windows Media Player can display photos individually or in a simple slide show, but your Pictures folder, described in Chapter 17, handles photos better. (Windows Media Player can't correct upside-down photos, for example, a feat done easily from within your Pictures folder.)

>> **Other Libraries:** Here you can find media appearing on other PCs in your Homegroup — a type of network I describe in Chapter 15.

After you click a category, Windows Media Player's Navigation Pane lets you view the files in several different ways. Click Artist in the Navigation Pane's Music category, for example, and the pane shows the music arranged alphabetically by artists' first names.

Similarly, clicking Genre in the Music category separates songs and albums by different types of music, shown earlier in Figure 16-5. Instead of just showing a name to click — blues, for example — the player arranges your music into piles of covers, just as if you'd sorted your albums or CDs on your living room floor.

TIP

To play anything in Windows Media Player, right-click it and choose Play. Or to play all your music from one artist or genre, right-click the pile and choose Play All.

TIP

YES, WINDOWS SPIES ON YOU

Just like your bank, credit card company, and grocery store club card, Windows 10's Music app and Windows Media Player both spy on you. Microsoft's 5,000-word online Privacy Statement boils down to this: Both players tell Microsoft every song, file, or movie that you play. Some people find that creepy, but if Microsoft doesn't know what you're playing, Windows can't retrieve that artist's profile information and artwork from the Internet.

If you don't care that Microsoft hums along to your music, don't bother reading any further. If you *do* care, choose your surveillance level in Windows Media Player: Click the Organize button in Windows Media Player's top-left corner, choose Options, and click the Privacy tab. Here's the rundown on the Privacy tab options that cause the biggest ruckus:

- **Display Media Information from the Internet:** If this option is selected, Windows Media Player tells Microsoft what CD you're playing and retrieves doodads to display on your screen: CD covers, song titles, artist names, and similar information.

- **Update Music Files by Retrieving Media Info from the Internet:** Microsoft examines your files, and if it recognizes any, it fills in the songs' tags with the correct information. (For more information on tags, see the "What are a song's tags?" sidebar.)

- **Send Unique Player ID to Content Providers:** Known in the biz as data mining, this option lets other corporations track how you use Windows Media Player when playing copy-protected music.

- **Cookies:** Like many other programs and websites, Windows Media Player tracks your activity with little files called cookies. Cookies aren't necessarily bad, because they help the player keep track of your preferences.

- **Customer Experience Improvement:** When enabled, this feature gives Microsoft your "player usage data," a generic term that could mean anything. I turn mine off.

- **History:** Windows Media Player lists the names of your recently played files for your convenience — and for the possible guffaws of your co-workers or family. To keep people from seeing the titles of music and videos you've recently played, remove all the check marks from this section and click the two buttons called Clear History and Clear Caches.

For more information about your privacy settings, visit Microsoft's privacy center online at `http://www.microsoft.com/privacy`.

Playing Music Files in a Playlist

Windows Media Player plays several types of digital music files, but they all have one thing in common: When you tell Windows Media Player to play a song or an album, Windows Media Player immediately places that item on your *Now Playing list* — a list of items queued up for playing one after the other.

You can start playing music through Windows Media Player in a number of ways, even if Windows Media Player isn't currently running:

» Click the File Explorer icon (shown in the margin) on your taskbar, right-click an album or a music-filled folder, and choose Play with Windows Media Player. The player jumps to the screen and begins playing your choice.

» While you're still viewing your own Music folder, right-click items and choose Add to Windows Media Player List. Your computer queues them up in Windows Media Player, ready to be played after you've heard your currently playing music.

» Place a music CD in your computer's CD drive tray and push the tray into your computer. Click the pop-up message that says, "Select to Choose What Happens with Audio CDs." When the second pop-up menu appears, choose "Play Audio CD," and Windows will automatically play future audio CDs as soon as you insert them.

» Double-click a song file, whether it's sitting on your desktop or in any folder. Windows Media Player begins playing it immediately.

To play songs listed within Windows Media Player's own library, right-click the song's name and choose Play. Windows Media Player begins playing it immediately, and the song appears in the Now Playing list.

Here are other ways to play songs within Windows Media Player:

» To play an entire album in Windows Media Player's library, right-click the album from the library's Album category and choose Play.

» Want to hear several files or albums, one after the other? Right-click the first one and choose Play. Right-click the next one and choose Add to Now Playing list. Repeat until you're done. Windows Media Player queues them all up in the Now Playing list.

» To return to a recently played item, right-click Windows Media Player's icon in the taskbar. When the list of recently played items appears, click your item's name.

» No decent music in your music folder? Then start copying your favorite CDs to your computer — a process called *ripping,* which I explain in the "Ripping (Copying) CDs to Your Computer" section, later in this chapter.

Controlling Your Now Playing Items

You can play music directly from the Windows Media Player Library: Just right-click a file, album, artist, or genre and then choose Play. Windows Media Player begins playing the music, but the program stays put, often filling the screen

To summon a smaller, more manageable player, click the Library/Player toggle button shown in the margin and summon the Now Playing window shown in Figure 16-6. (The Library/Player toggle button lives in the library's bottom-right corner.) Don't see the controls? Hover your mouse pointer over the Media Player window, and the controls appear along the window's bottom edge.

FIGURE 16-6:
The window's bottom buttons work much like the buttons on a CD player.

The minimalist Now Playing window shows what's currently playing, be it a video or artwork from your currently playing song. Onscreen controls let you adjust the volume, skip between listed songs or videos, or pause the action.

Windows Media Player offers the same basic controls when playing any type of file, be it a song, video, CD, or photo slide show. Figure 16-6 shows Windows Media Player open to its Now Playing window as it plays an album. The labels in the figure explain each button's function. Or rest your mouse pointer over an especially mysterious button, and Windows Media Player displays a pop-up explanation.

The buttons along the bottom work like those found on any CD player, letting you play, stop, rewind, fast-forward, and mute the current song or movie. For even more controls, right-click anywhere in the Now Playing window. A menu appears, offering to perform these common tasks:

- **»** **Show List:** Shows the playlist along the right side, which is handy for jumping directly to different songs.

- **»** **Full Screen:** Enlarges the window to fill the screen.

- **»** **Shuffle:** Plays songs randomly.

- **»** **Repeat:** Loops the same song.

- **»** **Visualizations:** Choose between showing the album cover, wavy lines, groovy spirals, dancing waves, or other freaky eye games.

- **»** **Enhancements:** Opens an equalizer, balance adjuster, playback speed, volume balancer, and other sound options.

- **»** **Lyrics, Captions, or Subtitles:** Display these items, if they're available, which come in handy when practicing for Karaoke night.

- **»** **Shop for More Music:** This option fills the Windows Media Player window with the music shopping page of the Windows Store app, ready for you to buy more music.

- **»** **Always Show Now Playing on Top:** Keeps the window above your other windows on the desktop.

- **»** **More Options:** Brings up the Options page, where you can tweak Windows Media Player's habits when ripping CDs, stocking your Windows Media Player Library, and other tasks.

- **»** **Help with Playback:** Fetches the Help program to deal with head-scratchers.

The Now Playing controls disappear from the screen when you haven't moved the mouse for a while. To bring them back, move your mouse pointer over the Now Playing window.

TIP

To return to the Windows Media Player Library, click the Library/Player toggle icon in the window's upper-right corner.

When you minimize Windows Media Player to the desktop's taskbar, hover your mouse pointer over the player's icon: A control pops up, letting you pause or jump between songs.

TIP

Playing CDs

As long as you insert the CD in the CD drive correctly (usually label-side up), playing a music CD is one of Windows Media Player's easiest tasks. Start by pushing the drive's Eject button, a rarely labelled button that lives next to or on the disc drive on the front of your computer.

When the drive tray emerges, drop the CD into your CD drive and push the tray back into the drive. Windows Media Player jumps to the screen to play it, usually identifying the CD and its musicians immediately. In many cases, it even tosses a picture of the cover art on the screen.

The controls along the bottom, shown earlier in Figure 16-6, let you jump from track to track, adjust the volume, and fine-tune your listening experience.

If for some odd reason Windows Media Player doesn't start playing your CD, look at the Library item in Windows Media Player's Navigation Pane along the left side of the window. You should spot either the CD's name or the words *Unknown Album.* When you spot the listing, click it and then click the Play button to start listening.

TIP

Press F7 to mute Windows Media Player's sound and pick up that phone call. Pressing Ctrl+P toggles the pause/play mode.

Want to copy that CD to your PC? That's called *ripping,* and I cover ripping in the "Ripping (Copying) CDs to Your PC" section, later in this chapter.

Playing DVDs

And now for a bit of bad news: Windows Media Player can't play DVDs. That news comes as a bit of a shock, considering that the Media Player in Windows 7 *could* play DVDs. What gives?

According to Microsoft, DVDs are old-school technology that's no longer needed. Today's ultrathin laptops and tablets don't even have DVD drives. Most people watch movies by streaming them to their computers over the Internet, Microsoft says. Or, they watch their DVDs on TV.

TECHNICAL
STUFF

Also, Microsoft no longer wanted to pay licensing fees to the companies owning the patents required for playing DVDs.

But although Windows Media Player can no longer play DVDs, Windows can still play DVDs with either of these solutions:

>> **Use the third-party DVD players provided by your computer manufacturer.** Most desktop PC manufacturers toss in a free trial version of a DVD player. If you like it, you can pay to upgrade to the full version.

>> **Download the free VLC media player from** www.videolan.org. Created by a nonprofit company based in France, it's not under United States jurisdiction.

Playing Videos and TV Shows

Many digital cameras and smartphones can capture short videos as well as photos, so don't be surprised if you find several videos in the Video library of Windows Media Player.

Playing videos works much like playing a digital song. Click Videos in the Navigation Pane along Windows Media Player's left side. Double-click the video you want to see and start enjoying the action, as shown in Figure 16-7.

FIGURE 16-7:
Move the mouse over the video to make the controls appear along the bottom.

PLAYING INTERNET RADIO STATIONS

Windows Media Player doesn't offer an easy way to play Internet radio stations. However, Windows offers you several ways to listen to music over the Internet:

- Head to Google (www.google.com) and search for *"Internet radio station"* to see what turns up. When you find a station broadcasting in MP3 or Windows Media Audio (WMA) format, click the website's Tune In or Listen Now button to load Windows Media Player and start listening.

- I like the stations at SomaFM (www.somafm.com). It offers about a dozen stations in a variety of genres, all playable through Windows Media Player.

- Install an app from an Internet streaming site, such as TuneIn Radio (http://tunein.com), which lets you tune into thousands of stations from around the world. Other people prefer dedicated music streaming apps like Pandora, available through the Windows Store.

Windows Media Player lets you watch videos in several sizes. Make it fill the screen by holding down Alt and pressing Enter, for example. (Repeat those keystrokes to return to the original size.)

>> To make the video adjust itself automatically to the size of your Windows Media Player window, right-click the video as it plays, choose Video from the pop-up menu, and select Fit Video to Player on Resize.

>> You can also toggle full-screen mode by clicking the Full Screen toggle in the video's bottom-right corner, shown in Figure 16-7.

>> When choosing video to watch on the Internet, your connection speed determines its quality. Broadband connections can usually handle high-definition videos, but slower connections and slower computers often have problems. You can't damage your computer by choosing the wrong quality of video; the video just skips and pauses while playing.

>> Windows Media Player's Recorded TV area only lists TV shows recorded by *Media Center,* a program available on earlier Windows versions. If you upgraded your PC to Windows 10, your recorded TV shows remain. (Media Center, however, isn't available for Windows 10, unfortunately.)

Creating, Saving, and Editing Playlists

A *playlist* is simply a list of songs (and/or videos) that play in a certain order. So what? Well, the beauty of a playlist comes with what you can *do* with it. Save a playlist of your favorite songs, for example, and they're always available for play-back with a single click.

You can create specially themed playlists to liven up long-distance drives, parties, special dinners, workouts, and other events.

To create a playlist, follow these steps:

TIP

1. **Open Windows Media Player and find the playlist pane.**

   Don't see a playlist hugging Windows Media Player's right edge? Click the Play tab near the top-right corner. Or when the player is in Now Playing mode, right-click a blank part of the Windows Media Player window and choose Show List from the pop-up menu: The list of currently playing items appears along Media Center's right edge.

2. **Right-click the album or songs you want, choose Add To, and select Play List.**

   Alternatively, you can drag and drop albums and songs onto the Playlist pane along Windows Media Player's right edge, as shown in Figure 16-8. Either way, Windows Media Player begins playing your playlist as soon as you add the first song. Your song choices appear in the right pane in the order you've selected them.

FIGURE 16-8:
Drag and drop albums and songs onto the Playlist pane.

3. **Fine-tune your playlist to change the order or remove songs.**

   Added something by mistake? Right-click that item from the playlist and choose Remove from List. Feel free to rearrange your playlist by dragging and dropping items farther up or down the list.

   Check the line at the bottom of the playlist to see how many items you've added to the playlist as well as your playlist's duration in minutes.

4. **When you're happy with your playlist, click the Save List button at the list's top, type a name in the highlighted box, and press Enter.**

   Windows Media Player lists your new playlist in the library's Playlists section, ready to be heard when you double-click it.

After you save a playlist, you can burn it to a CD with one click, as described in the next tip.

TIP

Make your own Desert Island Disc or Greatest Hits playlists and then burn them to a CD to play in your car or on your home stereo. After you create a playlist of less than 80 minutes, insert a blank CD into your CD burner and click the Burn tab. Take up the player's offer to import your current playlist and then click the Start Burn button.

TIP

To edit a previously created playlist, double-click the playlist's name in the Library's Playlists area. Rearrange, add, or delete items in the playlist and then click the Save List button.

Ripping (Copying) CDs to Your PC

In a process known as *ripping*, Windows Media Player can copy your CDs to your PC as MP3 files, the industry standard for digital music. But until you tell the player that you want MP3 files, it creates *WMA* files — a format that won't play on iPads, most smartphones, nor many other music players.

TIP

To make Windows Media Player create songs with the more versatile MP3 format instead of WMA, click the Organize button in the top-left corner, choose Options, and click the Rip Music tab. Choose MP3 instead of WMA from the Format drop-down menu and nudge the audio quality over a tad from 128 to 256 or even 320 for better sound.

To copy CDs to your PC's hard drive, follow these instructions:

1. **Open Windows Media Player, insert a music CD, and click the Rip CD button.**

   You may need to push a button on the front or side of your computer's disc drive to make the tray eject.

   Windows Media Player connects to the Internet; identifies your CD; and fills in the album's name, artist, and song titles. Then the program begins copying the CD's songs to your PC and listing their titles in the Windows Media Player Library. You're through.

   If Windows Media Player can't find the songs' titles automatically, however, move ahead to Step 2.

2. **Right-click the first track and choose Find Album Info, if necessary.**

   If Windows Media Player comes up empty-handed, right-click the first track and choose Find Album Info.

   If you're connected to the Internet, type the album's name into the Search box and then click Search. If the Search box finds your album, click its name, choose Next, and click Finish.

   If you're not connected to the Internet, or if the Search box comes up empty, right-click the first song, click Edit, and manually fill in the song title. Repeat for the other titles, as well as the album, artist, genre, and year tags.

Here are some tips for ripping CDs to your computer:

>> Normally Windows Media Player copies every song on the CD. To leave Tiny Tim off your ukulele music compilation, however, remove the check mark from Tiny Tim's name. If Windows Media Player has already copied the song to your PC, feel free to delete it from within Windows Media Player. Click the Library button, right-click the song sung by the offending yodeler, and choose Delete.

>> Windows Media Player automatically places your ripped CDs into your Music folder. You can also find your newly ripped music there as well as in the Windows Media Player Library.

Burning (Creating) Music CDs

To create a music CD with your favorite songs, create a playlist containing the CD's songs, listed in the order you want to play them; then burn the playlist to a CD.

I explain how to do that in the "Creating, Saving, and Editing Playlists" section, earlier in this chapter.

But what if you want to duplicate a CD, perhaps to create a disposable copy of your favorite CD to play in your car? No sense scratching up your original. You'll want to make copies of your kids' CDs, too, before they create pizzas out of them.

Unfortunately, neither Windows Media Player nor Windows 10 offer a Duplicate CD option. Instead, you must jump through the following five hoops to create a new CD with the same songs in the same fidelity as the original CD:

1. **Rip (copy) the music to your hard drive.**

   Before ripping your CD, change your burning quality to the highest quality: Click Organize, choose Options, click the Rip Music tab, and change the Format box to a lossless format like WAV, ALAC, or FLAC. Click OK.

2. **Insert a blank CD into your writable CD drive.**

3. **In Windows Media Player's Navigation Pane, click the Music category and choose Album to see your saved CDs.**

4. **Right-click the newly ripped album in your library, choose Add To, and choose Burn List.**

   If your Burn List already had some listed music, click the Clear List button to clear it; then add your CD's music to the Burn List.

5. **Click the Start Burn button.**

Now, for the fine print. Unless you change the quality to a lossless format when copying the CD to your PC, Windows Media Player compresses your songs as it saves them on your hard drive, throwing out some audio quality in the process. Burning them back to CD won't replace that lost quality. If you want the most accurate duplicates Windows Media Player can handle, change the Ripping Format to WAV (Lossless).

REMEMBER

If you do change the format to WAV (Lossless) in order to duplicate a CD, remember to change it back to MP3 afterward, or else your hard drive will run out of room when you begin ripping a lot of CDs.

A simpler solution might be to buy CD-burning software from your local office supply or computer store. Unlike Windows Media Player, most CD-burning programs have a Duplicate CD button for one-click convenience.

TIP

THE WRONG PLAYER KEEPS OPENING MY FILES!

You'd never hear Microsoft say it, but Windows Media Player isn't the only Windows program for playing songs or viewing movies. Many people use iTunes for managing their songs and movies because it conveniently drops items into their iPads and iPhones for on-the-road enjoyment.

But when your computer includes more than one media player, the players start bickering over which one handles your media-playing chores.

Windows settles these arguments with its Defaults area in the Settings area. To choose the player that should open each format, head for this chapter's earlier section, "Handing Music-Playing Chores Back to Windows Media Player." That section explains how to choose which player should handle which types of media files.

Chapter 17

Fiddling with Photos (and Videos)

or years, Windows graciously offered to import your photos as soon as you plugged in your camera. When Windows 10 arrived, though, that feature fell by the wayside. Now, with a year of updates under its belt, Windows 10 not only welcomes your camera again, but offers five ways to process your photos.

This chapter walks you through copying your digital photos from your phone or camera into your computer. From there, you can show them off to friends and family, email them to distant relatives, and save them in places where you can easily relocate them.

One final note: After you've begun creating a digital family album on your computer, please take steps to back it up properly by turning on File History, the automatic backup feature in Windows that I describe in Chapter 13. (This chapter explains how to copy your photos to a CD or DVD, as well.) Computers come and go, but your family memories can't be replaced.

Dumping a Camera's Photos into Your Computer

Most digital cameras come with software that grabs your camera's photos and places them into your computer. That software can be complicated and unwieldy, though. Thankfully, Windows can easily fetch photos from nearly any make and model of digital camera, as well as most smartphones. In keeping with Windows 10's theme of moving away from the desktop, Windows now lets the Photos app handle the job of importing and organizing your photos.

These steps work for most digital cameras and Android smartphones; iPhone owners must go through iTunes to copy their photos to their computer.

To import photos from your camera or smartphone into your computer, follow these steps:

1. Plug the phone or camera's cable into your computer.

Most cameras come with two cables: one that plugs into your TV set for viewing, and another that plugs into your computer. You need to find the one that plugs into your computer for transferring photos. (With smart phones, your USB charging cable handles the job.)

Plug the transfer cable's small end into your camera or smartphone, and plug the larger end (shown in the margin) into your computer's *USB port,* a rectangular-looking hole about ½-inch long and ¼-inch high. USB ports live on the back of the older computers, along the front of newer computers, and along the sides of laptops and tablets.

TIP

If the USB plug doesn't want to fit into the port, turn over the plug and try again. (It fits only one way.)

If you plug in an Android smartphone, be sure to tell it to connect in "Camera Mode" mode rather than "Media Device" mode. That lets Windows recognize your phone as a camera rather than a complicated phone.

If Windows doesn't recognize your digital camera, make sure that the camera is set to *display mode* — the mode where you can see your photos on the camera's display. If you still have problems, unplug the cable from your computer, wait a few seconds, and then plug it back in.

2. **Turn on your phone or camera (if it's not already turned on), wait for Windows to recognize it, and click the pop-up window that says Select to Choose What Happens with This Device.**

   If the pop-up window disappears before you can click it, turn your camera off, wait a few seconds, and turn it back on. The pop-up will reappear.

3. **When the second pop-up appears, choose Import Photos and Videos (Photos).**

   The second pop-up, named after your camera model, offers a plethora of options as shown in Figure 17-1. Depending on your camera's model, you may see these:

FIGURE 17-1:
The Import
Pictures and
Videos window
offers to copy
your camera's
files to your
computer.

- **Open Device to View Files (File Explorer):** This opens File Explorer, handy for manually selecting a few favorite photos and moving them to the folder of your choice. I explain how to move files with File Explorer in Chapter 5. (Digital cameras and smart phones always store their photos in a folder called DCIM, so navigate to that folder to find your photos.)

- **Get Your Stuff on your PC, Tablet and Phone:** This opens Windows 10's Phone Companion program, which is usually overkill. The Phone Companion can import photos, but it's designed mainly to install Microsoft's full suite of Windows apps onto your phone or tablet. And, unless you pay to subscribe to Office 365, the apps aren't fully featured.

- **Import Photos and Videos (OneDrive):** This copies your camera's photos and videos to OneDrive, your storage space on the Internet. I cover OneDrive in Chapter 5. *Tip:* If you install the OneDrive app on your phone, your phone can automatically upload every snapped photo to OneDrive. That's a simple way to not only backup your photos but to view them on your PC.

- **Import Photos and Videos (Photos):** Choose this and the Photos app appears, ready to import your photos and movies. Move to Step 4.

- **Take No Action:** Stumped by all the choices? Choose this to stop the import process, go outside, and get some fresh air.

TIP

If you prefer the old photo importer from earlier Windows versions, you can still find it. Open File Explorer and click This PC from the pane along File Explorer's left edge. When you spot your camera on File Explorer's right side, right-click the camera's icon. When the pop-up menu appears, choose Import Pictures and Videos. The old Import Pictures and Videos program appears, ready to import your photos, just as it did in previous Windows versions.

TIP

If you choose the wrong option at this step, it's not too late to fix things. Click the Start menu, click the Settings icon, and choose the Devices category. When the Devices page opens, choose AutoPlay from the left pane. On the right, beneath your camera's name, click the drop-down menu. There, you can choose any of the choices listed above. (I choose Ask Me Every Time so I can choose the method that I prefer for that particular session.)

4. **Decide which photos to import and click the Continue button.**

   The Photos app immediately searches your camera for new digital photos and videos, and then displays them, shown in Figure 17-2. The app sorts your photos by the month you snapped them.

   The app selects every new photo, ready to copy them all into your computer's Pictures folder. If you don't want to import a photo, click to remove the checkmark from the unwanted photo's upper right corner. To see more photos, use the scroll bar shown in Figure 17-2. (I cover scroll bars in Chapter 4.)

TIP

Only want to import a few photos? Then click the Clear All link. That removes all of the checkmarks, letting you place checkmarks next to the few photos you *do* want to grab. A Clear link next to each month lets you remove that month's photos from the import process.

5. **When the Start Importing Window appears, review your options and click the Import button.**

   The Start Importing window offers several options, as follows:

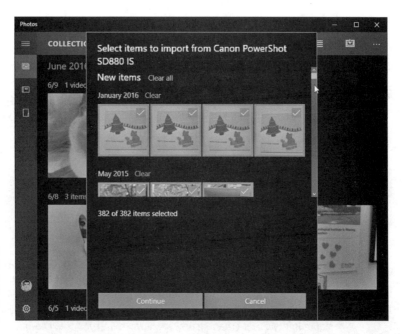

FIGURE 17-2:
The Photos app
displays groups
of pictures based
on the time you
took them.

- **Change Where They're Imported:** The Photos app normally places your photos into your easy-to-locate Pictures folder. To see it, open File Explorer and the Pictures folder lives in the Quick Access area, near File Manager's upper-left corner. Don't change this option unless you have a good reason: Most programs and apps, including Windows backup program, expect your pictures to live inside the Pictures folder.

- **Delete Imported Items from Camera After Importing:** Click this option, and Windows erases the camera's photos after importing them, which spares you the trouble of manually deleting them with your camera's awkward menus. If you don't click this option, your camera's memory card will eventually fill up, leaving you unable to shoot more photos down the road.

When you click Import, Windows imports your photos into the folder of your choosing, separating them into groups named after their year and month. For example, photos snapped in July, 2016 will appear in a folder named 2016-07.

When Windows finishes importing your photos, the Photos app remains onscreen to display your newly imported photos. The most currently shot photos always appear at the top. As you scroll down the app's list of photos, you go back in time, seeing older photos organized by month and day. I cover the Photos app later in this chapter.

Taking Photos with the Camera App

Most tablets, laptops, and some desktop computers come with built-in cameras, sometimes called *webcams.* Their tiny cameras can't take high-resolution close-ups of that rare bird in the neighbor's tree, but they work fine for their main purpose: snapping a quick headshot photo for use as an account photo on your computer, Facebook, or other websites.

To take a photo through your computer's camera with the Camera app, follow these steps:

1. **From the Start menu, click the Camera tile to open the app.**

2. **If the app asks permission to use your camera and microphone or location, decide whether to click Yes or No.**

    As a security precaution, Windows may ask permission to turn on your camera. That helps prevent sneaky apps from spying on you without your knowing. If you're using the camera app, then click the Yes button to give it permission.

The program might also ask for permission to access your precise location. That lets the program stamp your photo with its location information. That's handy to have when traveling, but it can be an invasion of privacy when at your house or that of a friend.

After you decide whether to allow access to your location, the camera window turns into a giant viewfinder, showing you exactly what the camera sees: your face.

If your computer or tablet includes two cameras (usually one in front and one in back), you can toggle between them by clicking the Change Camera icon, shown in Figure 17-3.

3. **Click the Camera icon to snap a photo or click the Video icon to begin recording a movie. (Click the Video icon again to stop recording.)**

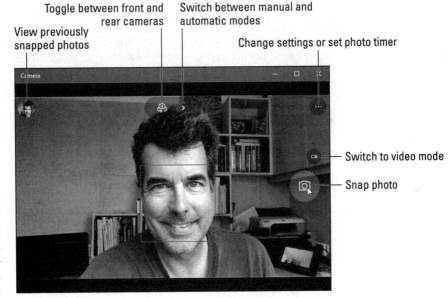

View previously snapped photos

Toggle between front and rear cameras

Switch between manual and automatic modes

Change settings or set photo timer

Switch to video mode

Snap photo

FIGURE 17-3: Choose your camera's options and then click the Camera icon for a snapshot or the Video icon for a movie.

When the camera detects a face, it places a square around the face, letting you know where the camera will focus. Yes, it's a little creepy.

TIP

The camera app saves all your snapped photos and videos in a folder named Camera Roll inside your Pictures folder. However, if you chose to use OneDrive when setting up your Microsoft account, your built-in camera's photos are also backed up on OneDrive. (I explain how to change OneDrive's behavior in Chapter 5.)

Viewing Photos with the Photos App

Microsoft's latest big update to Windows 10 added many features. But it also took a few away: The desktop's Photo Viewer, a Windows staple for nearly a decade, no longer appears on the Start menu.

When you want to view photos, Microsoft clearly plans for you to reach for the Windows 10 Photos app. It's a quick way to put your photos on display in different ways:

>> **Collection:** When opened, the Photos app appears in Collection mode. It displays *all* of your photos, sorted by the order you snapped them. Although it leaves nothing out, it's overkill unless you're ready to sit down and weed out the bad ones. (Right-click an unwanted photo and choose Delete to get rid of it.)

>> **Albums:** The Photos app takes a more curated approach here, breaking them down into photo sessions named after the day they were shot. It automatically weeds out duplicates, making for a short but sweet way to show off your highlights.

>> **Folders:** This simply lets you view your photos by their folders.

The next four sections explain how to make the most of the Photos app.

Viewing your photo collection

When opened, the Photos app automatically grabs your photos and places them on the screen in large thumbnails, sorted by the date you took them. That makes it easy to show off the latest vacation photos on a tablet, smartphone, or even a computer that's hooked up to a TV or large monitor.

The app automatically performs subtle photo tweaks when showing them, enhancing the highlights and straightening those tilted horizons. (All the tweaks happen only for display; your original photos remain untouched.)

To launch the Photos app and start showing off your photos, follow these steps:

1. **From the Start menu, click the Photos tile.**

   The Photos app quickly appears, shown in Figure 17-4. The Photos app searches for photos in your computer's Pictures folder, as well your OneDrive folders, and displays them as one group, all in the order they were taken.

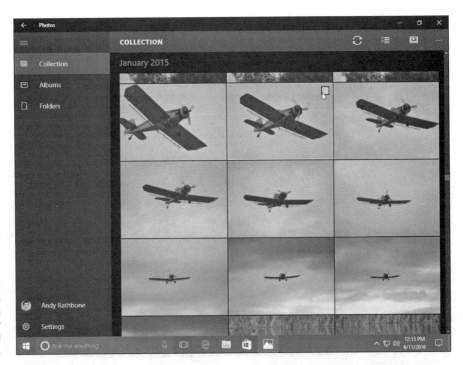

FIGURE 17-4:
The Photos app
displays photos
stored on your
computer as well
as on OneDrive.

The Photos app also appears when you open a photo on the desktop's File Explorer. (I explain how to browse your files with File Explorer in Chapter 5.)

2. **Scroll down to the photo you want to view or edit.**

The Photos app displays your photos in one long stream, without folders. Called simply *Collection,* the scrolling display places your most recently shot photos at the top, with the oldest ones at the bottom.

Scroll down with a mouse by using the scroll bar along the app's right edge. On a touchscreen, just slide your finger up or down the screen to see newer or older photos.

3. **Click a photo to see it full-screen and then choose any menu option to view, navigate, manipulate, or share your pictures.**

When a photo fills the screen, shown and labelled in Figure 17-5, sometimes the menus are hidden. You can bring the menus into view by either moving your mouse or clicking (or tapping) the photo. When the menus appear, you can control the app and photos in a variety of ways:

- **Next/Previous photo:** Move your mouse anywhere on the photo, and arrows appear on the photo's left and right edges. Click the right arrow to see newer photos or click the left arrow to see older photos. Don't see the arrows? Click the View Actual Size toggle until they appear.

Return to Collection view

Share Enhance Rotate More

File name Slideshow Edit Delete

DSC_8610.JPG - Photos

See next photo

FIGURE 17-5:
Click any of
these places
to do different
tasks while
viewing a photo.

See previous photo View actual size Zoom in

Zoom out

- **Return to previous view**: Return to viewing thumbnails of your photos by clicking the left-pointing arrow in the photo's top-left corner. (You may need to click or tap the currently displayed photo before the little arrow appears.)

- **Share the photo:** Click the Share button to share the photo with apps that can handle the job. (Chances are good that the Mail app appears, ready to email the photo to your destination.)

- **Slide show:** A click of this button clears the screen, and then the app begins cycling through all of your photos, showing each one for about five seconds before moving to the next. (Click any photo to stop the slide show.)

- **Enhance:** If possible, the Photos app automatically enhances your currently displayed photo to look its best. Click the Enhance button to turn off the enhancement if you think it looks better au naturel. (To save a photo with the enhancements, head for the adjacent Edit icon.) Don't see the Enhance button? Then the Photos app didn't find anything to fix automatically.

- **Edit:** This brings a new menu for editing the currently viewed photo. Click the X in the photo's upper-right corner to exit the editing menu.

- **Rotate:** This rotates your photo clockwise by 90 degrees; to rotate in the opposite direction, click it three times.

- **Delete:** If you spot a blurred photo, click this icon to delete it immediately. Weeding out the bad photos makes it easier to relocate the good ones.

- **More menu:** A click on these three dots fetches a new drop-down menu. This menu lets you copy or print the photo, open it in a new program, set it as your computer's lock screen or background, and see details such as the photo's name, size, date taken, resolution, and similar information.

- **Zoom:** Click these little buttons in the bottom, right corner to zoom in or out of the photo.

4. **To exit the Photos app, click the X in its upper-right corner.**

   The app clears itself from the screen.

Viewing photo albums

Everybody likes to take pictures, but only a meticulous few like to spend a few hours organizing them, weeding out the bad ones, and sorting them into easily accessible folders.

That's where the Photos app's robotically curated Albums mode comes in handy. When you turn on Album mode, the Photos app turns its robotic eye on all of your photos, weeds out the duplicates, finds a splashy one for the cover, and names it by the date of the photo session.

To view the Photos app's albums, follow these steps:

1. **From the Start menu, click the Photos tile.**

   The Photos app quickly appears, shown earlier in Figure 17-4, to show its Collection mode: a string of photos sorted by the order you shot them.

2. **From the Photos app's left menu, choose Albums.**

   The Photos app sorts your photos into albums that represent the best of your session and displays them, shown in Figure 17-6.

   From here, you can do several things:

   - **Click the Camera Roll tile:** Click the album called Camera Roll to view photos taken from your smartphone and automatically uploaded to OneDrive. It's a quick way to see how your life appears when seen through the lens of your smartphone.

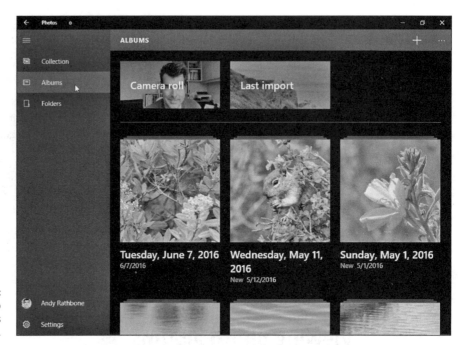

FIGURE 17-6:
Click Albums to
see your photos
sorted by session.

- **Last Import:** Click the Last Import album along the app's top edge to see your most recently imported photos.

- **Click a dated tile:** The app sorts each collection of photos by date. Click a date, and the Photos app shows you the best of that day's photos, shown in Figure 17-7.

3. **Click any photo to view it.**

   The Photos app fills the screen with the photo; to see more, click the Next or Previous arrows along the photos left and right edges.

TIP

FIXING ROTATED PICTURES

In the old days, it never mattered how you tilted your camera when taking the photo; you simply turned the printed photo to view it. Many of today's computer screens don't swivel, so Windows rotates the photo for you — if you figure out how.

The trick is to right-click any photo that shows up sideways. Then choose Rotate to turn your green cliffs back into grassy meadows. (The Photos apps Rotate button only rotates photos clockwise, so you must click the button three times to rotate a photo counter-clockwise.)

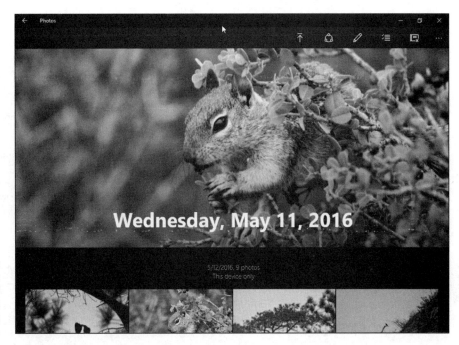

FIGURE 17-7:
Click a date to see
your best photos
from that day's
photo-shooting
session.

The Photos app takes its best guess as to which photos work best for each session. Taking mercy on the vacation-photo-saturated relatives sitting on your couch, the app leaves out a *lot* of your photos. That's usually a good thing, as it's smart enough to remove duplicates and blurry photos.

But if you want to change which photos should be included in an album, scroll to the bottom of the album's displayed photos. Then click the Add or Remove Photos button. There, you find check boxes next to all the day's photos, so you can pick and choose what should be included.

Viewing a slide show

Windows offers a simple slide show that displays one photo after another. It's not fancy, but it's a built-in way to show photos to friends crowding around your computer screen. Start the photos flowing across the screen in either of these two ways:

>> When in your Pictures folder, click the Manage tab and then click the Slide show icon (shown in the margin) from along the folder's top.

>> When viewing a photo in the Photos app, click the Slide show button from the row of six buttons along the photo's top edge.

Windows immediately darkens the screen, fills the screen with the first picture, and then cycles through each picture in the folder.

TIP

Here are more tips for successful on-the-fly slide shows:

>> Before starting the slide show, rotate any sideways pictures, if necessary, so that they all appear right-side up.

>> The slide show includes only photos in your currently viewed folder. It doesn't dip into folders inside that folder and show their photos, too.

>> Select just a few of a folder's pictures and click the Slide Show button to limit the show to just those pictures. (Hold down Ctrl while clicking pictures to select more than one.)

>> Feel free to add music to your slide show by playing, described in Chapter 16, before starting your show. Or, if you picked up a Hawaiian CD while vacationing on the islands, insert that in your CD player to play a soundtrack during your vacation slide show.

Copying digital photos to a CD or DVD

Your photos will be backed up automatically after you set up the Windows File History backup program, covered in Chapter 13. But if you just want to copy some photos to a CD or DVD, perhaps to share with others, stick around.

Head to the computer or office-supply store and pick up a stack of blank CDs or DVDs. Most newer computers can handle any type of blank CD or DVD except for Blu-ray discs.

Then follow these steps to copy files in your Pictures folder to a blank CD or DVD:

1. **Open your Pictures folder from File Manager, select your desired photos, click the Share tab from the Ribbon along the top, and click the Burn to Disc icon.**

Select the photos and folders you want to copy by holding down the Ctrl key and clicking their icons. Or, to select them *all*, hold down Ctrl and press the letter A. When you click the Burn to Disc icon, Windows asks you to insert a blank disc into your drive.

2. **Insert a blank CD or DVD into your writable disc drive's tray and push the tray shut.**

TIP

If you're copying a lot of files, insert a DVD into your DVD burner because DVDs can store five times as much information as a CD. If you're giving away a few photos to a friend, insert a blank CD instead because blank CDs cost less.

3. **Decide how you want to use the disc.**

Windows offers two options for creating the disc:

- **Like a USB Flash Drive:** Select this option when you intend for other computers to read the disc. Windows treats the disc much like a folder, letting you copy additional photos to the disc later. It's a good choice when you're backing up only a few pictures because you can add more to the disc later.

- **With a CD/DVD Player:** Select this option to create discs that play on CD and DVD players attached to TVs. After you write to the disc, it's sealed off so you can't write to it again.

4. **Type a short title for your backup disc and click Next.**

Type something short but descriptive. When you click Next, Windows begins backing up all of that folder's photos to the disc.

5. **Click the Burn or Burn to Disc button again if necessary.**

If you selected With a CD/DVD Player in Step 3, click Burn to Disc to start copying your photos to the disc.

If you didn't select any photos or folders in Step 1, Windows opens an empty window showing the newly inserted disc's contents: nothing. Drag and drop the photos you want to burn into that window.

Don't have enough space on the CD or DVD to hold all your files? Unfortunately, Windows isn't smart enough to tell you when to insert the second disc. Instead, it whines about not having enough room and doesn't burn *any* discs. Try burning fewer files, adding more until you fill up the disc.

Help!

Chapter 18

The Case of the Broken Window

S ometimes you just have a vague sense that something's wrong. Your computer displays an odd screen that you've never seen before, or Windows starts running more slowly than Congress.

Other times, something's obviously gone haywire. Programs freeze, menus keep shooting at you, or Windows constantly nags you with an incomprehensible error message every time you turn on your computer.

Many of the biggest-looking problems are solved by the smallest-looking solutions. This chapter points you to the right one.

TRY THIS FIRST

Sometimes a vague sense of frustration keeps growing stronger. Your wireless Internet isn't working right. The printer won't connect. A website takes forever to load. A program just won't cooperate. Dozens of problems start with small irritations like these.

Oddly enough, sometimes the simplest fix is to restart your computer:

1. **Right-click the Start button, choose Shut Down or Sign Out, and choose Restart from the pop-up menu.**

Your programs begin closing by themselves. If a program asks you whether you want to save your work, be sure to save it. Then your computer turns itself off. A second later, it rises from the dead to leave you at the lock screen, ready for another round.

Whether restarting your computer gives *you* a much-needed cooling off period or it really fixes the problem, a restart often works wonders. Give it try before spending too much time on the more strenuous fixes.

Toggling Between Tablet and Desktop Mode

Much of the confusion surrounding Windows 10 involves one thing: *Tablet mode*. With Tablet mode turned on, Windows 10 works much better on touchscreen tablets. Your fingers can easily find the larger buttons and menus.

But when a *desktop PC* runs in Tablet mode, confusion reigns. You may spot these symptoms:

>> Pressing the Start button won't bring the familiar Start menu to the screen's lower-left corner. Instead, clicking the Start button toggles between the full-screen Start screen and your most recently used app.

>> Apps and programs still run, but they consume the entire screen. The traditional desktop stays hidden because something always runs fullscreen on top of it.

>> In Tablet mode, the Start menu doesn't show you an alphabetically sorted list of tiles along the left edge.

Unless you know how to turn off Tablet mode on a desktop PC, Windows 10 won't make much sense.

To turn off Tablet mode and return to the regular desktop Start menu, follow these steps:

1. **Click or tap the Action Center icon (shown in the margin) near the taskbar's right end.**

2. **When the Action Center pane appears along the screen's right edge, click or tap the Tablet mode icon.**

    Your computer will toggle Tablet mode on or off with each press.

Press the Tablet mode toggle a few times so you can identify how the two Start menus behave in Windows 10. Then you'll know which switch to click when you're facing the wrong Start menu.

The Magic Fixes in Windows

For years, System Restore was the Windows go-to fix when your computer began running rough. System Restore lives on in Windows 10, as I describe in this chapter's later sidebar, "Restoring from a restore point." But Windows 10 offers several other powerful tools that bring an ailing computer back to health.

The following sections explain each tool, when to reach for it, and how best to make it work its magic.

Resetting your computer

When dealing with a particularly sick computer, sometimes reinstalling Windows is the only cure. In the past, reinstalling Windows took a lot of time and effort. And after reinstalling Windows, you still needed to copy your files and programs back onto your computer. It could take hours — even if you had the backups.

Windows 10 aims to solve that problem. By pushing a few buttons, you can tell Windows to reinstall itself onto your computer. And while installing a fresh copy of itself, Windows preserves everybody's user accounts and personal files. For Microsoft account holders, Windows preserves any apps they've downloaded from the Windows Store, as well and some of their most important computer settings.

TECHNICAL STUFF

Performing a reset saves settings from your wireless network connections as well as from your cellular connection, if you have one. The Reset tool also remembers any BitLocker and BitLocker-To-Go settings, drive letter assignments, and personalization settings, including your lock screen background and desktop wallpaper.

When your computer wakes up feeling refreshed with its new copy of Windows, you only need to reinstall your desktop programs. (The program politely leaves a handy list of those programs on your desktop, complete with website links, if possible, so you know exactly what to reinstall.)

TIP

The Reset tool can go one step further, if you like, by wiping your computer completely clean of *everything*: user accounts, data, and personal files. Then Windows 10 reinstalls itself, just as if it were on a new PC. That lets you either start from scratch or simply give away your computer to a relative or charity without worrying about leaking your personal information.

To reset your ailing PC, follow these steps:

1. **Click the Start button and choose the Settings icon from the Start menu.**

The Settings app appears.

2. **Click the Settings app's Update & Security icon. When the Update & Security window appears, click the Recovery option from the left pane. Then, in the section called Reset This PC, click the Get Started button.**

Windows displays the window shown in Figure 18-1, offering two ways to reset your computer.

TECHNICAL STUFF

If asked, insert your Windows disc, flash drive, or whatever else you used to first install Windows. Don't have a Windows installation disc or drive? Then click Cancel. You can't use the Reset option, unfortunately.

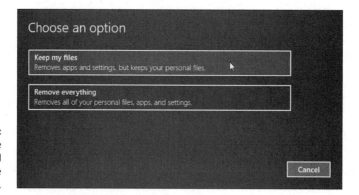

FIGURE 18-1:
Unless you have a very good reason, choose Keep My Files.

3. **Choose an option and click Next.**

The Reset tool offers two options:

- **Keep My Files:** The most widely used choice, this reinstalls Windows, but preserves everybody's user accounts and files. The only thing you lose are desktop programs, which must be reinstalled from their original discs or installation files. If you choose this option, jump to Step 5. (Windows 8 and 8.1 called this option Refresh instead of Reset.)

- **Remove Everything:** Only choose this when you want to wipe *everything* away from your computer, including everybody's user accounts and files, and reinstall Windows 10. Then you can start from scratch or safely give your computer to others. If you choose this, move to Step 4.

4. **Choose whether to just remove your files or to remove files *and* clean the drive.**

   Windows offers you two choices:

   - **Just Remove My Files:** Select this option only when your computer will stay within your family. Although this option is relatively secure, somebody with the right tools may be able to extract some previously erased information. (If your computer contains more than one drive, Windows asks whether you want to remove the files from both drives, or just the drive where Windows is installed.)

   - **Remove Files and Fully Clean the Drive:** Select this option when you intend to sell or donate your computer to strangers. This more time-consuming option removes your data and then scrubs the hard drive *extra* clean. That keeps out everybody but the most dedicated specialists who own expensive data recovery equipment.

   When you click an option and click the Reset button, Windows removes everything from your computer, fully cleaning the drive, if requested, then reinstalls itself to leave your computer with a "like new" copy of Windows 10. At that point, you're finished, and your computer's ready to start afresh or be given away safely.

5. **Take note of what desktop programs (and, possibly, drivers) will need to be reinstalled, then click Next, and click the Reset button.**

Windows reinstalls itself on your computer, which takes anywhere from 15 minutes to an hour. When your computer wakes up, it should feel refreshed and ready to work again. Expect any or all of the following things to take place when resetting your computer:

» When your computer wakes up and you sign in, you find a shortcut called Removed Apps waiting on your desktop. Click it, and your web browser displays a page with links to any desktop programs and drivers that you need to reinstall — if you decide you miss them, that is. (And if you do miss them, you need the program's installation discs to reinstall them.)

» Shortly after Windows wakes up, it visits Windows Update to download and install oodles of security patches, as well as updated copies of its bundled apps. Grab a good novel.

- After resetting your computer, reinstall your desktop programs one by one, restarting your computer after each new install. That gives you the best chance to weed out any misbehaving programs that may have caused the problems that messed things up.

- If you're connected to a network, you may need to tell Windows whether you're on a home network or a public network. You may also have to rejoin your homegroup, a simple task that I explain in Chapter 15.

WARNING

- If you inserted a Windows DVD into your computer in Step 2, be careful when your computer restarts. As it restarts, your computer may ask you to "Press any key to boot from disc." Don't press any key; instead, wait a few seconds until the message disappears. Then Windows loads itself from your computer's newly refreshed hard drive rather than the Windows installation DVD.

- If you've wiped your hard drive completely clean, you can use a File History backup, described in the next section, to restore the files that once lived in your Documents, Music, Pictures, and Videos folders.

Restoring backups with File History

The Windows backup program, File History, saves the files that *you've* created. It doesn't back up your apps and programs. After all, apps and programs can always be reinstalled. But many of the moments that inspired so many of your photos, videos, and documents can *never* be re-created.

RETURNING TO YOUR OLD WINDOWS VERSION

TIP

What if you upgrade to Windows 10, but decide later that you preferred your previous Windows version? Well, you can return to your older Windows version using another trick from the Windows 10 Recovery toolbox.

Head for the Settings app's Recovery section, as described in the first two steps of this chapter's previous two sections. Then, instead of clicking the Reset option, choose Go Back to a Previous Version of Windows. Then click the Get Started button to head back to your older, more comfortable Windows version. All your familiar files and programs should be waiting for you, and all of Windows 10's bundled apps will disappear.

Your timing is important, however: Thirty days after you've upgraded to Windows 10, this option disappears, and Windows 10 quietly disposes of its predecessor.

To keep your files safe, File History automatically makes a copy of *every* file in your Documents, Music, Photos, and Videos folders. It copies all the files on your desktop, as well. And File History automatically makes those copies *every hour.*

File History makes your backups easy to see and restore, letting you flip through different versions of your files and folders, comparing them with your current versions. Should you find a better version, a press of a button brings that older version back to life.

REMEMBER

File History doesn't work until you turn it on, a process I describe in Chapter 13. Please, *please,* flip back a few chapters and turn it on now. The earlier you turn it on, the more backups you'll have to choose from when you need them.

To browse through your backed-up files and folders, restoring the ones you want, follow these steps:

1. **Click the taskbar's File Explorer icon (shown in the margin) and then open the folder containing the items you'd like to retrieve.**

For example, click This PC in the folder's left pane to see your most commonly used folders, Desktop, Downloads, Documents, Music, Pictures, and Videos. Open any folder by double-clicking its name.

2. **Click the Home tab on the Ribbon atop your folder; then click the History button.**

Don't see the menu-filled Ribbon atop the folder? Then click the little upward-pointing arrow in the folder's upper-right corner, next to the blue Question Mark icon. (That arrow shows or hides the Ribbon.)

Clicking the History button, shown in the margin, fetches the File History program, shown in Figure 18-2. The program looks much like a plain old folder. Figure 18-2, for example, shows what happens if you click the History button in any folder and then click File History's Home button: That button lets you see the most recent backups of your folders.

The File History program shows you what it has backed up: your main folders, your desktop, your contacts, and your favorite websites.

Feel free to open the folders inside the File History window. You can also peek inside the files you find there to see their contents.

3. **Choose what you'd like to restore.**

Point and click your way through the libraries, folders, and files until you spot the item or items you'd like to restore:

- **Folder:** To restore an entire folder, open it so you're viewing its contents.

- **Files:** To restore a group of files, open the folder containing them, so the files' icons are onscreen.

Date and time of currently viewed backup

Move up one folder   Search available backups

Number of backups available   Home (See all backed up folders)

Settings

Saturday, June 11, 2016 11:54 AM | 28 of 28   Thursd

3D Objects   Contacts   Desktop   Documents   Downloads

Favorites   Links   Music   OneDrive   Pictures

Saved Games   Searches   Videos   CameraRoll   Documents

Music   Pictures   SavedPictures   Videos

19 items

View previous backup   View next backup   View as icons

Backed up folders   Restore the currently   View as list of files
viewed contents

FIGURE 18-2:
The File History
program lets you
restore backups
from any of your
main folders.

- **One file:** To restore an earlier version of a file, open that file from inside the File History window. File History displays that file's contents.

  When you've found the file or folder you want to restore, move to the next step.

4. **Move forward or backward in time to find the version you'd like to restore.**

    To browse through different versions of what you're currently viewing, choose the left-pointing arrow along the bottom, as shown in Figure 18-3. To see a newer version, choose the right-pointing arrow.

    As you move forward and backward through time, feel free to click open folders or individual files, peeking inside them until you're looking at the version that you want to retrieve.

Let's pull together and do this.

I have, myself, full confidence that if all do their duty, if nothing is neglected, and if the best arrangements are made, as they are being made, we shall prove ourselves once again able to defend our Island home, to ride out the storm of war, and to outlive the menace of tyranny, if necessary for years, if necessary alone.

See newer version   See older version

FIGURE 18-3:
Click the left or right arrow along the bottom to see newer and older versions of the file.

TIP

Not sure whether a folder contains your sought-after item? Type a word or two from your document into the Search box in File History's top-right corner.

5. **Click the Restore button to restore your desired version.**

   Whether you're looking at an individual file, a folder, or an entire library's contents, clicking the Restore button places that item back in the place where it used to live.

   That brings up a potential problem, however: What happens if you try to restore an older file named Notes into a place that already contains a file named Notes? Windows warns you of the problem with the window in Figure 18-4, which brings you to Step 6.

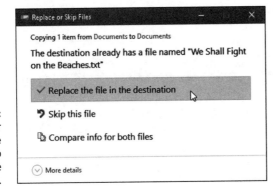

FIGURE 18-4:
Choose whether to replace the existing file, skip the file, or choose which file to keep.

6. **Choose how to handle the conflict.**

If Windows notices a naming conflict with the item you're trying to restore, File History offers you three ways to handle the situation, as shown in Figure 18-4.

- **Replace the File in the Destination Folder.** Click this option only when you're sure that the older file is better than your current file.

- **Skip This File.** Click this if you don't want to restore the file or folder. This option returns you to File History, where you can browse other files.

- **Compare Info for Both Files.** Often the best choice, this option lets you compare the files' sizes and dates before choosing which one to keep, the replacement file or the currently existing file. Or, if you want, this choice also lets you keep *both* files: Windows simply adds a number after the name of the incoming file, naming it Notes (1), for example.

7. **Exit File History by closing the window.**

You close the File History window just as you close any other window: Click the X in its top-right corner.

Want to know more about File History? Read on:

- >> In addition to backing up everything in your main folders and on your desktop, File History stores a list of your favorite websites, listed earlier in Figure 18-2 as Favorites. It also backs up the OneDrive files you've synced to your PC.

- >> I explain how to use File History to move an old computer's files to a new computer in Chapter 20.

- >> When buying a portable hard drive, flash drive, or memory card to create backups, don't skimp on size. The larger the hard drive you choose, the more backups you can save. File History comes in *very* handy.

TIP

TECHNICAL
STUFF

RESTORING FROM A RESTORE POINT

The new Recovery programs in Windows work wonders in resuscitating an ailing computer, and they're more powerful than the older System Restore technology. But in case you've come to rely on the System Restore programs built into earlier Windows versions, Windows 10 still includes System Restore — if you know where to find it.

To send your computer back to a restore point when it was working much better, follow these steps:

1. **Right-click the Start button and choose System from the pop-up menu. When the System window appears, click System Protection from the left pane. Finally, when the System Properties window appears, click System Restore.**

   The System Restore window appears.

2. **Click the Next button at the System Restore window.**

   The System Restore Point lists available restore points.

3. **Click a listed restore point.**

   You can see more available restore points, if available, by selecting the Show More Restore Points check box.

4. **Click the Scan for Affected Programs button to see how your chosen restore point will affect programs.**

   A handy touch, this feature lists programs you'll probably need to reinstall.

5. **Click Next to confirm your chosen restore point. Then click Finish.**

   Your computer grumbles a bit and then restarts, using those earlier settings that (hopefully) worked fine.

If your system is *already* working fine, feel free to create your own restore point, as I describe at the beginning of Chapter 13. Name the restore point something descriptive, such as Before House Sitting the Neighbor's Cat. (That way, you know which restore point to use if things go awry.)

Windows Keeps Asking Me for Permission

Like earlier Windows versions before it, Windows 10 offers both Administrator and Standard user accounts. The Administrator account, meant for the computer's owner, holds all the power. Holders of mere Standard accounts, by contrast, aren't allowed to do things that might change the computer or its settings.

But no matter which of the two accounts you hold, you'll occasionally brush up against the Windows version of a barbed-wire fence. When a program tries to change something on your computer, Windows pokes you with a message like the one shown in Figure 18-5.

Standard account holders see a slightly different message that commands them to fetch an Administrator account holder to type in a password.

FIGURE 18-5:
The Windows permission screens pop up when a program tries to change something on your PC.

Of course, when screens like this one pop up too often, most people simply ignore them and give their approval — even if that means they've just allowed a virus to settle comfortably inside their PC.

So, when Windows sends you a permission screen, ask yourself this question: "Is Windows asking permission for something *I* did or requested?" If your answer is yes, give your approval so Windows can carry out your bidding. But if Windows sends you a permission screen out of the blue when you haven't done anything, click No or Cancel. That keeps potential nasties from invading your PC.

If you don't have time for this bothersome security layer, and you're willing to suffer the consequences, you can find out how to turn off user account permissions by reading Chapter 11.

I Need to Retrieve Deleted Files

Everybody who's worked on a computer knows the agony of seeing hours of work go down the drain: You mistakenly delete a file.

The Windows File History backup program, described earlier in this chapter, is a lifesaver here. But if you never turned on File History — an easy task I explain in Chapter 13 — Windows offers another way to retrieve your deleted files: the Recycle Bin.

The Recycle Bin works because Windows doesn't *really* destroy your deleted files. Instead, Windows slips those files into your Recycle Bin (shown in the margin), which lives on your desktop.

Open the Recycle Bin with a double-click, and you find every file or folder you've deleted within the past few weeks. I cover the Recycle Bin in Chapter 3, but here's a tip: To restore a file or folder from the Recycle Bin, right-click the file and choose Restore. The deleted item magically reappears in its former home.

Fixing Broken Apps

NEW

Microsoft's latest update to Windows 10 makes it much easier to repair groggy apps. If your app no longer seems in good health and you'd like to reset it and start from scratch, follow these steps:

1. **Click the Start button and choose the Settings icon from the Start menu.**

   The Settings app appears.

2. **Click the Settings app's System icon (shown in the margin). When the System window appears, click the Apps & Features link along the window's left edge.**

   The Apps & Features window appears, listing your apps alphabetically along its right side.

3. **Click the malfunctioning app's name and, when the menu drops down, click the words Advanced Options.**

4. **When the Advanced Options settings appear, click the Reset button.**

Windows deletes and reinstalls the app from scratch, taking any of your preference settings and sign in details along with it. This isn't a big deal with say, the Calculator app. But more elaborate apps like Mail and Calendar may take some time to bring back up to speed with the right settings.

My Settings Are Messed Up

Sometimes you want to return to the way things were *before* you started messing around with them. Your salvation lies in the Restore Default button, which awaits your command in strategically placed areas throughout Windows. A click of that button returns the settings to the way Windows originally set them up.

Here are a few Restore Default buttons you may find useful:

>> **Internet Explorer:** When the age-old Internet Explorer program seems clogged with unwanted toolbars, spyware, or just plain weirdness, take the last resort of bringing back its original settings: In Internet Explorer, click the Tools

icon (shown in the margin) and choose Internet Options from the drop-down menu. Click the Advanced tab and click the Reset button.

WARNING

Resetting Internet Explorer wipes out nearly *everything,* including your toolbars, add-ons, and search engine preference. If you also select Internet Explorer's Delete Personal Settings check box, clicking the Reset button even kills your browser history and saved passwords. Only your favorites, feeds, and a few other items remain.

» **Apps:** Released one year after Windows 10 arrived, the Anniversary update adds a reset button that restores malfunctioning apps back to their original working condition. I describe how in the previous section, "Fixing Broken Apps."

WARNING

» **Firewall:** If you suspect foul play within Windows Firewall, bring back its original settings and start over. (Some of your programs may need to be reinstalled.) From the desktop, right-click the Start button and choose Control Panel. When Control Panel opens, choose System and Security and open Windows Firewall. Click Restore Defaults in the left column. (Be careful with this one, as you may need to reinstall some apps and programs.)

» **Media Player:** When the Media Player Library contains mistakes, tell it to delete its index and start over. In Media Player, press and release the Alt key, click Tools, choose Advanced from the pop-out menu, and choose Restore Media Library. (Or if you've accidentally removed items from the Media Player Library, choose Restore Deleted Library Items instead.)

» **Groove Music app:** Sometimes even the Groove Music app becomes confused. If it's leaving out some of your music or leaving ghosts of music you've deleted, try resetting it: Click the Settings icon (shown in the margin) in the left pane, just to the right of your account name. When the Settings pane appears, click the words, Delete Your Playlists and any Music You've Added or Downloaded from the Groove Catalog. When the Groove Music app wakes back up, it relocates all of your music and adds it back into the app's catalog.

» **Colors:** Windows lets you tweak your desktop's colors and sounds, sometimes into a disturbing mess. To return to the default colors and sounds, right-click the Start button and choose Control Panel. In the Appearance and Personalization section, choose Change the Theme. Then choose Windows from the Windows Default Themes section.

» **Fonts:** Have you tweaked your fonts beyond recognition? Return them to normal by opening the desktop's Control Panel, clicking Appearance and Personalization, and then clicking Fonts. In the left pane, click Font Settings and then click the Restore Default Font Settings button.

» **Libraries:** In Windows 10, libraries are hidden by default. (I explain how to turn them on in Chapter 5.) When turned on, libraries appear in every folder's Navigation Pane. But if one of your libraries is missing (say, the Music library), you can put it back. Right-click the word Libraries along the right side of any folder and choose Restore Default Libraries. Your default libraries — Documents, Music, Pictures, and Videos — all reappear.

>> **Folders:** Windows hides a slew of switches relating to folders, their Navigation Panes, the items they show, how they behave, and how they search for items. To mull over their options or return them to their default settings, open any folder and click the View tab on the Ribbon menu along the top. Click the Options icon; when the drop-down list appears, click Change Folder and Search Options. The Folder Options window appears, which lists a Restore Defaults button on each of its tabs: General, View, and Search. (Click Apply after each change to make it stick.)

Finally, don't forget the Reset option in Windows, described at the beginning of this chapter. Although it's overkill for many problems, it resets most of your settings to the default.

I Forgot My Password

When Windows won't accept your password at the Sign In screen, you may not be hopelessly locked out of your own computer. Check all these things before letting loose with a scream:

>> **Check your Caps Lock key.** Windows passwords are case-sensitive, meaning that Windows considers OpenSesame and opensesame to be different passwords. If your keyboard's Caps Lock light is on, press your Caps Lock key again to turn it off. Then try entering your password again.

>> **Use your Password Reset Disk.** I explain how to create a Password Reset Disk for a Local account holder in Chapter 14. (The disk doesn't work for Microsoft account holders.) When you've forgotten the password to your Local account, insert that disk to use as a key. Windows lets you back into your account, where you can promptly create an easier-to-remember password. (Flip to Chapter 14 and create a Password Reset Disk now if you haven't yet.)

>> **Let another user reset your password.** Anybody with an Administrator account on your computer can reset your password. Have that person head for the desktop's Control Panel (see Chapter 12), click User Accounts and Family Safety, and click User Accounts. There, she can click the Manage Another Account link to see a list of every account. She can click your account name and click the Change the Password link to create a password you can remember more easily.

Note: If you've forgotten the password to your *Microsoft account*, none of the preceding suggestions will work. Instead, open any web browser and visit www.live. com. The site leads you through the steps to reset your password.

TIP

MY PROGRAM IS FROZEN!

Eventually, one of your programs will freeze up solid, leaving you in the cold with no way to reach its normal Close command. Should you find yourself facing this icy terrain, these steps will extricate the frozen program from your computer's memory (and the screen, as well):

1. **Right-click the Start menu, and select the Start Task Manager option from the pop-up menu.**

   The Task Manager program appears, listing the names of currently running programs.

2. **Click the frozen program's name.**

   If you don't spot your program's name, clicking the More Details link reveals everything currently running on your PC.

3. **Click the End Task button, and Windows whisks away the frozen program.**

   If your computer seems a bit groggy afterward, play it safe by restarting it.

If none of these options works, you're in sad shape, unfortunately. Compare the value of your password-protected data against the cost of hiring a password recovery specialist. You can find a specialist by searching for *recover windows password* on Google (www.google.com).

My Computer Is Frozen Solid

Every once in a while, Windows just drops the ball and wanders off somewhere to sit under a tree. You're left looking at a computer that just looks back. None of the computer's lights blink. Panicked clicks don't do anything. Randomly tapping the keyboard does nothing, or worse yet, the computer starts to beep at every key press.

When nothing onscreen moves (except, perhaps the mouse pointer), the computer is frozen up solid. Try the following approaches, in the following order, to correct the problem:

>> **Approach 1:** Press Esc twice.

 • This action rarely works, but it's a quick first salvo that can't hurt anything.

» **Approach 2:** Press the Ctrl, Alt, and Delete keys simultaneously and choose Start Task Manager from the menu that appears.

- If you're lucky, the Task Manager appears with the message that it discovered an unresponsive application. The Task Manager lists the names of currently running programs, including the one that's not responding. On the Processes tab, click the name of the program that's causing the mess and then click the End Task button. You lose any unsaved work in that program, of course, but you should be used to that. (If you somehow stumbled onto the Ctrl+Alt+Delete combination by accident, press Esc to quit Task Manager and return to Windows.)

- If that still doesn't do the trick, press Ctrl+Alt+Delete again and click the Power icon (shown in the margin) in the screen's bottom-right corner. Choose Restart from the pop-up menu, and your computer shuts down and restarts, hopefully returning in a better mood.

» **Approach 3:** If the preceding approaches don't work, turn off the computer by pressing its power button. (If that merely brings up the Turn Off the Computer menu, choose Restart, and your computer should restart.)

» **Approach 4:** If you keep holding down your computer's power button long enough (usually about 4 to 5 seconds), it eventually stops resisting and turns off.

Chapter 19

Strange Messages: What You Did Does Not Compute

E rror messages in *real* life are fairly easy to understand. A blinking digital clock means you need to set the time. A parked car's beep means that you've left your keys in the ignition. A spouse's stern glance means that you've forgotten something important.

But Windows error messages may have been written by a Senate subcommittee, if only the messages weren't so brief. The error messages rarely describe what you did to cause the event or, even worse, how to fix the problem.

In this chapter, I've collected some of the most common Windows error messages, notifications, and just plain confusing attempts at conversation. Find a message that matches what you're experiencing and then read how to handle the situation as gracefully as Windows will allow.

Add Your Microsoft Account

Meaning: You must sign in with a Microsoft account to perform several tasks in Windows. If you don't have a Microsoft account, you see the message in Figure 19-1. As described in Chapter 2, Microsoft accounts let you reap the most benefits from Windows.

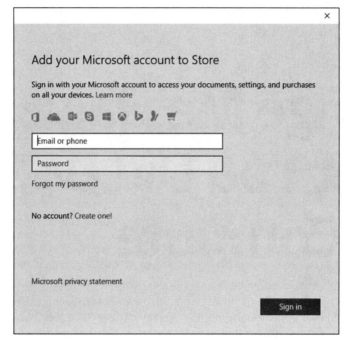

FIGURE 19-1:
To take advantage of many Windows features, you must create a Microsoft account.

Probable cause: You may have tried to use the Windows Store or OneDrive, which both require a Microsoft account.

Solutions: Sign up for a free Microsoft account, as I describe in Chapter 2.

Choose What Happens with This Device

Meaning: When the window in Figure 19-2 appears in your screen's bottom-right corner, click it to tell Windows what to do with the item you've just connected to your computer.

When you click the window in Figure 19-2, the window in Figure 19-3 appears in the screen's *top*-right corner.

Probable cause: You just slid a *flash drive* (a stick of memory) into your computer's USB port, attached a camera, or connected another device to your computer.

Solutions: Choose how you want Windows to react when you reconnect that device in the future. You can always change this decision by visiting the Settings app's Devices area and choosing the AutoPlay category from the left pane. There, Windows lists all of your devices and how Windows currently handles their arrival. Click any device, and a drop-down menu lists all of your choices. (I prefer the Ask Me Every Time option so I can choose the action I need at the time.)

Did You Mean to Switch Apps?

Meaning: Your currently viewed app is trying to open another app. Windows shows you the message in Figure 19-4 to make sure the app's not trying to do anything evil.

Probable Cause: You've clicked a link inside one app that requires another app to handle the job.

FIGURE 19-4:
Click Yes unless
you think
the app is trying
something
sneaky.

Solutions: Unless you think the app is trying to install a virus or do something bad, click the Yes button to approve the job.

Do You Want to Allow This App to Make Changes to This Computer?

Meaning: Are you sure that this software is free from viruses, spyware, and other harmful things?

Probable cause: A window similar to the one shown in Figure 19-5 appears when you try to install downloaded software or a driver for one of your computer's parts.

FIGURE 19-5:
Do you think this
software is safe?

Solutions: If you're sure the file is safe, click the OK, Yes, or Install button. But if this message appears unexpectedly or you think it may not be safe, click the Cancel, No, or Don't Install button. I cover safe computing in Chapter 11.

Do You Want to Save Changes?

Meaning: Figure 19-6 means you haven't saved your work in a program, the program is about to close, and your work is about to be lost.

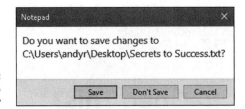

FIGURE 19-6:
Do you want to
save your work?

Probable cause: You're trying to close an application, sign out, or restart your computer before telling a program to save the work you've accomplished.

Solutions: Click the Save button to save your work and let the program close. I cover saving files in Chapter 6. Don't want to save the file? Then click Don't Save to discard your work and move on.

Found Some Malware

Meaning: When the built-in Windows antivirus program, Windows Defender, finds a potentially dangerous file on your computer, it lets you know with the message in Figure 19-7. Windows Defender then removes the file so it can't harm your computer or files.

FIGURE 19-7:
Windows
Defender has
found and
removed a
potentially
dangerous file on
your computer.

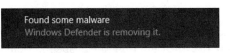

Found some malware
Windows Defender is removing it.

Like most notifications, this one always appears in the screen's bottom-right corner.

Probable cause: A dangerous file — *malware* — probably arrived through email, a flash drive, a networked computer, or an evil website. Windows is removing the file so it can't do any harm.

Solutions: Windows Defender is already removing the offender, but try to remember what action forced Windows Defender to clean up the problem. Then remember not to repeat that action. It wouldn't hurt to tell Windows Defender to give your computer a scan, and to scan any storage device you just connected. (I explain Windows Defender in Chapter 11.)

How Do You Want to Open This?

Meaning: The window in Figure 19-8 appears the first time you open a new type of file on the desktop.

FIGURE 19-8: Windows doesn't know what program should open this file.

Probable cause: Windows apps and programs often fight over the right to open your files. To make sure that the right program is opening your file, Windows displays this message for you to confirm that the correct program is handling the job.

Solutions: If the right program is opening your file, click OK. Windows won't bug you the next time you open that type of file. The message reappears the next time you open a *different* type of file, however. If the wrong program is trying to open the file, choose the correct program from the message's list.

If Windows doesn't offer any valid suggestions, however, click the option Look for an App in the Store. (I cover this problem in Chapter 6.) To open that file, you may need to download or buy an app from the Windows Store.

Let This App Use Your Precise Location?

Meaning: An app is asking permission to know your current physical location, as shown in Figure 19-9, and Windows wants to know whether you want to allow that.

FIGURE 19-9: Click Yes to let the app know your location.

Probable cause: An app needs your location to do something, perhaps to give you information about your immediate surroundings.

Solutions: If you trust the app and feel comfortable letting it know where you're currently sitting or standing, click Yes. That gives the app permission to always know your location without having to ask again. If you think the app is being too nosy, click No. However, the app will probably ask for permission again the next time you open it.

Reconnect Your Drive

Meaning: The message in Figure 19-10 tells you that the Windows backup program, File History, has stopped working.

FIGURE 19-10: Your backup drive or card isn't plugged in to your computer.

Probable cause: File History was saving your files on a portable hard drive, flash drive, or memory card that's no longer plugged in to your computer.

Solutions: This message appears most often on laptops and tablets after you've taken them on the road, leaving your backup drive at home. So, find your portable hard drive, flash drive, or memory card and plug it back into your computer. (If File History doesn't begin working again, revisit the File History section in Chapter 11 to make sure the settings are correct.)

Once you plug the drive back into your computer, File History thoughtfully makes a fresh backup of everything that hasn't yet been saved.

There Is No Email Program Associated to Perform the Requested Action

Meaning: The particularly cryptic message in Figure 19-11 means you're trying to send email from the desktop, but you haven't installed a desktop-based email program.

FIGURE 19-11:
You need to install an email program onto the desktop.

Probable cause: Here's where the split between the traditional desktop programs and Microsoft's new apps becomes irritating. Microsoft doesn't allow Windows desktop programs to use the Mail app. If you click any desktop program's Send This or E-Mail This option, this message appears until you install a *desktop*-based email program.

Solutions: Download and install a desktop email program. To keep things simple, you'll have to decide between using the Mail app, or a traditional desktop-based email program. It's often difficult to run more than one email program on the same computer. I describe choosing and setting up email in Chapter 10.

You Don't Currently Have Permission to Access This Folder

Meaning: If you see the dialog box in Figure 19-12, it means Windows won't let you peek inside the folder you're trying to open. (The folder's name appears in the message's title bar.) A similar message appears when Windows won't let you peek inside a file.

FIGURE 19-12:
Find somebody
with an
Administrator
account to open
the folder or file.

Probable cause: The file or folder belongs to somebody with a different user account.

Solutions: If you hold an Administrator account, you can open files and folders from other people's user accounts by clicking Continue. If you don't have an Administrator account, however, you're locked out.

Chapter 20

Moving from an Old PC to a New Windows 10 PC

When you bring home your exciting new Windows 10 computer, it lacks the most important thing of all: The stuff from your *old* computer. How do you copy your files from that dusty old PC to that shiny new Windows PC? How do you even *find* everything you want to move?

Before Windows 10, Microsoft solved the problem by including a virtual moving van called Windows Easy Transfer. The Windows Easy Transfer program grabbed not only your old computer's files but its settings (your browser's list of favorite websites, for example).

Unfortunately, Microsoft discontinued Windows Easy Transfer in Windows 10, complicating the process of moving to a new PC. This chapter explains your current options for moving your information from your old PC to your new PC.

TIP

Here's a time-saver: If you're just *upgrading* your old Windows 7 or 8.1 PC to Windows 10, you can skip this chapter. When you upgrade, Windows 10 leaves all your personal files and programs in place.

Hiring a Third Party to Make the Move

Microsoft may have walked out on the automated PC file transfer business, but third-party vendors are happy to do the job. In fact, Windows XP and Windows Vista owners have no other choice — Microsoft doesn't offer *any* transfer solutions for those older Windows versions.

That leaves you two third-party options: computer upgrade software or taking your PC to a professional.

The following sections cover the pros and cons of each.

Buying Laplink's PCmover program

The PCmover software suite of programs from Laplink (www.laplink.com) transfers not only your old PC's files and settings but some of its programs, as well. That's more work than Microsoft's old Easy Transfer program ever attempted. The PCmover suite works on every Windows version from Windows XP to Windows 10. (It *doesn't* work with Windows RT, released on some inexpensive tablets.)

However, the powerful transfer programs come with a staggering array of potential complications, which isn't surprising: Moving from one PC to another is fraught with possible mishaps. (On the positive side, Laplink helps you move by offering free, 24-hour tech support in United States, Canada, Australia, and the United Kingdom.)

Your first job is choosing which PCmover software you need: PCmover Home or PCmover Professional. Both let you transfer information only from *one* old PC to *one* new PC. That's usually not a problem, but keep in mind that you can't give the program to a friend after you've transferred your files.

>> **PCmover Home:** This minimalist package moves files, settings, and user profiles to your new PC. However, it won't move apps and programs.

>> **PCmover Professional:** The more popular (and more expensive) option, this software copies apps and programs to the new PC, as well as files, settings, and user profiles.

Both programs copy your old PC's files, settings, and some programs to your new PC, as shown in Figure 20-1. However, neither package guarantees to copy *all* of your programs. Because of technical reasons, some programs can transfer, but others won't. (The reasons behind those potential problems come with their own fine-print section too detailed to list here.)

FIGURE 20-1:
PCmover
Professional
helps you move
from an old PC to
a new one.

If you plan to transfer your files over a network, you can buy and download your chosen PCmover program from Laplink's website. Most people, however, find a better deal by buying the PCmover Ultimate boxed program from Amazon (www. amazon.com). That package includes PCmover Professional *and* a transfer cable, and it costs less than the version on Laplink's website.

The PCmover programs are copy-protected, so you need a working Internet connection before you can begin using them. Also, depending on the amount of information on your old PC — and the way you connect your computers — the transfer process can take several hours.

TIP

ZINSTALL'S WinWin10 PRO

PCmover may be the least expensive third-party file transfer solution, but it's not the most comprehensive. Zinstall's WinWin software costs more than twice as much as the competition. Depending on your situation, though, it might do a more thorough job, especially when transferring desktop programs from your old PC to your new one.

For more information about Zinstall's products, visit the company's website at www. zinstall.com.

In short, the PCmover software works best for somebody who's not only patient but also experienced enough with computers to know how to talk with tech support people if something goes wrong. (Tech support people usually speak very, well, *technically*.)

Visiting a repair shop

Almost all local computer repair shops can move your old PC's information to your new PC. (Call first to see whether they want the PC alone, or the PC, monitor, keyboard, and mouse.) Repair shops that make house calls are even better because you won't have to unplug any cables and drop off your PCs at the shop.

Check with your neighbors — they've probably already found a favorite local computer shop or technician.

The prices at local computer repair shops vary widely, and they probably charge more than the price of buying file-transfer software. But if something goes wrong, *they're* the ones talking to tech support, not you.

TECHNICAL STUFF

MOVING THE MICROSOFT WAY

According to Microsoft, moving from an old PC to a new PC is easy. First, you log in with a Microsoft account on both your new and old PCs. Then you copy your old PC's Documents, Music, Pictures, and Videos folders to OneDrive, your online storage space.

When you step over to your new computer and sign in with that same Microsoft account, your settings travel automatically to your new PC. And, because Windows 10 includes OneDrive built-in, your old PC's files and folders are waiting for you.

However, Microsoft's method works only with PCs running Windows 8, Windows 8.1, or Windows 10; earlier Windows versions don't support Microsoft accounts as well. Copying files and folders to and from OneDrive can take a lot of time and effort, as well. When you move your files to OneDrive, Microsoft is banking that you'll simply keep everything stored there. As soon as you fill up your allotted OneDrive storage space, you need to pay Microsoft a monthly fee for more storage.

If you know how to find all of your old PC's files, and if they all fit onto OneDrive, and if you're well-versed in file management chores with File Explorer, OneDrive might meet your needs. But that's a lot of "ifs." Simply put, Microsoft's method isn't the best for people who aren't experienced with computers.

A repair shop can probably transfer your files even if your old computer no longer turns on or has trouble running. Chances are good that your old computer's hard drive still works, and it still has all of your files. Techies at the repair shop can usually transfer your files from your old computer's hard drive directly to your new PC.

Even if you hate throwing in the towel and calling a professional, remember, you need to transfer your old PC's information only *once.* And, if the techie who does the job seems friendly and competent enough, grab a business card. It may come in handy down the road.

Transferring Files Yourself

You can transfer files yourself if you're moving from a Windows 7, 8, 8.1, or 10 PC. You can do this with a combination of a Microsoft account and the built-in File History backup program in Windows. You tell the program to back up your old PC's files, and then you tell your new PC's program to restore the files.

However, you need a portable hard drive for this to work. Portable hard drives are fairly inexpensive, usually costing less than $100. But there's a bonus: When you're through transferring the files, the drive works perfectly for backing up your *new* computer.

To transfer files from an old Windows 7, 8, 8.1, or 10 computer to a new Windows 10 computer, follow these steps:

1. **If you're running Windows 7 on your old PC, upgrade it to Windows 10.**

   For many Windows 7 owners, this is probably a deal breaker. Unless, of course, you took advantage of the free Windows 10 upgrade offer that ended July 29, 2016. Now that the deadline has passed, Windows 7 owners might be better off by buying a file transfer program discussed earlier in this chapter.

   If you're running Windows 8, 8.1, or 10 on your old PC, move ahead to Step 2.

2. **If you've already been using File History on your old PC, jump to Step 5. Otherwise move to Step 3.**

3. **Sign in with your Microsoft account on your old PC.**

   When you sign in with a Microsoft account, Microsoft remembers many of your settings and services so it can duplicate them on other PCs you sign into.

4. **Plug the portable hard drive into your old PC and then set up File History to save your files onto the portable hard drive.**

File History comes built into Windows 8, 8.1, and 10. I describe how to set it up and turn it on in Chapter 13. It could take anywhere from a few minutes to a few hours to back up your files for the first time.

While File History backs up your files, it shows the statement "File History is saving copies of your files for the first time." (It also lists the word *Stop* in case you want to stop the backup.)

When File History has finished backing up your files to the portable drive, those words change to say "Files last copied," followed by the date and time it finished backing up your files, as shown in Figure 20-2. At that point, move to Step 5.

FIGURE 20-2:
The File History
window lists the
backup's date
and time.

5. **Sign into your new Windows 10 PC with the same Microsoft account you used on your old PC. Then plug the portable hard drive into your new computer.**

By signing in with your Microsoft account, your settings automatically transfer to your new PC. (The wallpaper on your new PC quickly changes to match your old PC, letting you know that something is happening.)

6. **Open File History and direct your new Windows 10 PC toward your old File History backup.**

On your new Windows 10 PC, click the Start button and type **File History** into the Search box and press Enter. The Control Panel's File History window appears, as shown in Figure 20-3.

Click the check box labeled I Want to Use a Previous Backup on this File History Drive. A window drops down, listing the backup you've made on your old PC. Click its name, and click the Turn On button.

Your new PC begins backing up its files for the first time, but these incoming files won't damage your old PC's backup.

7. **Choose Restore Personal Files from the File History window's left pane.**

   The window shown in Figure 20-3 appears.

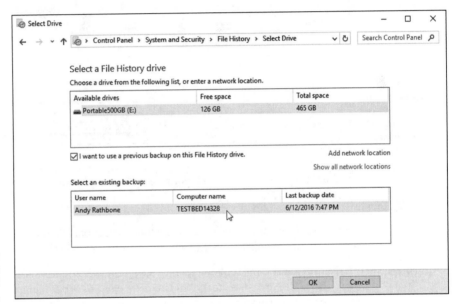

FIGURE 20-3: Choose the backup you'd like to restore.

8. **Choose the files and folders to restore and then click the green Restore button.**

   Click the Forward or Back arrows next to the big green button along the window's bottom until you find the date and time of the files you'd like to restore.

   For example, if you used File History on your old PC for the first time in Step 4, click the Back arrow (on the left) until you're at the Number 1 backup.

   If you've been using File History on your old PC all along, click the Forward arrow (on the right) to move to your most recent backup.

   When you're viewing the files or folders you want to restore, click the green button found on the window's bottom edge, shown in Figure 20-4. File History begins copying your old PC's files and folders onto your new PC.

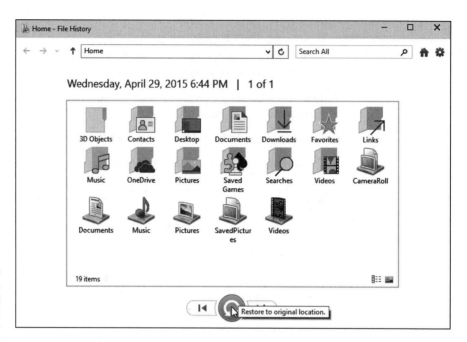

FIGURE 20-4:
Click the green
button to restore
the files and
folders.

If there are no complications, your new PC should soon have the files and folders from your old PC.

>> If you'd already been using File History on your old PC, all of your old PC's backups should still be available to you on your new PC.

>> Your new PC will continue to back up your new computer's files to your portable hard drive. Keep the hard drive plugged in permanently. (Or, if you bought a new laptop or tablet, plug it in frequently so your computer can keep your backups current.)

>> If you've just borrowed a friend's portable hard drive, you can unplug it at this point and give it back. But you should really have your own portable hard drive so you can begin backing up your new Windows 10 PC.

>> Your Microsoft account and File History can transport your settings and files to your new PC. However, you must still install all of your old desktop programs onto your new PC.

>> If you're moving to Windows 10 from a Windows 8 or 8.1 PC, you can find your apps waiting for you in the Windows Store: Click your icon near the Store app's upper-right corner and choose My Library from the drop-down menu. There you can find and download your old apps to your new PC.

Chapter 21

Help on the Windows Help System

D on't bother plowing through this whole chapter for the nitty-gritty. What you find here are the quickest ways to make Windows dish out helpful information when something on the desktop leaves you stumped:

>> **Press F1 when on the desktop:** Press the F1 key from within Windows or any desktop program.

>> **Start menu:** Click the Start button and click the Get Started tile.

>> **Question mark:** If you spot a little blue question mark icon near a window's top-right corner, pounce on it with a quick click.

In each case, Windows fetches help, either by going online, fetching built-in instructions, or leading you to a tutorial built into Windows 10.

This chapter explains how to take advantage of the help Windows 10 has to offer.

Getting Started with Windows 10

The Windows 10 Get Started app offers a short guided tour to Windows 10. It appeals mostly to the same people who enjoy reading book introductions: They set the mood for what's coming.

 To open the app, click the Start button and click the Get Started icon (shown in the margin) from the Start menu. The app fills the screen, shown in Figure 21-1.

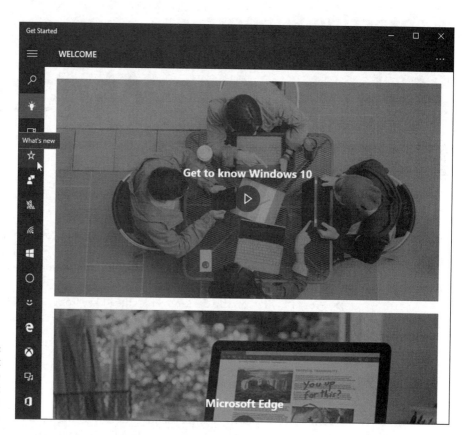

FIGURE 21-1:
The new Get Started app offers a short introduction to Windows 10.

 Like most apps, the Get Started app lists icons along the left edge. Can't see the icons' labels? Then click the hamburger menu icon (shown in the margin) in the app's upper-left corner. Clicking that icon in any app expands the app's left pane, letting you see labels next to the mysterious icons. You can also hover your mouse pointer over an icon and a pop-up reveals its name.

Click the What's New icon, shown in Figure 21-1, to see a quick explanation of the biggest changes in Windows 10.

Feel free to click any of the other categories along the left and browse the offered options. However, the Get Started app serves as a very brief introductory guide to Windows 10. It's definitely not a problem solver.

In fact, the Get Started app has its own problem: Many portions work only when you're connected to the Internet. If you're not connected, the app simply displays an error message.

Contacting Support

Windows 10 comes with a new app designed to make it easy to find just the type of help you need for your particular problem. Called simply, Contact Support, the app works much like those phone robots that make you press different numbers on your phone until you're finally routed to the proper department.

The app, like most things in Windows these days, requires you to log in with a Microsoft account. Microsoft began basing Windows around Microsoft accounts with Windows 8, and without one, you'll find Windows to be increasingly difficult. (To be fair, Apple and Google also require their own accounts.)

To summon the Contact Support app and begin routing yourself to somebody or something that can help you with your computer's particular problem, follow these steps:

1. **Click the Start button, click the All Apps icon, if necessary, and click Contact Support (the icon is in the margin).**

   The Contact Support program appears, shown in Figure 21-2, and immediately starts to break your problem into manageable categories.

2. **Click the applicable category, and continue clicking through the menus until you find your preferred method of support.**

   Clicked the wrong category? Click the backward pointing arrow (shown in the margin) in the window's upper, left corner to return to the previous screen.

   As you click through the categories, you notice that Microsoft's support options fall into these main categories:

   - **Online:** Some categories simply take you to a website for more help. To its credit, the app usually routes you to the correct place more quickly than you could have done yourself by searching on the Internet. But this option won't help you if you're having trouble connecting to the Internet.

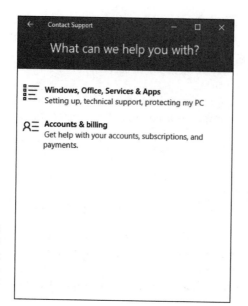

FIGURE 21-2:
The Windows 10
Contact Support
program routes
you to the correct
department.

- **Chat Online with a Microsoft Answer Tech:** A good place to start, this begins as a free chat, where you type messages back and forth with a Microsoft representative. Depending on the severity of your computer's problem, though, it may move to a paid service.

- **Schedule a Call, Call Me As Soon As Possible:** These options provide variations on a common theme: paid support. I describe Microsoft's paid support options in this chapter's next section.

- **Ask the Community:** Perhaps your best bet, this involves posting your question in an online forum at answers.microsoft.com. I describe it in this chapter's last section.

I recommend trying the Online option first. Sometimes reading a website's Frequently Asked Questions will clear up a common problem. I cover the other two options, paid support, and Ask the Community, in the next two sections.

Microsoft's paid support options

Microsoft offers two main types of paid services, broken down into these categories:

>> **Assure Software Support Plan:** For a $149 annual fee, Microsoft offers one year of help by online chat or phone (and personal training, if you live close by to a Microsoft Store). For people who constantly take their PC to repair shops or call in-home tech support companies, the annual support plan may save some money.

>> **Premium Software Support:** If you only need help with Microsoft's own software like Windows or Office, you can pay $99 for an hour's worth of online chat or phone support. That $99 is per hour, however. And the charge is for each session, which shows why the Assure Software Support Plan might be a better deal for problems that occur frequently.

If you've purchased your computers directly from Microsoft's online or retail stores, Microsoft offers extended service and warranty plans. By paying in advance, you can take advantage of Microsoft's support plans without having to pay a per-incident charge or hourly fee.

If you live close to a Microsoft Store, you find better support by taking your computer to the store, where they can help you in person. To find the Microsoft Store nearest you, visit www.microsoftstore.com.

Microsoft's free support options

For free support, your best bet is the Microsoft Answers forum. It's an online gathering place for confused owners, knowledgeable tech enthusiasts, and an occasional Microsoft employee.

You visit the website, choose your category, type in your question, and wait. Sometimes a Microsoft employee will answer, but more often than not, somebody with a similar problem will chime in. The more people that respond, the more likely everybody will find a solution to a common problem.

Remember, though: The forums are for Microsoft products. If you're having problems with software from another company, you're limited to that other company's technical support.

To visit the free Microsoft Answers forum, follow these steps:

1. **Visit the Microsoft Answers website at** answers.microsoft.com **and choose Windows from the Browse the Categories section.**

2. **Choose your Windows version from the Browse by Version section.**

3. **Sign in with your Microsoft account.**

   Like most things involving Microsoft these days, you need a Microsoft account to access the Microsoft Answers Forum.

   The forum's website appears, shown in Figure 21-3.

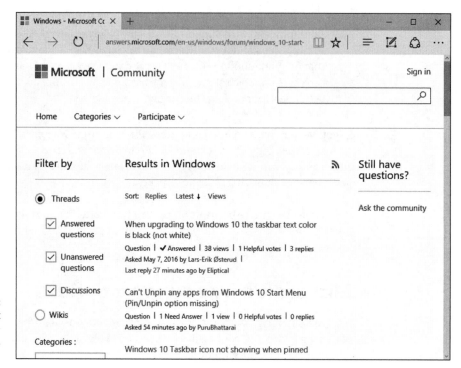

FIGURE 21-3:
The Microsoft
Answers online
forum provides
free tech support.

4. **Search the forum for previously answered questions.**

If something about your computer isn't working correctly, it probably isn't working for others, either. Type a few key words describing your problem in the Search box, located in the window's upper, right corner, and press Enter.

When the website lists the results, spend some time browsing them to see if any solutions work for your computer's particular problem. If not, move to Step 5.

5. **Type in your question, fill out a title, problem description, and category. Then click the Submit button.**

To ask a question, click the Ask a Question link. The website presents a form, shown in Figure 21-4, for you to fill in a title and details about your computer's problem.

Don't forget to fill out the Category drop-down lists at the bottom of the form. They let you choose your Windows version, as well as narrow down your question by topic. Those little chores help others find your question, and possibly provide answers, when they visit later on.

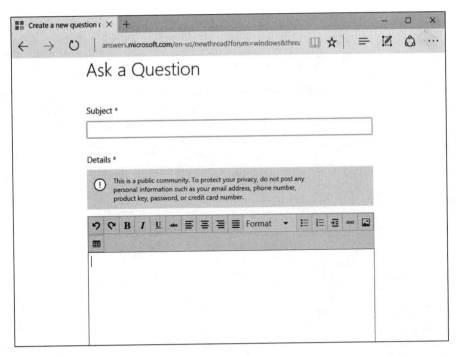

FIGURE 21-4:
Type a title for
your question.

And then, you wait. When somebody responds, a notice appears in your email with a link to your posted message and the response. Click the emailed link to revisit the forum, where you can begin a correspondence that may solve your problem.

The Answers Desk is free, and although it's not guaranteed to provide an answer, it's definitely worthwhile.

TIP

For the best results, keep these tips in mind when posting a message on the Answers Forum:

>> Don't rant. Remember, most forum visitors aren't paid. Many of them are confused souls trying to piece together solutions, just like you. Many computer nerds also hang out there. They're actually interested in solving problems, and they're persuaded more by logic than emotions.

>> To attract the best responses, be as descriptive as possible. If you see an error message, list it in its entirety, without typographical errors. Type in your computer's exact make and model.

>> If possible, list the exact steps you take on your computer to reproduce the problem. If your problem is reproducible on other people's computers, it's much easier to solve.

>> Most of the best answers don't come from Microsoft's paid technicians. They come from strangers who have your same problem, perhaps even the same make and model of computer, and who want to swap tips to make things better for you both.

>> Keep an eye on your email Inbox, and respond to people who try to help. The information you're exchanging will live on for years. Even if you're not able to solve your immediate problem, you're leaving a trail that can help others solve that problem down the road.

7

The Part of Tens

Chapter 22

Ten Things You'll Hate about Windows 10 (And How to Fix Them)

You may find yourself thinking Windows 10 would be perfect if only . . . *(insert your pet peeve here)*.

If you find yourself thinking (or saying) those words frequently, read this chapter. Here, you find not only a list of ten of the most aggravating things about Windows 10 but also the best ways you can fix them.

I Don't Want Windows 10!

Microsoft gave away Windows 10 as a free upgrade during its first year of release. As the deadline for the free upgrade approached, Microsoft grew more aggressive in promoting Windows 10. Messages appeared out of the blue, telling people to schedule their update. Some people upgraded to Windows 10 simply because they couldn't figure out how to avoid it.

Don't get me wrong: Many people love Windows 10. Others hate it, and still more simply wish Microsoft had made Windows 10 an optional, informed choice rather than something to wake up to in the morning.

If you've found yourself with an unwanted upgrade to Windows 10, here's how to return to the charms of your previous Windows version:

1. **Click the Start menu, click the Settings icon, and, when the Settings app appears, click the Update & Security category.**

2. **When the Update & Security page appears, click Recovery from the left pane.**

3. **From the right pane, find the Go Back to a Previous Version of Windows section and click the Get Started button.**

Your computer will grumble a bit before restarting. Eventually, after enough grumbling and restarting, you'll return to your older, more familiar version of Windows. Your files and programs should be waiting for you, as well.

After 30 days, however, this option disappears. Once that happens, you're stuck with Windows 10. Remember, though, Microsoft constantly updates Windows 10. It's grown increasingly easier to use during the past year. You might learn to like it.

I Want to Avoid the Apps!

With Windows 10, Microsoft continues its switch from the old-and-weary world of desktop programs to the mobile-friendly land of apps. After a year of updates, apps are more difficult to avoid than ever.

Some people love apps. They're designed for touchscreen tablets, as well as for phones, with limited screen real estate. They lack complicated menus and aim for touch-friendly simplicity. Other people hate apps, preferring to run programs on their desktop. After all, they've been doing it that way with a mouse and keyboard for two decades.

If you find Microsoft's focus on apps to be misguided and annoying, here's how to avoid them. Follow the tips in these sections to remove apps from the Start menu and your PC, keeping your focus on the desktop.

Pruning apps from the Start menu and your PC

Windows 10 stocks the Start menu's right edge with app tiles. Windows 8 and 8.1 owners may be accustomed to Microsoft's new app-loving lifestyle, but apps may be new and unwanted for Windows 7 upgraders.

Luckily, you can prune those tiles fairly easily. To remove a Start screen tile, right-click it and, when the pop-up menu appears, choose Unpin from Start. Repeat with all the other tiles until they're gone, gone, gone.

That removes the app tiles from the Start menu. But the apps still remain on the Start menu's All Apps alphabetical list. And it doesn't remove the apps from your PC.

To go one step further and *uninstall* the apps, follow these steps:

1. **Click the Start button and choose the Settings icon from the Start menu.**

   The Settings app appears.

2. **Click the Settings app's System icon (shown in the margin). When the System window appears, click the Apps & Features link along the window's left edge.**

   The Apps & Features window appears, listing your installed apps along its right side, as shown in Figure 22-1.

3. **To remove an app, click its name, click the Uninstall button that appears below its name. Then click Uninstall again when Windows asks whether you're sure you want to delete the app.**

   Windows deletes the app from your computer, removing it from the Start menu along the way. Not all apps can be deleted, unfortunately. If the Uninstall button is grayed out, that app can't be uninstalled.

You can reinstall a mistakenly deleted app by visiting the Windows Store, searching for the app in the Store's Search box, and reinstalling it. (It's also listed when you click your account icon near the upper-right corner of the Windows Store and choose My Library from the drop-down menu.) I describe how to install apps from the Store in Chapter 6.

Telling desktop programs, not apps, to open your files

Some people don't mind apps, as long as the apps don't intrude on chores normally handled by their traditional desktop programs. But in Windows 10, apps often want to open your desktop files. Clicking a music file from the desktop's File Explorer, for example, normally fetches the Groove Music app rather than Media Player, which has held the reins for years.

To hand the chores back to your desktop programs, follow these steps:

1. **Click the Start button and click the Settings icon from the Start menu.**

    The Settings app appears.

2. **When the Settings app opens, click the System category (shown in the margin) and then click the Defaults Apps option from the left pane.**

    The Choose Default Apps screen appears.

3. **For each type of file, choose the program that should open it.**

    In the Music Player section, for example, click the currently listed program. When the Choose an App screen appears, showing apps and programs capable of playing music, choose the desktop player you want to handle the job.

Repeat for other program categories until you've replaced any Start menu apps with their desktop equivalents.

I Want to Avoid the Desktop!

A touchscreen tablet entices you to stick with apps for their finger-sized tiles and easy-to-touch icons. Smartphone owners have enjoyed the app lifestyle for years. Easily downloadable apps offer help for nearly every niche, from bird-watching to car repair.

A tablet's lightweight yet large screen makes it easy to read digital books, newspapers, and magazines. You can browse your favorite websites while away from your desk. The newly beefed-up Settings app in Windows 10 makes it easier than ever to avoid the desktop.

But staying nestled within the world of apps can be more difficult than it appears. No matter how hard you try to avoid the desktop and its pin-sized controls, you'll find yourself dragged there when you do any of the following things from the Start menu:

>> **Manage gadgetry:** The Devices area of the Settings app lists all the devices connected to your computer, from printers to mice to portable hard drives. But it shows only their names; to change the settings of many of those devices requires a trip to the desktop's Control Panel.

>> **Run Desktop Programs:** If you install or run any older programs designed for the desktop, you're back in the old-school land of the desktop and its mouse-central design.

>> **Manage files:** You can access your photos and music files from the Photos and Music apps, respectively. But if you need to visit your OneDrive files or do more advanced tasks — sorting files by creation date, for example — it's time to visit the desktop.

In short, the apps in Windows 10 handle most simple computing tasks, but when it comes to fine-tuning your computer's settings or performing maintenance work, you find yourself returning to the desktop or its Control Panel.

TIP

If you constantly return to the desktop for certain tasks, visit the Windows Store to search for an app that can handle the job. Microsoft stocks the store with more apps every day, and as the apps fill more niches, you'll find yourself relying on the desktop less often.

Until the apps catch up with the desktop, tablet owners might want to pop a portable Bluetooth mouse (covered in Chapter 12) into their gadget bags for those inevitable trips to the desktop and its tiny buttons and menus.

TIP

When running Windows on a tablet, make sure you're in Tablet mode: Slide your finger inward from the screen's right edge. When the Notifications pane appears, make sure the Tablet mode button is highlighted. If it's not highlighted like the adjacent buttons, tap it to switch back to Tablet mode.

I Don't Want a Microsoft Account

Microsoft wants *everybody* to sign in with a Microsoft account. To Microsoft's credit, Windows 10 is much easier to use with a Microsoft account. Many services require one. Without a Microsoft account, you miss out on the handy OneDrive online storage space, as well as downloading new apps from the Store. Your *child* even needs to sign in with a Microsoft account if you want to track his computer usage.

But if you don't want a Microsoft account, you don't need one. Just sign up for a Local account instead. However, Local account holders limit themselves to the "old school" world of life on the desktop. For many people, the desktop works just fine.

A Local account lets you use your desktop and desktop programs, just as they've worked on Windows 7 and earlier Windows versions.

You'll just have to avert your eyes whenever you see the OneDrive entry built-in to the desktop's File Explorer.

I explain how to create both Local and Microsoft user accounts in Chapter 14.

Windows Makes Me Sign In All the Time

The power-conscious Windows normally blanks your screen when you haven't touched a key for a few minutes. And, when you belatedly press a key to bring the screen back to life, you're faced with the lock screen.

To move past the lock screen, you need to type your password to sign back in to your account.

Some people prefer that extra level of security. If the lock screen kicks in while you're spending too much time at the water cooler, you're protected: Nobody can walk over and snoop through your email.

Other people don't need that extra security, and they simply want to return to work quickly. Here's how to accommodate both camps:

To keep Windows from asking for a password whenever it wakes back up, follow these steps:

1. **Click the Start button, and click the Settings icon.**

   The Settings app appears.

2. **Click the Accounts icon from the Settings app, and click Sign-in Options from the left panel.**

3. **Click the Require Sign-In Options drop-down menu, and change it to Never.**

Taking these steps leaves you with a more easy-going Windows. When your computer wakes up from sleep, you're left at the same place where you stopped working, and you don't have to enter your password anymore.

Unfortunately, it also leaves you with a less-secure Windows. Anybody who walks by your computer will have access to all your files.

To return to the safer-but-less-friendly Windows, follow these same steps, but in Step 3, select the When PC Wakes Up From Sleep option. Your changes take place immediately.

TIP

If you hate signing in, you're a perfect candidate for Windows Hello. Instead of having to type in a name and password, you simply slide your finger over a fingerprint reader. Windows immediately greets you, and lets you in. I describe how to set up Windows Hello in Chapter 14.

The Taskbar Keeps Disappearing

The taskbar is a handy Windows feature that usually squats along the bottom of your desktop. Sometimes, unfortunately, it up and wanders off into the woods. Here are a few ways to track it down and bring it home.

If your taskbar suddenly clings to the *side* of the screen — or even the ceiling — try dragging it back in place: Instead of dragging an edge, drag the entire taskbar from its middle. As your mouse pointer reaches your desktop's bottom edge, the taskbar suddenly snaps back into place. Let go of the mouse and you've recaptured it.

Follow these tips to prevent your taskbar from wandering:

» To keep the taskbar locked in place so that it won't float away, right-click a blank part of the taskbar and select Lock the Taskbar. Remember, though, that before you can make any future changes to the taskbar, you must first unlock it.

» If your taskbar drops from sight whenever the mouse pointer doesn't hover nearby, turn off the taskbar's Auto Hide feature: Right-click a blank part of the taskbar and choose Settings from the pop-up menu. When the Taskbar settings page appears, turn off the toggle switch called Automatically Hide the Taskbar in Desktop Mode. (Another toggle keeps the taskbar from hiding in Tablet mode, as well.)

I Can't Line Up Two Windows on the Screen

With its arsenal of dragging-and-dropping tools, Windows simplifies grabbing information from one window and copying it to another. You can drag an address from an address book and drop it atop a letter in your word processor, for example.

However, the hardest part of dragging and dropping comes when you're lining up two windows on the screen, side by side, to swap information between them.

Windows offers a simple way to align windows for easy dragging and dropping:

1. **Drag one window against a left, right, top, or bottom edge.**

   When your mouse pointer touches the screen's edge, the window reshapes itself to fill half the screen.

NEW

   Windows 10 also lets you drag windows to corners, which is your way of telling the windows to reshape themselves to fill one-quarter of the screen. By dragging a window into each corner, you can align four windows neatly on the screen.

2. **Drag the other window against the opposing edge.**

   When your mouse pointer reaches the other edge, the two windows are aligned side by side.

You can also minimize all the windows except for the two you want to align side by side. Then right-click a blank spot on the taskbar and choose Show Windows Side By Side. The two windows line up on the screen perfectly.

Try dragging windows to each position on the desktop, including the corners, so you'll be prepared when you need to view several files onscreen simultaneously.

It Won't Let Me Do Something Unless I'm an Administrator!

Windows gets really picky about who gets to do what on your computer. The computer's owner gets the Administrator account. And the administrator usually gives everybody else a Standard account. What does that mean? Well, only the administrator can do the following things on the computer:

>> Install programs.

>> Create or change accounts for other people.

>> Start an Internet connection.

>> Install some hardware, such as digital cameras and MP3 players.

>> Perform actions affecting other people on the PC.

People with Standard accounts, by nature, are limited to fairly basic activities. They can do these things:

>> Run previously installed programs.

>> Change their account's picture and password.

If Windows says only an administrator may do something on your PC, you have two choices: Find an administrator to type his or her password and authorize the action, or convince an administrator to upgrade your account to an Administrator account, a simple task I cover in Chapter 14.

I Don't Know What Version of Windows I Have

Windows 10 comes in several versions. Not sure exactly what version of Windows lives on your computer? Windows doesn't really shout it out, but a little probing forces it to reveal that information. Specifically, you need to look at the System window.

Follow this step to see what version of Windows is installed:

1. **Right-click the Start button and choose System from the pop-up menu.**

   Chances are good that you're running Windows 10 Home or Professional version.

If you're running an earlier version of Windows, follow these steps:

1. **From the Desktop, click the Start button.**

2. **Right-click the menu item named either Computer or My Computer and choose Properties from the pop-up menu.**

   When the System Properties window appears, read the information to discover your version of Windows, and whether it's 32-or 64-bit.

If your desktop doesn't have a Start button, you're running Windows 8.

My Print Screen Key Doesn't Work

Contrary to its name, the Print Screen key doesn't shuttle a picture of your screen to your printer. Instead, the Print Screen key (usually labeled PrintScreen, PrtScr, or PrtSc) sends the screen's picture to the Windows memory.

From there, you can paste it into a graphics program, such as Paint, letting the graphics program send the picture to the printer.

If you want to capture an image of the entire screen and quickly save it as a file, press ⊞+PrtScr.

That shortcut tells Windows to snap a picture of your current screen and save it as a file. Windows saves those pictures in your computer's Pictures folder within a folder called *Screenshots.* Screenshot files are in the PNG format, a favorite with many graphics programs. The screenshot includes your mouse pointer, as well. Subsequent screenshots include a number after the name, as in Screenshot (2) and Screenshot (3).

When saved, your screenshot can head for your printer when you right-click the file and choose Print from the pop-up menu.

Some tablets can also take and save a screenshot if you hold down the volume down toggle and press the tablet's built-in Windows key. Other tablets require different key combinations, so check your tablet's manual to see how it takes screenshots.

When something on your computer screen looks confusing or broken, take a screenshot. Sending the screenshot file to a tech support person lets them see exactly what you're seeing, which increases his chance of fixing it.

Chapter 23

Ten or So Tips for Tablet and Laptop Owners

For the most part, everything in this book applies to deskbound PCs, laptops, and tablets. Windows 10 offers some exclusive settings for the portable crowd, however, and I cover those items here.

Designed for travelers, it explains how to toggle Airplane mode in a hurry, connect to yet another Wi-Fi hotspot, and toggle an uncooperative tablet's autorotate feature.

If nothing else, please read the section on backing up your laptop or tablet before traveling. It's easier and more essential than ever.

Turning on Tablet Mode

When in Tablet mode, Windows 10 switches to its finger-friendly mode: The Start menu fills the entire screen. Your apps fill the screen as well. Because tablets are often smaller than desktop monitors, seeing one program at a time makes it easier to focus on the essential information.

When running in Tablet mode, Windows even adds extra space to a list of menu items, making it easier to poke the desired option with a fingertip.

However, Tablet mode isn't always easy to define. When you plug a keyboard into your tablet, for example, do you want to turn off Tablet mode and return to the desktop and its less-touch-friendly menus? The same question arises when you plug in a mouse.

The new convertible laptops that switch between a laptop and a tablet with a folding motion complicate matters. Windows 10 sometimes can't tell which mode you want.

Fortunately, it's easy to see whether or not you're in Tablet mode and to toggle the setting on or off.

To toggle Tablet mode on a touchscreen tablet, follow these steps:

1. **Slide your finger inward from the touchscreen's right edge.**

   The Action Center pane appears.

2. **When the Action Center pane appears, tap the Tablet Mode button.**

   The Action Center pane shows at least four toggle buttons along the bottom. The highlighted buttons are turned on; the others are turned off.

Some tablets may switch automatically depending on the devices plugged into it. When your tablet senses a change — perhaps you've removed it from a docking station — it sends you a message in the screen's bottom right corner, asking whether you want to switch to Tablet mode. If you'd like to toggle Tablet mode, approve the message, and Windows switches accordingly.

If your tablet toggles to Tablet mode at inappropriate times, give it a little supervision: Tap the Start button, tap the Settings icon, and, when the Settings app appears, tap the System icon. The Tablet Mode section, found on the left side of the System page, gives you these options:

>> **When I Sign In:** Tap this, and a pop-up menu lets you choose how Windows should behave when you sign in to your account. Windows can automatically send you to your preference of desktop or Tablet mode. Choose the other option, Use When Appropriate for my Hardware, and your PC defaults to its manufacturer's recommendations, handy with some combination laptop/tablets.

>> **When this Device Automatically Switches Tablet Mode On or Off:** Here, a pop-up menu lets you fine-tune your computer's discretion in automatically toggling Tablet mode. If your tablet already chooses Tablet mode correctly, Choose Don't Ask Me Before Switching. If your tablet needs more supervision, choose Always Ask Me Before Switching.

>> **Hide App Icons on the Taskbar When in Tablet Mode:** This toggle lets you choose whether to see app and desktop program icons on your taskbar. Some tablet owners prefer to remove the icons to reduce clutter. (Tablet owners can always see which apps are running in the background by tapping the taskbar's Task View icon, shown in the margin.)

>> **Automatically Hide the Taskbar in Tablet Mode:** There's little need for a desktop in Tablet mode, so there's even less need for the taskbar, that once essential strip along the desktop's bottom edge. Choose this option to toggle it off when in Tablet mode. If you prefer the safety net of the taskbar, toggle this back on.

Choose any option, and the change takes place immediately; you don't need to click an OK or Yes button to approve the changes.

Switching to Airplane Mode

Most people enjoy working with their tablets or laptops during a long flight. Portable devices are great for watching movies and playing games while pretending to catch up on some work.

But most airlines make you turn off your wireless connection while the plane is in flight, referred to in airport lingo as *Airplane mode.*

To turn on Airplane mode, follow these steps:

1. **Click or tap the Action Center icon near the clock in the screen's bottom-right corner.**

   The Action Center pane appears.

2. **Tap or click the word Expand above the row of buttons.**

   The Action Center pane normally shows four buttons along its bottom edge; tapping or clicking Expand reveals a row of hidden additional buttons.

3. **Click or tap your Airplane Mode icon (shown in the margin).**

   When the button is highlighted, Airplane mode is on, which turns off your tablet's radios: Wi-Fi, Bluetooth, and GPS.

To turn off Airplane mode and reconnect to the Internet, repeat these steps. This time, however, you toggle *off* Airplane mode, which reactivates your Wi-Fi, Bluetooth, and GPS.

TIP

Airplane mode not only puts your tablet and laptop in compliance with airline safety rules, but it conserves battery life, as well. Feel free to keep your computer in Airplane mode even when you're not on an airplane.

Airplane mode turns off not only your computer's wireless but its cellular gear, as well, if you have a cellular data plan. It's a handy way to shut *off* all your computer's radio activity with one switch.

Connecting to a New Wireless Internet Network

Every time you connect to a wireless network, Windows stashes its settings for connecting again the next time you visit. But when you're visiting a wireless network for the first time, you need to tell your computer that it's time to connect.

I explain wireless connections more thoroughly in Chapter 15, but here are the steps for quick reference:

1. **Turn on your laptop's wireless adapter if necessary.**

   Most adapters stay on continuously unless your computer is in Airplane mode. If so, turn off Airplane mode, as described in the previous section.

2. **Click your taskbar's wireless network icon, shown in the margin.**

   You can reach the taskbar's wireless network icon even when Tablet mode is turned on.

   Windows lists any wireless networks it finds within range.

3. **Connect to a wireless network by clicking its name and clicking the Connect button.**

   At many places, clicking Connect may connect your laptop to the Internet immediately. But if your laptop asks for more information, move to Step 4.

   WARNING

   Never connect to a wireless network listed as an *ad hoc* connection. Those connections are usually set up in public places by thieves hoping to rip off unsuspecting visitors.

4. **Enter the wireless network's name and security key/passphrase if asked.**

   Some secretive wireless networks don't broadcast their names, so Windows lists them as Hidden Network. If you spot that name or Windows asks for the network's security key, track down the network's owner and ask for the network's name, known as its *SSID* (Service Set Identifier) and security key or passphrase to enter here.

   When you click the Connect button, Windows announces its success. Be sure to select the check box labeled Connect Automatically. That tells your computer to remember the password and connect automatically the next time you come within range.

If you sign in with a Microsoft account, your Wi-Fi passwords travel with your account. If you log on to a Wi-Fi network with your laptop, you can automatically log on with your tablet, as well.

Toggling Your Tablet's Screen Rotation

Most Windows tablets are meant to be held horizontally. But if you pick them up, they automatically rotate to keep your work right-side up. Turn your tablet vertically, for example, and your desktop becomes long and narrow.

Autorotation comes in handy when you're reading a digital book, for example, because the longer, thinner pages more closely resemble a printed book. It's also a convenient way to rotate photos on a tablet when showing them off to friends. But when the screen rotates unexpectedly, autorotate becomes a bother.

TIP

Most tablets come with a rotation lock button along one edge. (The rotation button is usually near the power button for some reason.) Pressing that toggle button either locks the screen in place or lets it rotate freely.

You can also toggle autorotation directly from the desktop by following these steps:

1. **Click the Action Center icon near the clock in the screen's bottom-right corner.**

   On a touchscreen, slide your finger inward from the screen's right edge.

   The Action Center pane appears.

2. **Tap or click the word Expand above the four buttons.**

   The Action Center pane normally shows four buttons along its bottom edge; tapping or clicking Expand reveals the hidden buttons.

3. **Tap or click the Rotation Lock button.**

   When the button is highlighted, Windows stops the screen from rotating automatically. Tap it, and the highlight disappears, letting the tablet stay right-side up no matter how you move the tablet.

Repeat these steps to toggle autorotate on or off.

Choosing What Happens When You Close Your Laptop's Lid

Closing the laptop's lid means that you're through working, but for how long? For the night? Until you get off the subway? For a long lunch hour? Windows lets you tailor exactly how your laptop should behave when you latch your laptop's lid.

To start tweaking, follow these steps:

1. **From the desktop, right-click the Start button and choose Power Options from the pop-up menu.**

2. **From the left pane of the Power Options window, click Choose What Closing the Lid Does.**

   Shown in Figure 23-1, Windows offers several lid-closing options for whether your laptop is plugged in or running on its batteries: Do Nothing, Sleep, Hibernate, or Shut Down.

FIGURE 23-1:
Change your laptop's reactions when plugged in or on batteries.

TIP

Generally, choose Sleep because it lets your laptop slumber in a low-power state, letting it wake up quickly so that you can begin working without delay. But if you have another preference, you may choose it here.

Also, you can choose whether your computer should require you to enter a password when it's turned back on. (Passwords are always a good idea.)

3. **Click the Save Changes button to make your changes permanent.**

Adjusting to Different Locations

PCs don't move from a desktop, making some things pretty easy to set up. You need to enter your location only once, for example, and Windows automatically sets up your time zone, currency symbols, and similar things that change over the globe.

But the joy of a tablet or laptop's mobility is tempered with the annoyance of telling the thing exactly where it's currently located. This section supplies the steps you need to change when traveling to a different area.

Follow these steps to let your laptop know you've entered a new time zone:

1. **From the desktop, right-click the clock in the taskbar's bottom-right corner.**

   A pop-up menu appears.

2. **Click Adjust Date/Time.**

   The Settings app opens to the Time & Language section.

3. **Click the Time Zone option and then select your current time zone from the drop-down list.**

   That changes your time zone, which is all most travelers need. Extended-stay travelers may opt to change region-specific items — the region's currency symbol, for example, or the date, time, and number formats — or to add foreign characters to their keyboard. If you're deeply embedded in a foreign zone, move to Step 4.

4. **Change your date and time formats, as well as regional and language preferences to match your current country's customs.**

   The Settings app's Time & Language section lets you change all of the regional settings in Windows:

   - **Date & Time:** This is the section you changed in Step 3. There's no need to revisit unless you erred in that step.

   - **Region and Language:** Choose this option, located just below the Date & Time option, to tell your apps what country you're visiting. (That lets the apps display local content that matches your location.) Choose the adjacent Add a Language button to add another language so you can read and type in that language.

   - **Speech:** Click here to fine-tune the speech recognition in Windows.

5. **Close the Settings app, if desired.**

   To exit the Settings app, click the X in its top-right corner.

Backing Up Your Laptop Before Traveling

I explain how to back up a PC in Chapter 13, and backing up a laptop or tablet works just like backing up a desktop PC. Please, please remember to back up your laptop before leaving your home or office. Thieves grab laptops and tablets much more often than desktop PCs. Your laptop and tablet can be replaced, but the data inside it can't.

Keep the backed up information at *home* — not in your laptop's bag.

Theft is why I don't recommend storing any sort of backup memory card inside your tablet or in your tablet's carrying case. When the thief takes your tablet, he takes your backup, as well.

Microsoft's OneDrive, built into Windows 10, lets you store your information on the Internet quite easily, providing an automatic backup. I explain how to set up OneDrive in Chapter 5.

Accessing the Mobility Center

Introduced in Windows 7, the Mobility Center lives on in Windows 10. It's a collection of frequently accessed settings for portable devices.

To access the Mobility Center, right-click the Start button and choose Mobility Center from the pop-up menu. The Mobility Center appears, as shown in Figure 23-2.

FIGURE 23-2:
The Mobility Center places laptop and tablet settings in one easy-to-reach location.

Different manufacturers offer different settings, but almost all of them offer quick ways to toggle screen brightness, sound volume, rotation, battery plans, and ways to connect to monitors and projectors.

Index

X

Z

About the Author

Andy Rathbone started geeking around with computers in 1985 when he bought a 26-pound portable CP/M Kaypro 2X. Like other nerds of the day, he soon began playing with null-modem adapters, dialing computer bulletin boards, and working part-time at Radio Shack.

He wrote articles for various techie publications before moving to computer books in 1992. He's written the *Windows For Dummies* series, *Microsoft Surface For Dummies*, *Upgrading & Fixing PCs For Dummies*, and many other computer books.

Today, he has more than 15 million copies of his books in print, and they've been translated into more than 30 languages. You can reach Andy at his website, www.andyrathbone.com.

Author's Acknowledgments

Special thanks to Dan Gookin, Matt Wagner, Tina Rathbone, Steve Hayes, Colleen Diamond, Virginia Sanders, and Ryan Williams.

Thanks also to all the folks I never meet in editorial, sales, marketing, proofreading, layout, graphics, and manufacturing who work hard to bring you this book.

Publisher's Acknowledgments

Executive Editor: Steve Hayes

Project Manager: Colleen Diamond

Development Editor: Colleen Diamond

Copy Editors: Colleen Diamond
and Virginia Sanders

Technical Editor: Ryan C. Williams

Editorial Assistant: Serena Novosel

Sr. Editorial Assistant: Cherie Case

Production Editor: Kumar Chellappan

Cover Photo: Vladitto/Shutterstock